MORE PRAISE FOR BRETT BUTLER'S
KNEE DEEP IN PARADISE

"Butler's writing is incisive and her wit is razor-sharp . . . [*Knee Deep in Paradise*] is a well-written and compelling story about overcoming fantastic odds, and everyone likes a fairy tale, especially a true one."
—*Associated Press*

"A surprisingly introspective and stylishly literate autobiography."
—*Houston Chronicle*

"The real surprise in *Knee Deep in Paradise* lies not in the stories Butler tells, but in how exceedingly well she tells them."
—*St. Petersburg Times*

"The most remarkable aspect of comedian Brett Butler's autobiography, *Knee Deep in Paradise,* is how well-written it is. She has a command of felicitous phrases and the ability of a true raconteur."
—*Ft. Lauderdale Sun Sentinel*

"*Knee Deep in Paradise,* sharply and evocatively written, has an easy time towering over the joke collections turned into bestsellers by fellow standup comedians."
—*Dallas Morning News*

"Butler is a graceful, sardonic stylist . . . "

—*Minneapolis Star Tribune*

"In *Knee Deep in Paradise*, Butler memorably grounds this melodramatic outline with her distinctive smarts and cool wit." —*Atlanta Journal Constitution*

"Brett Butler is a bona fide writer—[*Knee Deep in Paradise*] isn't a book to be left on the plane. It's one to be read, dog-eared, given a place on the bookshelf, loaned to a best friend, and re-read from time to time."

—*Cincinnati Post*

"[Butler] is everything fans of her stand-up and sitcom would expect her to be: Intelligent, funny, well-spoken and down to earth." —*Birmingham News*

". . . in this surprisingly graceful autobiographical memoir . . . Butler recalls the ups and downs of her life in prose that is sometimes melancholy, sometimes poignant, ultimately triumphant." —*Columbia State*

"A heartfelt, eloquent, even lyrical account of how she survived a nettlesome life." —*Columbus Dispatch*

Knee Deep
in Paradise

To Dave
with all best wishes
and gratitude to
such warm
folks in LA

Knee Deep
in Paradise

Brett Butler

Brett [signature]

HYPERION

New York

The following quotations are reprinted by permission:

Maya Angelou (page 3) from *The Complete Collected Poems of Maya Angelou*. Reprinted by permission of Hirt Music, Inc. Copyright © 1969.

James Agee (page 49) from "Knoxville Summer 1915," in *A Death in the Family*. Reprinted by permission of the James Agee Trust.

Denise Levertov (page 203) reprinted by permission of New Directions Publishing Corporation.

E. E. Cummings (page 371) from "my father moved through dooms of love," in *Complete Poems: 1904–1962* by E. E. Cummings, edited by George J. Firmage. Copyright 1940, © 1968, 1991 by the Trustees for the E. E. Cummings Trust. Reprinted by permission of Liveright Publishing Corporation.

F. Scott Fitzgerald (pages 373–377) from *The Letters of F. Scott Fitzgerald*, edited by Andrew Turnbull. Reprinted with permission of Scribner, a Division of Simon & Schuster Inc. Copyright © 1963 by Frances Scott Fitzgerald Lanahan. Copyright renewed © 1991 by Joanne J. Turnbull, Joanne T. Turnbull, Frances L. Turnbull, and Eleanor Lanahan, Matthew J. Bruccoli, Samuel J. Lanahan, Sr., Trustees u/a dated 7/3/75, created by Frances Scott Fitzgerald Smith.

Gioconda Belli (page 391) from *From Eve's Rib*. Reprinted by permission of Curbstone Press. Copyright © 1989 Gioconda Belli. Translation © 1989 Steven F. White.

Use of the material from *Blood on the Dining Room Floor*, (page 279) copyright © 1933, 1948 by Gertrude Stein. Granted by permission of The Estate of Gertrude Stein.

All photographs courtesy of the Brett Butler Collection.

ISBN 0-7868-8914-4

FIRST MASS MARKET EDITION

1   3   5   7   9   10   8   6   4   2

Original book design by Claudyne Bianco Bedell

For Ken

WHOSE FAITH, KINDNESS, WIT,
BRAINS, AND HUMILITY PROVE
THAT OPPOSITES ATTRACT.

KNEE DEEP
IN PARADISE

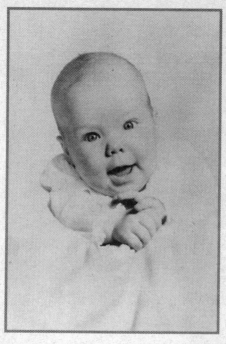

Mom calls this her "Gerber baby".
To me, it resembles a photograph
of a drooling softball.

Montgomery, '58

MY LIFE HAS BEEN ONE GREAT BIG
  JOKE
A DANCE THAT'S WALKED
A SONG THAT'S SPOKE
SOMETIMES I LAUGH UNTIL I CHOKE
WHEN I THINK ABOUT MYSELF.

–*Maya Angelou*

Prologue

Surrendering an autobiography before the age of forty is best left to geniuses or martyrs. Since geniuses are too busy and true martyrs never speak of it, that leaves celebrities. On the other hand, I always reckoned that my life was interesting even before I "amounted to anything."

Unlike recollections that are privately sentimental, writing about one's life and the people who inhabit it can be a perilous thing. It's tempting to describe a cloudy day as sunny, or a confused soul as a cruel one.

But thirty-seven years of breathing somehow creates proportion, and truth ends up typing itself. Minimizing the outrageous or magnifying the mundane is not caprice on my part. Sometimes I just remembered things that way. All of it is important and none of it is.

If my career had stopped where this book ends—around the age of thirty-two—then the story would have been complete, ending well in that the author lived to tell it. However, it might have been harder to sell. Millions of people overcome adversity, whether self-inflicted or externally administered, and we have the reward of our own evolution. But the act of survival does not require an audience. I'm only thankful that I didn't have one when I was doing it. When someone becomes famous, anything they stepped in along the way becomes part of their legend. I'm not naïve enough to resent my colorful past or ashamed enough to deny it. The good news, to me, is that I started writing this years before I stumbled upon fame. (Or it stumbled upon me—I haven't figured that out yet.) When someone famous writes an autobiography the very preciousness of the act begs for interference. Curious bystanders pace and camp out at literal and figurative doors. And you worry that it can all be undone. . . .

But being coy did not make me famous. I am not leaving out what happened that got me here. My "discovery" is at the beginning of this book for reasons that will become apparent by the end of it. You know you've lived a hell of a life when stardom is anticlimactic. Sort of.

After nearly twelve years of doing stand-up comedy and being about the seventh-most-booked woman comedian on the circuit, I was "found." Without a series of favors, flukes, and fine omens combining on one night in October of 1992, I might be performing parts of this book in an obscure Manhattan performance showcase instead of writing it down. The whole thing was an accident—if you believe in such things. If Cary Hoffman, the owner of Stand-Up New York, had not suggested that a certain producer watch me, David Tochterman of the Carsey-Werner Company wouldn't have seen me and I probably wouldn't be starring in my own television show.

Not only did I not know what they were "looking for," I tried not to let myself care. Years of not being what they were seeking made me relatively immune to such dreams. On a good night I was happy if I made people laugh, even if they included the talent scouts in the crowd. My reasons for this were numerous: I didn't want to be in a sitcom; I was afraid to try serious acting even though I desperately wanted to; and I had just about decided that writing was going to be my career, no matter how impoverished I'd be for its duration.

I mention my nonchalance, feigned or otherwise,

for a reason. I hoped for nothing and that night in October 1992 roundly disappointed those expectations. Lots of other women were on that showcase and, at the age of thirty-five, I was the oldest one there. It would have been a great night for casting a show called *Me and My Funny Daughters.* Even though I had fun on stage, I didn't think the set went well. I told my manager, "I'll do better next time," as I was leaving. But I was still tickled because I'd started out stiff and then loosened up my act and the room, breaking away from the fear about being seen by Someone Powerful. I just did it for me.

The next morning, my managers called and said to get over to the Ritz-Carlton Hotel *quickly.* I was in no mood to have another carrot dangled in front of me, because I'd already been to a terrible audition that day. One of the major networks had brought me in to read for a new show about a bus trip across America with five strangers. They thought it would be a comedy.

First, everyone else in the room was about seven and I wondered how they expected infants to improvise. For the "audition," I was asked personal and subjective questions. The man and woman who were interviewing us were like eager therapists that might have missed a few classes. Original answers confused them, and I recall that they were particularly delighted with a young man who sat in a chair on his head. I did not have high hopes for being chosen. The man leaned across the desk with an earnest expression and said, "Brett, what do you consider to be your most interesting qualities?" Lord. I said, "I like calves' liver and want to kill the boy sitting on his head." They said they would call me.

So now I was being told that this guy Tochterman was excited about my show from the night before and to hurry over right away. I got in a cab and went to meet him. My manager Christine Martin was there, too. We sat, ordered coffee, and Tochterman said, "This is big." I said, "Yes?" He said, "We are doing a new show and have been looking everywhere for the right person for it. You are so . . . good." I looked at him. He wore an expression of polite excitement and I felt slower than usual. He wasn't like the clowns I'd met that morning.

I asked, "What are you saying?" "Well, Brett, we might want you for this show." I looked at my manager. She'd borrowed his expression. It's still funny to me that they were both more excited than I, and I was a pretty excitable gal. "What?" I asked. "As the wacky next-door neighbor? They always want a Southern girl saying things like, 'I wouldn't let him butter my dog's grits,' and then they tease up her hair and send her home." David said, "No, we're looking for the lead role."

Then I remembered that Carsey-Werner were the people who produced *The Cosby Show* and *Roseanne*.

They let me absorb that for a moment, and then spoke about the logistics of the next few days. Christine and I walked away and were going down the street chatting about nothing. Ten blocks later, I suddenly grabbed her arm and said, "My God. That was a good meeting, wasn't it?"

When we got back to their office, the other half of my management team, David Martin, Christine's husband, was there, too. Our mood was jubilant although we had nothing signed, promised, or delivered. We just sat and grinned at one another.

David said, "Brett, do you remember the first thing you said to Chris and me when we met?" I did. They'd approached me at a club in Manhattan, years before, and said that they were in personal management and wanted to speak to me about representation. I'd been through some flutterings of fame before I was ready and had left LA for good, I thought, returning to New York to work on my stand-up.

Although David and Christine appeared sincere and intelligent, I barely said hello before issuing this edict: "I am *never* moving to LA and I am *never* going on a sitcom." Neither of them batted an eye. They said, "Great. How visionary. So what *do* you want to do?" They somehow said that without a trace of sarcasm, which impressed me greatly.

I answered them sincerely. I said that I wasn't sure that LA wanted someone like me, that I'd worked hard to get good on stage, but that doing stand-up wasn't as rewarding as it used to be. I thought my comedy was perishing somehow, but I still wanted to write something with characters and dialogue—whether fiction or plays. I basically wanted everything except, in a manager's opinion, something to make money. They signed me anyway.

For years David and Christine had to hear not just rejections of me, but colorful, specific things about what was wrong with my act, persona, material, and they never once tried to get me to do anything just for money or that compromised the goals I set for myself. They fought for the most challenging bookings, trying for places that didn't think I was "hip" enough to play, and, most importantly, worked with me in the unprofitable arena of putting together a one-person show. So when we got the call a few days later for me to go out to LA and meet Tom Werner and Marcy Carsey about this show, it was happening to all of us.

I flew into LAX, rented a car, and drove to Studio City, missing the exit for my hotel. Fearful of being late for such an important meeting, and regretting not taking the offered limo, I was hurrying toward the right off-ramp, and saw a woman next to the road with a sign saying, "PLEASE HELP. HUNGRY CHILDREN." She looked like me if I hadn't quit drinking or never came indoors, except her hair was naturally blond. I slowed down for the light and saw two children about four and five years old sleeping beneath a cardboard lean-to by a tree.

Here I was, scrambling to get to a first-class hotel in a rented Cadillac, perfumed and listening to the Isley Brothers really loud. When I saw her, I turned off the music, reached into my purse, and pulled out a bunch of twenties. I passed them to the woman's brown, ragged hand as I rolled by. She started to say, "Thank you," and then when she saw that I had given her more than a few one-dollar bills, the rest of the niceties ended up as a garbled animal cry, resounding pitifully in my ears until I pulled up at the hotel and heard the valet say, "Good day. Will you be staying with us, ma'am?" I didn't know if I had tithed for luck or to stave off the fear that always traveled with me.

I don't repeat this to garner kudos for my alleged humanity. I do it to illustrate the dread I felt at this incipient break in my career. When I met Ken, who later became my husband, I felt the same way. I thought that anything so wonderful must have been a cosmic mistake and braced myself for its removal. Dreams that do come true can be as unsettling as those that don't. When I saw that woman on the off-ramp, I saw every misstep I'd ever taken, and it took me a moment to realize that I wasn't her anymore. I kept thinking, There but for the grace of God, not knowing that the phrase would actually mean something to me in the near future.

I used to stay up late at night, especially after I moved to New York in 1984, writing stories. They were mostly thinly disguised versions of my past. It seemed like a good, albeit subconscious, way to figure out where I'd been. When writing, I could call myself back from the darkness, rest and reclaim things I'd let go of long ago. Like many people going through momentous episodes in their lives, sometimes it was hard for me to tell whether angels or devils prevailed at the time. Vital parts of me had been up for grabs. I think that sin, in and of itself, is really quite simple, and its effects are as varied as those of us who choose them. But somehow I got saved: from things, myself, the devil, from whatever you want to call it.

So, from the brief repose of knowing where I've been and how I got here, I submit yet another book from somebody famous. It will fall far short of other books, words, and ideas that have inspired me, if for no other reason than I learned it the hard way and wasted a lot of time in getting here. Writing such a book is a pretentious excursion, implying validity where mere excuses would suffice. All I did was stay alive long enough to do something I loved and get recognition for it. I guess I'm trying to say it's just a bloody book and I didn't even know how many punchlines were in it until I wrote it all down.

"Little Roland" with "Little Julia",
his mother. In nearly every
picture, he seems to be looking
away.

Tuskegee, circa 1940

1.

I spent the first twenty years of my life waiting for two men I was reasonably certain would never come back—my daddy and Jesus Christ. I don't wait for them anymore. My dad, anyway. And at least with Jesus I didn't spend all that time thinking he was gone because of something I did.

I was born on January 30, 1958, in Montgomery, Alabama, at exactly six o'clock in the evening. I would have been born in Tuskegee, where we lived, had the town not been too small to accommodate a hospital.

Later I would ask my mother, after we moved to Georgia and I was teased about being born in Alabama (the
world is never too small for regional rancor), if I was
conceived in Georgia. She would answer, "Why, yes.
Tell them it happened in Atlanta." Everyone who
made me was Southern, stretching back, it would seem,
into infinity. On my father's side, there was inescapable
pride in this; on my mother's, benign resignation. In
any event, I'm so Southern I'm related to myself.

We were surrounded by believers in the New Testament, the Gospel of Jesus Christ. My mother held the
fort of our agnosticism as best she could, but it was
nearly an impossible fight. When we were small and
had to fill out forms in school that asked for our religion, I'd ask my mother what to write. She pursed her
lips and said, "Put 'Protestant.' " Then she gave a technical explanation and added, "But I'm not even sure
that that's what we are because I can't answer for my
children and I'm not going to tell y'all what to believe.
All I can do is try and convince you that being a good
person is better than not being one." I wasn't so sure
what to do about a mother who didn't quote Bible
verses or scare me with Revelation. Once, when I was
about ten, I asked my mother what religion she was.
After pausing a moment, she said, "I'm a pantheist.
That means that God is in everything." I liked that
idea. It cleared things up for me.

When I was eight, I had a friend down the street

named Mary Catherine. She was my age and attended Catholic school, wearing a uniform every day. We played together when we got home, and one day she came to her door in tears, saying that she couldn't come outside. I went by every afternoon for a week and begged her to at least come over to my house for a while. When she asked permission to leave, I saw that her mother had been crying, too. I asked what was wrong and, after much coaxing and promises that I would not tell anyone—which I suppose I'm breaking now—Mary Catherine filled me in. "My parents just got divorced," she said, sniffling. I couldn't understand. I told her, "But your dad's out back cutting the grass. My mom got divorced and that means your father doesn't live with you anymore."

Her little face still raw from crying, Mary Catherine continued. "He still lives with us because it's a secret. You don't understand. It's against the church. In the eyes of God we are sinners." I told her that I'd heard everybody was a sinner, but didn't mention that I knew only a general meaning of the word. Apparently, at her house, sinning was taken quite seriously. "Don't you see? If people find out, then we'll be excommunicated." She started weeping even harder and I joined in, believing she had said that her family would be "executed." By the time I was old enough to understand the difference between the two words, I didn't care.

If you believed in Jesus, there were lots of catchy ways of saying so. Some of the expressions are as colorful as the South itself: Saved! Born again! And my personal favorite: Washed in the blood. Later in my life, whenever anyone asked me if I had been saved, I told them not really, but that I had a terrible first marriage—I had been washed in the blood.

From time to time, revivals came to town. I went because there wasn't much else to do. I didn't go because I was scared of hell. I was just afraid I'd miss something. To me, boredom is worse than hell any day.

I should have known then that I was an addictive personality. Or at least destined for show business. I used to get saved all the time. When the minister asked those of us who wanted to embark on the journey of Jesus to come forward, I always marched to the front. At the time, it wasn't very different from a magician asking for an assistant from the audience. I can still see the crushed look on my mother's face when someone would tell her that I had gotten saved again.

Church signs advertising the coming week's sermons regulated our lives as much as headlines. Our town was small and conservative. People said "Hey" to each other on the street, and we took this as proof of our goodness. In many ways, we were right. We collectively eschewed the larger intellectual concepts of the world and found biblical reinforcement for our provincialism. Integration, for example, was more of a concept than a reality, and closer to profanity than an ideal. It certainly was not a goal.

There were always those who could find various passages—even from the Old Testament, which was considered a last resort among aficionados of The Word—that promoted segregation. These versions of the gospel were tailor-made to hide hate, which, in turn, covered an even deeper fear—the fear of change. "It says in the Bible that He don't want us mixin' with the colored." Period. If you asked exactly where that was located in the "Good Book," you were considered trouble. Among the more intelligent, it was deemed backward to openly resist integration, if only because it was inevitable. Besides, people like Lester Maddox, the governor of Georgia who was famous for passing out ax handles to keep blacks out of his restaurant, were such undiluted rednecks that many people were afraid to imitate him. Segregation became unfashionable before it became unjust.

Progress howled at us Southerners, chasing us and cornering us like the dogs we had sicced on runaway slaves not that long ago. I could count the black children who were in class with me on one hand, and that was for the entire time I was in school. The absence of black people in our family's life was not deliberate, unlike our avoidance of racists. Since our mother had protected us from bigots, I assumed that we just didn't know any. The first time I experienced bigotry was so subtle that I almost missed it. Since I'd been in elementary school, I'd seen the newsreels of blacks being mowed down by fire hoses and German shepherds, and I thought all hatred had to be that brazen. But my first incident, up close, seems so minor, comparatively, that it almost doesn't bear mentioning, yet the fact that I recall it so well makes me think otherwise.

I was about ten years old, attending a big new Methodist Church with my best friend. I was fidgeting in my seat, half listening to the sermon, when the preacher mentioned integration. I stopped yawning long enough to hear his oratory. My mother believed in integration and, by happy conversion, so did I. The reverend spake, "Now I believe our colored brethren deserve a place to worship, but over where *they* live, not among us." I actually heard smatters of applause and felt sick to see my friend's father grunting in agreement. I wanted to pull off my "red rose of the visitor," which ensured that I would be greeted kindly later on, amid steely questions of "When can we expect to see your mama here with us one Sunday?" I never went back to the service.

We were not churchgoers. When we were young, we'd sometimes attend with our cousins. The pressure of dressing up for church and having to get up early on a weekend made the experience a bleak one. When I did go, I was fond of the pictures of Jesus and the little children around him. What happened at Sunday school and the boring service was another story. I learned the Lord's Prayer and songs and was once given a Bible for memorizing verses. I am not sure why I thought the words in that Book differed from the experience of church, but it did. Jesus was so big that even his tiniest sentences grew, for me, past the church and the town. Church was just another place to feel alone and out of place. My mother never went with us either. We were packed in cars with well-meaning relatives and just taken there as if going would fix us once and for all.

We went to the Baptist Church if we went with our cousins and to the Methodist Church if I was with my girlfriend who lived next door to my grandparents. I was too young to tell the difference in religions and had only been told that I was christened in an Episcopal Church somewhere in Alabama when I was six months old. I liked knowing that my salvation had been taken care of in advance. It made more sense to me than the part about Jesus dying for our sins and earning our way back. Since my own father was long gone and had made no attempt to contact us, I thought we were lucky to have God and Jesus. I saw God as a Father who wouldn't split. And I saw Jesus as the ultimate Big Brother who cared about me no matter what. My feelings toward Jesus haven't changed in all this time. Despite the fact that I've seen him used as a weapon by many against many, as happens with any deity, I always liked him. His trait of complete kindness outweighed every fiery teaching and judgment I ever heard.

I kept seeing the same four or five paintings of Jesus throughout my childhood. It was almost as if some huge multinational goyim conglomerate had a monopoly on images of Christ. He was the benevolent Caucasian with arms outstretched to sinners and children alike. Although I've seen him portrayed in more varied forms over the years, I still feel the same love when I think about Jesus. Images of the Son of God, the really handsome Jesus Christ Superstar, the man who would make things right between us and our Father twice removed, was a comfort to me. The sense of belonging cushioned the pangs of growing breasts, pending menses, and waiting for the next father to go away.

I don't know. In a way, after the first father leaves, the rest are easy.

Memaw, Uncle Mickey and Mom
Atlanta, circa 1940

Mom seems alone here —
and she's looking in the same
direction as my dad in the
picture with his mom, taken
at almost the same time.

2.

My father's name was Roland Decatur Anderson, Jr. When he was growing up, he was known as Little Roland so he would not be confused with his father, Roland, Sr. This was his mother's idea. Her name was Julia Holmes Powell Anderson. The day after they got married, my father's parents moved in with Julia's parents, Mr. and Mrs. Richard Holmes Powell. Julia's father was hardly ever called by his given name, either. He was known as "Big Dad" or "Senator" even after his term in the Alabama state senate expired. It was not unusual for overly deferential relatives to address him as "Senator" to show their regard for his once lofty position.

The nicknames did not end there: Big Dad had a wife named Julia, and that was what they named their second daughter. In the Deep South, that long ago, there were actually little-girl juniors running around named after the woman fine enough to bring them into the world. So living in the same house were Big Dad, Big Julia, Big Roland, and Little Julia bringing up my father, who would eventually ask to be called "Andy" to avoid the diminutive of anything.

My Grandfather Roland used to say that he fell in love with Julia the first time he saw her while she was attending Florida State College for Women. "I was there visiting a cousin and saw Julia's ankles first and then her calves and I wanted to marry the rest of her before she finished walking down the stairs." Big Roland played Triple A baseball in Tallahassee when he and Julia began dating, and was a good enough catcher to have big-league scouts buying him drinks from time to time. Whether love for Julia or lack of ambition stalled his career, I cannot say, but Roland followed his gal back home to Alabama and they married soon after.

Big Dad hated his daughter's new husband, who was roundly thought to be of "inferior stock and inclination." Julia was a plain, slender woman who had married a rugged, uneducated man, in my great-grandfather's eyes. It was hard for her to win her father's forgiveness for this sin, but she eventually did, with the birth of her first child, who was my father.

When my father was very young, Big Dad bailed Big Roland out of a scandal involving misuse of gas-company funds. Now that proof of his inferiority was set in stone, their attention could be turned to the "raising of the boy." When I heard these stories for the first time and then heard them corroborated exactly by other relatives, it always sounded like something that had happened hundreds of years before, so antiquated were the expectations and emotions of those involved. They abided the dismal marriage of their only child for her sake and that of their only grandchild, who was the apple of their collective eye.

And, as if one internal estrangement wasn't enough, Julia herself was subject to lifelong scorn for surviving the scarlet fever that killed her younger sister at twenty months of age. Julia's mother, Nana, always told Julia that the "pretty child" had died. Still, they were always polite; voices were never raised, and the propriety of the Senator's home would be honored at all costs.

My mother, conversely, was being raised a few hours away in Marietta, Georgia, a town to the north of Atlanta. Carol Jean Parker was the second child of Eugene Robinson Parker and his wife, née Elizabeth Jewel Mitchell. Everyone called them Gene and Judy.

Their lives were "normal" and it suited them just fine. Both sides of my maternal grandparents' families came from the outskirts of Great Britain—Ireland, Wales, and Scotland. They were politically more progressive than the rest of the family, lifelong "yellow dog" Democrats, which means that they would vote for a canine over a Republican if that was the only choice available. Sometimes they went to the First Baptist Church, but they were never fanatical about that.

One of my favorite stories about my Grandmother Judy—we called her Memaw—happened when my mother was sixteen. A bunch of women from the First Baptist Church Ladies Auxiliary, as devout and arbitrary a bunch of women as you could hope to find in Cobb County, came to my grandmother's house for what appeared to be social reasons. In several minutes, they mentioned that my mother's hand-me-downs were the subject of their call. One of them said, quite sweetly, "Judy, we understand that you are giving Carol's old clothes to the colored maid's girl and we think they are nice enough to give to one of the white girls over at the school." My grandmother's response was a less profane version of "Don't let the screen door hit you in the ass on the way out." She and my grandfather never went inside a church again unless they were attending a wedding.

About the only thing the Andersons and the Parkers had in common was that both matriarchs, Judy and

Julia, had graduated from college while neither of their husbands had. It impresses me that both of my grandfathers married women with brains, women who sought an education when it was not required or, in some cases, even considered attractive.

When Gene and Judy would eventually meet my father, the man who would soon marry their eldest daughter and make her life a living hell, his elitism would horrify them. My father was openly contemptuous of the fact that some of my mother's relatives came to America after the Revolutionary War. He branded them parvenus in his generous moments and "shanty Irish" when he and my mother were alone. He quoted his illustrious genealogy from his family tree back to Jamestown. Whether my father knew it or not, the residents of that founding colony were also the first North Americans to import slaves from Africa. My father thought of blacks as "helpless inferiors," yet he was openly contemptuous of white people who said "nigger." However, the older generations from both sides of my family, maternal grandparents notwithstanding, did not think it wrong to say "nigra" and "them" through clenched teeth when referring to the race of people they had owned as recently as eighty years before.

In fairness to several of my relatives, not in my immediate family, I've seen their attitudes change over the years, or perhaps they're just careful not to say certain words around me anymore. I have an older relative who was a lifelong segregationist, yet a devout believer in the gospel according to Jesus Christ. He used to tell horrid ethnic jokes, laughing heartily at their punchlines, and in the next breath would quote the Bible. At the age of sixty, he had a sudden and intense realization that racism was—in his own words—a "sin." He stopped telling the jokes and using "pet names" for minorities. Recently he hired a black woman to run his office.

For the first eighteen years of his life, my father was filled with the noblesse oblige of his grandfather and the sugar-coated praise of his mother. The result was that he felt he was heir to a large and shiny piece of the American dream and that God Himself would see to it that nothing stood in his way.

~

My father got an ROTC scholarship, which was canceled when the Navy found out he had asthma. His failure to graduate from Vanderbilt was his first major disappointment in life. So he went back to Alabama, began to call himself "Andy" instead of Roland, and enrolled in the University of Alabama at Tuscaloosa. Almost before he chose his courses, he phoned home with the exciting news that he was joining the same fraternity to which William Faulkner had once belonged—

Sigma Alpha Epsilon. The SAE initiates were mostly young, white, and fashioned out of the same excited cloth of self-importance. Hell, they were mostly snobs. My father's uniqueness lay in the fact that he had a better notion of what he wanted from life than he did about how to participate in its retrieval.

My mother used to tell us a story that my dad told her about when he was in college. Andy and a pal drove over to Oxford, Mississippi, to see William Faulkner. When they got to his home at Rowan Oaks, the woman who answered the door told them to go away, that the great man was a busy recluse and for them not to bother him again. My father said that he certainly understood, and would the woman be kind enough to give Mr. Faulkner a gift from two admirers. She agreed and took the present inside. Several minutes later, William Faulkner came outside laughing and thanked my father and his friend for the wonderful present, which, he said, he planned to use right away. My father had given him a gift-wrapped copy of *Gone With the Wind* with a matchbook taped to the cover.

Julia used to tell us a different anecdote about her only child. "Oh, sugah, I'll never forget the time. Your daddy was just three years old and I took him to the grocery store. When we got home, I opened the back door to get him and the grocery sacks. I looked in the car, and as I sit here, he had opened a carton of eggs and broken every single one of them right there on the seat." She smiled as she continued, "You know I was furious, but then he just looked up at me with those sweet big eyes and said, 'No harm done!' Well, I nearly died laughing right then and there. Wasn't that the cutest thing you ever heard?" Our mother would mutter, "Not really," for no one in particular.

Carol Jean Parker, my mother, graduated from high school the same year that my father graduated from college. The photographs of her in her school annuals are so beautiful that I used to get jealous looking at them. Why couldn't I be as pretty as she was? I would wonder. I hoped that I would acquire some of her features with the passing of time or at least be as slender as she so effortlessly appeared to be.

Her smile was radiant and clear. (It still is.) It was not the "say cheese" variety, the kind that some striking women perfect in order not to wrinkle the eyes. There are local ads in her high school annual that used students as models. In one of them, my mother is standing in front of a brand-new high-fidelity television set in an evening gown. The sweetness in her face is immediate and real and it makes me sad that she ever got less than that in return.

She was in the chorus and had a three-octave voice that landed her a scholarship at Peabody College. But instead of the asthma that halted my father's first educational plans, she had another health contingency to deal with. At the tender age of eighteen, she made what was delicately called "a mistake." She was driven down to Florida by her father and dropped off at a home for unwed mothers. Mom said that Granddaddy hardly spoke a word during the entire trip, but his jaws were clenching and unclenching the whole time. It took them years after that to become friends.

The expressions used to describe what happened to her are too sugary for the truth of it: My mother was on a date with a boy who wouldn't stop when she begged him to and he raped her. In that light, terms like "getting into trouble" or "visiting a relative" were nothing but the sounds of a family and a reputation shattering like mirrors with parallel myths of bad luck. After seven and a half months of pregnancy, my mother miscarried a son, then returned home as if nothing had happened. Even now, nearly forty years later, there are still small-town big mouths who speculate as to the nature of my mother's fall from decency.

Once my mother was living with her parents again, she got a job assisting a doctor in Atlanta. Not long after that, she met my father through mutual friends. Their first date was on the telephone and they spoke for hours. Before their planned meeting, my mother caught pneumonia and Andy came to see her during her recuperation. He fell in love at first sight. As for my mother, she said, "I thought it was love. He wasn't like any boy I'd known. He was exciting and funny and the smartest person I'd ever met. I just added those things up and it seemed like love."

They were married three months after they met. Although signs of discord were already there, the nuptials were planned and rushed along for a strange reason. Memaw tried to talk to Mom about the unsuitability of her fiancé by saying she thought he had a mean streak and would make her unhappy. Andy's coarse sarcasm, which passed for wit among those he deemed worthy of his company, was deeply felt at my mother's house. My mother was too caught up in feelings to pay any heed. After a particularly bad evening, my grandmother said, "I don't want him coming around here anymore. If the two of you are getting married, do it now."

But there is no evident strife in their wedding photos. I get such a kick out of looking at them. My mother's sweetness, intelligence, and an electric innocence shine in her expression. Ever since I was little, when I looked at the pictures for the first time, I've been struck at how different she looked from the other women there. The bridesmaids looked just the way they were supposed to look in the Deep South in 1957. Their bonnets of hair are coiffed sternly with lacquer atop their soft young faces. But my mother looks like she's getting married in Paris or New York twenty years later. Her gown is white satin without a stitch of lace, and there was a Nehru collar on her neck, a full decade before anyone else was wearing them. The sleeves come to a point on her wrist, and right below that is her bouquet of a single giant white orchid tied with little white ribbons streaming down. Her black hair is but a feathered cap upon her head, barely two inches long. Once, when I was little, I asked her why she had short hair and no one else there did. She said, "I saw Gina Lollobrigida wearing hers that way in a magazine, and I liked it." It might not sound very rebellious, but I've always appreciated her uniqueness and lack of vanity from that single, simple act.

And there is one photo of my mother and father that is quite telling. They are clasping hands, grinning large, but only my mother looks directly into the camera. My father seems to have one eye looking straight ahead and the other looking off into the distance somewhere. I have tried to imagine what he was trying so hard to see . . . or what he saw that no one else did.

Carol Jean Parkes, at 15, posing
for a local jewelry store ad!
My sister Katy got her sweet
face.

            Marietta, '53

IT DOESN'T MATTER WHO MY FATHER
WAS; IT MATTERS WHO I REMEMBER
HE WAS.

—*Anne Sexton*

3.

I have seen pictures of Andy only when he was young.
I do not know if any others were ever taken.

My memories of him are scattered and fleeting. Perhaps if I'd known that the day we finally left was the
last time I'd ever see him, I might have paid more attention. Although I was only four, I can recall parts of
the day so clearly that perhaps I did have a premoni-
tion of sorts. The arbitrary glimpses I've saved are
friendly enough. The cruelty he exhibited toward my
mother was often of the icy variety, difficult to under-

stand when one is young. All I could sense was the tension, until right before the end when he did not care who witnessed his violence.

My father used to say that he was allergic to all sorts of things. He would frequently lean backward over the side of the bed to put in nose, eye, or ear drops. Such benign images stand apart from the times his rage spewed forth. And then it was never directed at us, his children, but at our mother.

When I was four, Andy took a job as one of the vice-presidents of public relations for the Humble Oil Company in Houston. He told everyone that this was his "big break," the one he'd been waiting for all his life. Other than being away at college, it was also the only time he would ever live away from home. It was all very sudden. We packed what we needed in the car, and headed to Texas in the rain. Before we arrived, we'd been through a large part of Hurricane Carla.

Not long after finding an apartment, Andy began a vicious cycle of shopping, drinking, check-bouncing, and alienating anyone who might be considered friendly. Whenever our mother became acquainted with anyone, even another young mother in our complex, he soon humiliated both of them, making further connections impossible. From Thanksgiving to the spring of the next year, nearly four months, none of us were allowed out of the apartment at all.

Memaw, appalled at the turn of events, came all the

way from Georgia to see us. While she was there, I remember a flash of a moment when my father's hands
went around her neck. Memaw asked him, in a voice
both calm and stern, to let go. He did and Memaw left.
Within a week, she sent us tickets to come back to Marietta.

My mother says it was a coincidence that the date we
left him was April 1st in 1962.

I have gone over that day repeatedly in my mind. It's
hard to tell whether it stands out because of the rarity
of young memory or because of the significance of the
event. It was morning and my sisters were all dressed
up in outfits my mother had sewn. The gold zigzag
strips on the hem and sleeves are still clear to me. Even
small children know when Something Big is happening, so all of us were quietly watching and waiting for
whatever that might be.

Usually, my mother was the placating one, kind and
trying to put a good face on things. At his worst, my
father was the opposite—imperious, manic, and, occasionally, cruel. That day they seemed to swap person-
alities. My mother's jaw was set, and she moved with
determination and efficiency. Andy was obsequious
as he interjected timid pleas for her to stay. He seemed
most concerned about my mother's imminent departure and did not seem to see me and my two little sisters lined up in our good clothes by the door. Mother
got the last bag, set it beside her, and said, "Girls, kiss

your daddy goodbye." He stooped down to hug us. I had just turned four, and I think it was the biggest hug he'd ever given me. It was also the last.

My father was eccentric, peculiar, and unprepared for reality. This worked out fine, because reality and my father were rarely on speaking terms. He thought that an average life, one that was typical and not extraordinary, was a thing to be abhorred and avoided at all costs. Even his name—Roland Decatur Anderson, Jr.—was one of those liquid, poetic ones, reminiscent of generals and great expectations, the sort of name that happens only in the South. The South is often noted for its eccentric characters, both real and fictional, and I was there long enough to know that "normal" either becomes a divine ambition or a malediction. For my father it was a private war, a cause to be won, and he fought it on a grand scale. And because he fought alone, he was both the victor and the casualty.

My father's mother, Julia, told us—in a rare moment of indiscretion—that she had given birth to her only child in the parlor of her home in Tuskegee. I suppose that was a piece of information designed to make the listener feel connected, somehow part of history. In the year my father was born—1933—home births were the norm, so that in itself wasn't newsworthy. What made it titillating and later amusing was her addendum: "The birth was quite difficult. The doctor had to give me an ether enema for the pain." Being a baby cast out into the air of this world is traumatic enough, I reckon, without the added waves of a mother's screams and being surrounded by one of the weirder items on the Chart of Elements emanating from a Very Private Place. After the recounting, it is not hard to forgive my father for virtually anything he did in his life.

In any case, he was an adored, coddled, smart boy who was told time and time again of his genetic, ancestral, downright predestined superiority among men. Saturate a child with that, add some Southern Episcopalianism and an upbringing in a town no larger than three thousand people, and then try not to imagine some deeply disturbing side effects. I have a photograph of my father at the age of ten studying at home, his little pale face and arms bent over his books. His skin was almost translucent, a result of his severe asthma and of being kept indoors almost obsessively by his mother. He would stay near home and believe in his "specialness" until it was too late.

I remember my father reading constantly, playing records, and talking. He also liked to watch television. Things were happy then. When it was dark, we'd all watch TV together. *Bonanza* would come on and my dad would start cracking jokes when we knew the scenes weren't funny. We knew this because the music would get slow and sad and people would be crying. My mother would be saying, through hysterical laughter, "Hush, Andy. Just watch the show!" But we could tell she didn't really want him to hush. I didn't mind not understanding what he was joking about. It was enough that it made my mother so happy. It made him happy, too. He wanted to perform and Mom was the best audience he would ever know.

My sisters and I started doing impressions of people when we were quite young. Tana, who is fifteen months younger than I, came into the living room once wearing a man's hat and a strange expression on her face. My father hooted, "Oh, Christ! She's doing Eliot Ness!" We'd watched Robert Stack so often that Tana had figured out how to imitate him. She was all of three years old at the time.

I had two imaginary friends until I was six. Their names were Mr. Promise and The Don Don. Mr. Promise, my mother tells me, is the one I talked about. She said that I referred to him in terms of what adventures I had. The Don Don was different. He was behind the door and she says that I would open the door, look up about seven feet in the air, and ask him things. I sought his advice and wanted to know if Mr. Promise and I could do certain things.

I have heard it said that imaginary friends are the continuance of relationships from previous lives. I don't know about that. My mother and father both got a kick out of them. When I made a certain dish for these friends—called *merchecar*—I was allowed to go into the kitchen and use real ingredients. I remember Worcestershire sauce, lemons, and sugar. One of my earliest memories is of being in the kitchen with Andy and of how he talked to me like a grown-up, handing me the necessary items for my special dish. It is a nice memory and an apt one. My father helping me make food for people who weren't really there. He used to have nicknames for me, too. He called me Pervis and Doomer. I don't know why.

I had a book lying around as long as I could remember. (I've since lost it somewhere and feel like hell about it.) It was a book about perspective in drawing, and the author was Earnest Norling. On the title page there was an inscription: "To my dearest Brett, on her first birthday. With much love, Your Uncle Earl Long." I asked my mother who Earl Long was, and she told me that he was an insane man who'd once been the governor of Louisiana. She described his colorful and scandalous life, adding that he was probably a historical footnote compared to his older brother Huey. So, until I was in my teens, I told people that I was related to the Longs. I thought that was a nice way to be connected to the famous without the burden of dubious sanity. When I was nearly sixteen, Mom overheard me telling someone about my Uncles Earl and Huey. She said, "Where on earth did you get that idea?!" I said, "Well, he gave me a book when I was one. For my birthday." She rolled her eyes. "That was from your father. It was a joke." How was I supposed to know? Who else would tell jokes to a baby, for Christ's sake?

From the time we left Andy until I went away to college at the age of seventeen, my mother's parents let us stay with them for varying lengths of time. Staying with Memaw and Granddaddy was one of the finer and more sane parts of my whole life. When we went there, it was as if we'd come in from a storm. I'm sure it wasn't raining every time we entered their house through their large, warm kitchen, so the inclemency I recall was probably only our lives.

Their home was set back on a shady street, with a big sloping yard out front. Trees were everywhere. It was a house made for children. Among the things I loved most were the flour and sugar canisters with chefs' faces on them; little porcelain bees on the noses of the chefs made them wince. They were the first things I checked going in the door. If they were still there, it was like I was there, too.

We felt secure there and didn't mind having to go to bed on time or the rules against our chronic back-talking. We rose early and, if it was winter, we went to the kitchen to warm ourselves in front of the heating vents beneath the cupboard. My grandfather used to put our breakfast plates there the night before so that they'd be warm for the food, and we shared the space. The adults stayed in the back of the house, and my sisters and I would get up and watch Tarzan movies and read their big books. The two I remember best were H. G. Wells's *Outline of History,* and an art book with one hundred paintings in it. The painting called "Senecio" by Paul Klee was my favorite and I tried to draw it in crayon about a hundred times.

The description of my grandparents' house in such prosaic terms is not accidental. Everything they gave us in our lives, from love to shelter to financial support in the years to come, was never random, manic, or conditional. I'm grateful to them for taking us in and happy that my mother realized how good they were for us. I was young, and the impact of a sheerly ordinary life, even in scattered doses, was pronounced. Also, it was such a contrast to the home of my other grandparents that I needed to know there were such places, such families on earth. I measured the difference only in my heart.

Our other grandparents did not struggle to see us, so the shuttling back and forth was minimal. As a matter of fact, Julia and Big Roland never came to see us at all. Since Marietta was only a couple of hours away from Tuskegee, perhaps my father's parents imagined that we were right down the street. It was almost thirty years before I found out that their unavailability wasn't the result of a personal grudge.

Memaw, silently and not asking for applause, would occasionally take us to see them. She packed the three of us in the car so that we could see the grandparents we called by their first names. There was no malice in that, either. Julia said that she did not like to be called Grandmother. Big Roland seemed glad, in a sad sort of way, when we came by. He always seemed to have a lot on his mind and even more smoke pouring out of his face. We would get kisses, hugs, and small talk since we were small people. Then we would go away until the next time. They appeared, without being rude, to be relieved that we were going. As Gertrude Stein once said of her older brother, with whom she had many disagreements sputtering down into nothingness: "Little by little we never met again."

My thoughts on this now are just that we—the grandchildren—were the second half of a mess that Julia and Big Roland never quite knew how to clean up. Smiles, kisses, and kindness were easy to administer in small doses for short whiles, since someone else actually took care of us when we were sick or needed new shoes.

When I was five we moved to a little apartment complex called Pine Forest. It's hard to meet anyone who's from Marietta and struggled financially for any length of time who did not live there; it was close to public housing in terms of quality and its transient residents. While we lived there, Mom started to date a very tall man who was nice to us all. He seemed so normal, in fact, harmless, that he did not bear further scrutiny. One night, he woke us all up, piled us into the car, and drove us to the hospital. Mom was sick and had to lie down in the backseat. She was moaning and crying.

Soon after that, we were at my grandparents' house, and I noticed that my mother was wearing the same kind of expression she did on the day that we left my father. The difference, this time, was that I had not seen the pain preceding it. My grandparents' dining-room table was covered with silver, china, and ceramics. Mom was greeting people as they came in, and, one by one, the pieces left the house and my mother put the bills in her purse. Little was said between my mother and Memaw during these transactions. Granddaddy was nowhere to be seen. Pain and stubbornness were in the air, and all I could do was sense it. Later, when I was grown, my mother told me about the scary ride to the hospital. She'd nearly died of a botched illegal abortion. While she was still in the hospital, her mother had visited and words were spoken—unkind ones— and my mother decided to move us all to Miami. She thought the climate would be better for my little sister Toren's asthma.

So we packed up our little old Fiat and said good-bye. Memaw made me repeat her phone number to her the entire morning. She said it was in case something happened, an "emergency," but she asked me so often that I finally became frightened. Then we drove off.

Tiny pieces of the floorboard were missing beneath my feet, and I watched slivers of the road almost the whole time on the trip down to Miami. I thought that unless I watched the road as my mother drove we would have a wreck. I actually believed that until I was old enough to drive myself. At the time I didn't know what hyper-vigilance was. I only knew that it was exhausting to feel that way and still be too young to do anything about it. From that time on—until I was past thirty—it felt like the entire family was my responsibility. No one else knew. I couldn't admit such a ridiculous emotion, much less describe it, to the people who took care of me. And the one person who could have helped me the most was my mother, but I didn't want to bother her when she had so many problems of her own.

Roland Jr's good old days:
a crisp tux, champagne and
his best friend to toast. This is
my godfather, Robert Brannon.
The pretty woman, Marilyn,
would later become an
accomplished artist and
Bobby's wife.　　Tuscaloosa, '56

SLEEP, SOFT SMILING, DRAWS ME UNTO
HER: AND THOSE RECEIVE ME, WHO
QUIETLY TREAT ME, AS ONE FAMILIAR
AND WELL-BELOVED IN THAT HOME:
BUT WILL NOT, OH, WILL NOT, NOT
NOW, NOT EVER; BUT WILL NOT EVER
TELL ME WHO I AM.

—James Agee

4.

When we got to Miami, we moved into a housing project and were virtually the only Anglos there. It was 1963, and thousands of Cubans were fleeing Havana by the boatful and arriving with more fear and poverty than any of us from merely broken homes could imagine: they were coming from a shattered country. I didn't know about the politics, just that they had left. In my young mind, I thought the circumstances precipitating their exodus were like a tornado or a flood.

There was an air of both desperation and relief in the complex where we lived.

One family at the project had a little girl whose head was stuck, turned all the way around to one side and would not move. Her father carried her so that she could see from her resting place on his shoulder. She was a year or so younger than I was and I thought her father was so kind to worry. Most of our neighbors could not speak English, and the ones who did often did not know enough for us to understand one another. I began to learn a form of mime to communicate with them, picking up a few Spanish words along the way.

Mom got a job assisting a Miami cardiologist. Since she left for work each morning dressed in white, I thought she was a nurse. When the ragged Fiat finally broke down, we took buses to get around the city. Miami was the hottest, brightest place I'd ever seen, taking on the quality of a strange dream. Even the buildings seemed to glare with their own light source as if they were made from reflective concrete.

One day, Mom was trying to take us off a crowded bus by the back door and, before I could step down, the doors closed in front of me. The driver couldn't hear my screams and I could only see my mother and sisters getting smaller behind us. My grandmother's phone number was swirling in my head. Finally, a block or so away, but seeming much longer in time and distance, the driver stopped. I can still see my mother running toward me, carrying my sisters and dropping groceries behind her on the pavement. An old man helped me off and waited for the next bus until he was sure we were all right. He spoke only Spanish, but I know he understood my mother's fervent thanks.

Our baby-sitter was a young woman named Mercy. She was eighteen and beautiful. She was sweet to us and comforted me when I cried, which was often. One day, the old woman who lived upstairs from us was hysterical about something. Mercy explained that a solar eclipse was going to happen that day. She said that if you looked at it you would go blind. I was so scared that I gathered my two sisters and hid us all beneath the blankets with the blinds drawn. A couple of hours later I awoke to find my sisters gone. Screaming bloody murder, I ran out into the hallway and Mercy ran to meet me. "Where are they? Are they dead?" In my hysteria, I was trying to speak Spanish, too. Mercy laughed and tried to soothe me. They had been cleaning the house during the whole thing.

Sometime after that, my sisters and I were playing outside when suddenly the women at the project all ran outdoors at once, sobbing and clutching at one another. I looked for Mercy, who was always the picture of calm, but her skin was light green and she had to hold on to the banister to stop from falling. I couldn't understand the Spanish they were speaking as we were led inside

to the great god television. I thought it might be another eclipse, except everyone seemed so sad. I couldn't
figure it out. My mother came home early and tried to
explain who President Kennedy was and why someone
had killed him.

I began to worry about everything. I was getting sick
of life, and I was only five. It was more than seeing the
road through the bottom of the car, more than being
left on a bus by accident, or even the moon momentarily
hiding the sun. This was also the time of the Cuban
Missile Crisis. The anxiety about that seemed to reach
from Washington, D.C., all the way down to Miami,
where the war, the grown-ups said, would happen. I
kept hearing things, born either of superstition or truth,
that made a child curious about her prospects. Since I
tried not to let my mother know about my concerns,
they grew and magnified in me until my dreams were
littered with apocalyptic debris.

Since I was too young to understand politics, as-
tronomy, or assassins, I had the feeling that something
very large that didn't love me was after us and that if I
tried hard enough, we could escape it. And we closed
the blinds so the eclipsing sun wouldn't fry our eyeballs
and I prayed that the bombs wouldn't really explode
and that my baby sisters would be fine and no more
presidents would be shot. It was too much, too much,
and the rottenest year I'd had.

But then I met a kid who could cope. I met Irving.

We all played in a communal sandbox at the complex. Irving was the meanest kid there, the meanest kid I'd ever seen, even in the movies. He lived with his mother, too, and didn't know where his father was either. He punched and kicked and threw things, and had a mouth so vile his language was as incomprehensible as that of the refugees around us. One day I heard him call another child a "shitass." I could tell from the reaction of the other kids that this was not a harmless thing to say. I liked it nonetheless, thinking it possessed a poetry not found in "dummy" or "stupid head." Although correct, I was disabused of its acceptability after returning home and trying it out on my sister. So when we got really mad, we simply called each other "the word that Irving said." We stayed in the sandbox to hear many more things and got ringworm and sunburn and waited for our mother to come home.

My mother was a kind and enthusiastic parent. She read to us and always had a big roll of paper so we could color and draw. She answered questions patiently and was never too tired to answer them. How we felt and what we learned were important to her. And she was careful to balance her time between us, and respect our individuality. In retrospect, I am sure she was pretty sad about being a thousand miles away from any adult who knew or cared about her, but she put on a good show. We loved to make her laugh and did plenty of it. But then she began to date and I resented it. I was young and couldn't understand why she needed more than us to make her happy. Pretty soon I realized that her dating was serious and I prayed against it with all my strength. I was beginning to make the connection between the advent of men and disaster. My loathing of my mother's dates increased in strength and sophistry through the years until they created misery for everyone. I was not angry at any man for loving her, but for taking her away from us. It seemed that once a man left us, he took parts of us with him.

So when she brought home someone who was special, I hated him most of all. His name was Joe. Mom would greet him, then walk us upstairs to Mercy's apartment, where we'd stay during their date. Mercy always watched *The Outer Limits,* which had the scariest music I'd ever heard. I still get chills when it comes on. I tried not to cry when it was time for Mom to leave, so I had, instead, an awful lump in my throat. My sisters were younger and seemed to manage fine. I didn't know what would be worse—them being scared, too, or me being that way all by myself and feeling like such a baby. Then the dates started happening more and more, and one day we moved away from the girl whose neck would not turn and the cussing Irving and Mercy and into a house with a daddy and another life.

Our new house was a big beautiful place on Biscayne Boulevard. The yard had hibiscus flowers and kumquats growing, and there was beautiful wallpaper and rooms with curtains that matched the spreads. My mother got pregnant, and the fact that Joe was already married with three children of his own didn't seem to mar anyone's happiness. Once, when my mom was very sick during her pregnancy, we went to stay with Joe's wife. I thought she was kind of mean at the time, but I didn't know that she was still married to him, either. Oh, she fed us and made sure we were clean and put us to bed on time, but I got the feeling she didn't really like us. Looking back, I cannot believe her kindness.

Then our last name became Butler. Mom said she almost didn't change our names because she knew she'd be saddling me with the insufferable and unlikely moniker by which I've been known for the past thirty years or so. Sure enough, the taunts began at once. In my elementary-school years they called me things like "bread and butter," and other things that delighted children when confronted with the prefix "but." Later, obvious comparisons to one of the characters in *Gone With the Wind* were frequent and annoying.

My mother named me for the character Lady Brett Ashley in a book I was too young to read or understand. She told me that Hemingway, the author, was a "good writer" and that Lady Brett was "an interesting woman." (When I would finally read *The Sun Also Rises* at age thirty-three—the same age as Lady Brett in the book—I found that my namesake was an alco-

holic and a veritable nymphomaniac, making the Lady
part of her name quite ironic. I began to wonder if
my mother had the gift of prophecy.) By the time I
began performing under my current name, I wanted
to change it back to Anderson, but it seemed like too
much trouble. Besides, my "stage" name was easy for
people to remember.

Right after we moved into our new house, my
mother and Joe had a daughter, giving them four children apiece. Maybe fertile people just find each other.
My new sister's name was Kristen and, like the rest of
us, she had no middle name. When Mom brought her
home, she let me hold the new baby. Kristen was beautiful and had giant purple birthmarks on the top and
sides of her head. When she was less than a year old,
they were removed. The stitches looked worse than the
birthmarks did. She looked like she'd been in a sword
fight. Who knew she would become so beautiful after
being born with giant purple polka dots.

Around the time I turned six, I came down with a
fever and Mom took me to the pediatrician. Both of
them looked worried after I got there, and I heard the
word "injection." I asked Mom what it meant. The
next thing I knew, I was in the hospital having a spinal
tap. Two days later I had a second one. They said I had
spinal meningitis, and then our relatives flew down to
see me. I wanted to see my family, but not because I
was ill. Then one day I woke up and I was well. One

doctor called it a miracle. Another said it was a misdiagnosis. In any case, they let me go home.

While I was still in the hospital, my new stepdad, Joe, came by to see me. I was lonesome because Mom was with the new baby, and he brought me dozens of colored pipe cleaners and ribbons and showed me how to make little animals out of them. He stayed to play and talk with me for hours. Another time, a couple of years later, my sisters and I were visiting our grandparents in Marietta, because our mother was ill and couldn't get out of bed for a few months. While we were there, Joe wrote me a letter that went in circles on pink paper. In all the years I knew my stepfather and all the unhappiness we shared, I still remember these two episodes gratefully. He was overwhelmed by life, just like we were. And because he was a man, he felt like he had more of a load to carry than anyone. He was an only child and told us stories about being given coal in his Christmas stocking because he had been a "bad boy." I guess he had to dig his daddy stuff out of thin air. My own father, my real father, was becoming more and more distant, and his face faded further and further from my mind.

It was decided that we'd all move back to Marietta, where Joe would get another job selling insurance. Then one day, just a month after school started, my second-grade teacher came to our house and said that my sister Tana and I could skip a grade. The next day

I went into the third grade and Tana went to the second. Tana, always smarter than I, had learned everything I did because I came home every day and read aloud to her. She actually learned to read upside down from standing in front of me, leaning over while I pointed to the words.

We got back to Georgia and I was happy to see my grandparents again. My teacher in Miami was the only thing I missed about the place, and my new teacher was awful. Her name was Mrs. Bill. She used to make kids take gum out of their mouths and wear it on their noses. Since I hated gum, it wasn't a problem to me, but she seemed to enjoy humiliating the children who were caught. Hating her became an avocation. I would draw caricatures of her and wonder what made her. Once, when I tried to hyphenate a word at the end of a line, and did it improperly, she criticized me for it. I said, "Well, I saw it in a book." She laughed at me and said that I was wrong, that there was no such thing. Her ignorance was as unsettling as her cruelty, but there was nothing for a seven-year-old to do.

Besides my new teacher, I was also learning to hate math. I loved almost every other subject. Science didn't thrill me, but at least I could memorize the facts and not have to show my work. Since we were transferred to the school in which Memaw taught fourth grade, it was hard to hand out the "baby sister ate my homework" excuse. Mrs. Bill would simply ask my grandmother about it in the teachers' lounge and then come back and nail me in front of everyone. Our enmity blossomed.

Merely having a rotten teacher was a refreshingly ordinary problem to have. We lived near grandparents who loved us, as well as the rest of our large family. Even the name of our school—Allgood Elementary—was typical. But, by the time we moved there, I'd already spent my whole young life moving around. Suddenly finding myself on a street with shuttered homes and green lawns was comforting, if bizarre. The good part was that I made friends and lived near grandparents who loved us, as well as near various aunts, uncles, and cousins.

When I was nine, I came home from school one day to find a brochure on the kitchen counter. The title was "Having Your Baby." I picked it up, ran into the den, and fairly screamed at my mother, "Are you pregnant?!" In the fourth grade I sounded like the shrillest advocate of Planned Parenthood. My mother answered me. Yes, she was pregnant. It's pretty funny now that I think about it. I looked at her as a parent would have looked at a teenager who'd gone out and done the same thing. My mother was thirty when she had her fifth child. After naming the rest of us rather unconventional names—Brett, Tana, Toren, and Kristen—she named my new baby sister Catherine Elizabeth. We called her Katy.

I began to realize that my mother and stepfather weren't going to make it together. Unlike the time we were with my real father, their fights were not loud. The house just became quiet. Joe's diminished respect for my mother and the sneers behind her back were painful to behold. He grew openly apathetic to me and my other two sisters who were not his "real" children. Once at night I heard my mother whisper for him to just leave if that was how he felt. The next day, my stepfather acted as if nothing had happened. The sadder my mother got, the happier Joe became. I wanted to be as pretty as his other daughters from his first marriage or the sisters he and my mother had together. Failing that, I began to hate him. I mentioned it to my grandparents, but they were silent. I guess they thought he was an improvement over my own father, who was still nowhere to be seen.

My mother's engagement portrait
Atlanta, January '57

5.

While Mom was expecting, Memaw and Granddaddy
bought a house for us. Since Grandmother was a
teacher and Granddaddy worked for a lumber company, the money they spent for the house was not exactly disposable income. It was a nice three-bedroom
brick affair on a street called Sunny Lane. After living
in rented houses for the whole time we were a family,
suddenly we had a place of our own. The Monkees
sang a song written by Carole King called "Pleasant
Valley Sunday." We were living it. The daddies all

came home at six o'clock and the mommies waited for them. We were in suburbia.

Soon after we moved in, our stepfather began to get calls from a woman. Before long, she was brave enough to leave her name, and I took the messages. I would hiss at Joe that "Sissy" had phoned and watch him for any sign of discomfort. I began to understand yet another adult problem—the other woman. At the age of ten, I failed to see the irony that my mother had been both the usurper and the usurped in this category. The affair began to shadow our lives. It was like there was a bomb ticking away and none of us knew where it was hidden. I wondered when Mom would get mad enough to do something about it.

Several months before, when Mom was pregnant with Katy, she and I were in a car accident, hit from behind. Mom reached over to grab me and the steering wheel hit her hip, breaking it. Her convalescence, coupled with the depression that was to pretty much become our roommate, was the beginning of the end of her second marriage.

One day I was reading in the living room and my stepdad stuck his head in the door. I said, referring to a word I didn't know, "Hey, Daddy, what's 'invalid' mean?" He laughed and said, "Your mother is an invalid." I still didn't learn what the word meant, but could measure his contempt for her by the way that he said it.

The security and ease of suburban living began to put its hands around our necks. We lived on the tantalizing rim of prosperity. Weekend visits to the local country clubs with friends and the advent of "rich" subdivisions made us all thirsty for the leisure and possessions of a higher class. It was doubly painful because I thought these feelings were unique. I actually believed I was the only young girl who wanted nicer clothes and to stop hearing the whispers about money. We used to have to stand in a separate line at school to get the discount lunch tokens. It's a lovely system, really, when children can be stratified before they are even able to vote. When we learned about the "food chain" at school, I thought they meant rich kids and poor kids.

My stepfather had dreams as large as anyone's. Such illusions are contagious. Since he was prepared to work to make them happen, this made him very different from my own father. Joe would gather us up on weekends and take us to see the newly built homes in the big rich subdivisions. These fancy housing "projects" had names that overlapped like names from soap operas: Indian Hills, Fox Hills, Post Oaks, etc. Since the South was the last place the love of the monarchy died, the villages within villages began to retrace its steps, beginning with glorious names. Riding schools and polo fields cropped up where vacant lots and drive-ins once stood.

Joe would pull up in front of one of the houses and walk ahead of the real-estate agent, showing us all where our new rooms would be. "And you can have this one, Brett." I would gaze in, sniffing the new paint, and imagine where my ruffled bed would go. These fantasy excursions did not last long. For every pound my mother gained after her accident and the birth of my youngest sister, for every nap she took, he seemed to come home an hour later at night, or we'd get yet another call ending in a hang-up. Pretty soon, after these final months of dreaming, he left. Except for my mother's deepening melancholy, I was glad.

When my stepdad left, I began to have that old dream about my father. I dreamt it for the first time about a week after we went away from Andy. The images of the dream were probably from movies I watched on TV, mainly Howard Keel musicals at that. From an aerial view, I saw a river, wide, dark, and blue, like I imagined the Columbia to be. On either bank there were tall evergreen trees. Hundreds of logs were flowing downstream, and a few dozen of them were tied together in a raft. My father was standing on that raft looking up at me. He wore blue jeans and a flannel shirt, things he'd never worn in real life, and he was waving to me. Since I'd never been in a plane or helicopter, the sensation of rising above him, slowly and quietly, was surreal. It was as if he wanted me to come back and get him and I could not.

The mood of the dream was the strangest part of it. I did not really want to get him, and both of us—through telepathy or something similar—seemed to accept the situation for what it was. I was just going away and there was nothing to be done about it. He got smaller and smaller until there was nothing left to see but the sun glinting off a blue ribbon on the earth. I would have this dream every six months or so, interrupted only by the birth of siblings or other momentous events. Sometimes it would come in those moments right before sleep and I would chase it away. I'd have the dream about once a year until I was twenty-seven and moved in with Ken, my second husband. It all but disappeared after that. Until I started thinking about my father for this book.

When I was eleven, my mother's favorite uncle died, casting her further into depression. He and his family had taken my mother in during her teenage pregnancy, and she missed him. I heard her crying in the living room late at night, and I would wonder when we'd be happy and what we'd done not to be for so much of the time. Notice I said "we." I took on my mother's feelings without invitation or permission. Soon after that we got a letter telling us that Big Roland had died, too. I didn't feel anything. I didn't know him at all. We had stopped hearing from that side of the family completely, except for Julia's birthday cards.

One of the great things about my childhood was when I signed up for summer softball when I was ten. I had no brothers or father to foster such abilities in me, and when I hit or pitched a ball, no one was more surprised than I when it went over the fence or crossed the plate for a strike. When I arrived at the games, I was ecstatic to hear the other players saying, "Oh, good, Brett's here." When I was at bat, the outfield players used to back up. I felt passionate about it, much larger than the circumstances required. From the time I was seven I had been reading about Lou Gehrig and wanted to be a baseball player more than anything in the world. Of course, by the time I was eight, I realized the impossibility of such a dream, but that didn't stop me from playing. The only thing I couldn't do was run. My coach used to laugh when he watched me. The first day he saw me trying to beat the ball to first, he thought I was kidding around. I told him I had never run so fast in my life. He said, "Well, maybe they'll let us use pinch runners." I was embarrassed, but instead of trying to run faster, I just tried to hit the ball farther to avoid the necessity of stopping at single bases. My nickname was T.B., for "Turtle Butler."

⁂

Our street was the same and as different as anyone's. There were mothers that were sweet to us and who asked about our family and who helped with large and small things. There were moms who were polite in that Southern way, who said, "Hey," but in tones designating us Daughters of the Divorced Woman in the

Neighborhood. I remember Jeannette Miller, who lived across the street from us and was married to a Baptist preacher. She was unrelentingly kind and cheerful, defying the homemade logic we possessed about religious people being judgmental. One Christmas my mother was shopping at Kmart—because we could—and someone took her billfold out of her purse with all of her Christmas cash. Jeannette came over and gave Mom more than she'd lost. Mom said, "Oh, that's so sweet, but I only lost fifty, Jeannette." Jeannette would not take the difference and told Mom that her own Christmas would be even better now. My mother cried, and as Mrs. Miller walked away, I thought we'd had an angel in the house.

There were rednecks on the street who drove fast, loud cars and whose children were miniature versions of themselves. They were the first to burn their Beatles albums after John Lennon made his remark about the Beatles being bigger than Jesus Christ. But none of them were as mean as I wanted to believe they were. It turned out they were just country people living on their first paved roads—literally and metaphorically. But they said "nigger" and "ain't" so I fancied that we were superior to them.

There were other mothers who never came outside at all. When you are a child you think the only pain there is is the one you know. But only now, so many years later, do I remember the red, puffy eyes of some of my friends' mothers and the sniffles behind their closed doors.

One of the mothers on our street got a job selling makeup and started to make a lot of money. She left the father and we all talked about her pink Cadillac, and it put a tiny river of fear into the whole street. What if all of the mothers . . . Oh, never mind. And one of the mothers was out-loud crazy and loved her strange sons, who did not seem to care that they were thought of as strange, so secure were they in their mother's affection. We used to ring their doorbell and run away, and the woman's husband loved her so much. She was a screamer and a doer. Another woman was a pretty widow who'd married the handsomest man. He loved her and adopted her two daughters, and I thought if God would only send the same new dad to us, I'd be good forever. There was the mother who screamed at her dog and her daughters, and her husband had the tiredest smile and the slowest walk from his car to the house when he came home from work. They were neighbors. We knew everything and nothing about them, and we could sleep with unlocked doors. There might have been sadness inside the houses, but we were safer then in many ways. I hope everyone turned out all right.

∾

An innocent antagonism rose up between my mother
and her parents. It was as if they were past disappointment in her and wanted Things to Be Right. We
all did, but were at a loss as to how that might happen.
From the ages of ten to fourteen, I went to class, stud-
ied minimally, and made good grades. I started missing school because I learned to make myself sick in the
mornings. The truth was that I was too afraid to leave
home. I thought I was the thing that held it together.
Delusions like that need a firm hand to discourage
them, and there just wasn't one around.

Staying home from school was my part-time job.
Sometimes I mustered up a severe case of hives, so
grand that I was practically disfigured from them. The
first time I got them they scared me. The swelling was
so immense it looked as if I had walked into a beehive.
Mom would call the pediatrician and he would send
over some antihistamine. By the time it took effect, I
would also be drowsy, so I just stayed in for the rest of
the day.

I forged my mother's signature so well on absentee
notes that one day, when she'd actually written one, the
school called our house to verify it. I was faking the
physical ailments to make up for the cataclysmic emotions that circled me. I was sad and anxious. Just thinking about my mother and younger sisters at home by
themselves would give me fever, nausea, or the won-
derfully visual accompaniment of hives. I'm sure it

bothered my mom, but not to the extent that she could do anything about it. Only once, when I was fifteen, did a teacher ask, "Brett, what is your problem?" I didn't like the way she said it. Even more, I disliked being called on my absentee status. I said, "My grades are fine, right? Then leave me alone!"

The good thing about cutting class was that mid-morning, when I'd suddenly start to feel better, I'd get to watch television. Mike Douglas, Merv Griffin, and *The Hollywood Squares* came on during the day. At night, especially if I knew that I was going to be "sick" the next day, I stayed up late and watched Johnny Carson, too. That's when I fell in love with comedy. None of the comedians were Southern and only a few were women, but I related to them more than the Miss Georgia contestants and singers or anyone else. I wanted to be Jack E. Leonard or Jonathan Winters and didn't think there was anything weird about it. Later, I loved acts like George Carlin and Robert Klein, and I thought heaven was a place where Mike Douglas cried with happiness, saying, "We'll be right back!" I would then be led over to a seat, and even the commercials would be good.

The first time I did stand-up comedy was at a school Christmas pageant when I was eight. Everybody was doing something, and since I never learned to play the piano, I decided to do some of George Carlin's act from *The Ed Sullivan Show*. I came home from school and told my mother that was what I wanted to perform in the pageant. She acted like every eight-year-old girl in the world wanted to be a comedian. She helped me remember and write down some of Carlin's jokes, and she even gave me some of her own. For years she'd been sending in funny things my little sisters had said to the *Reader's Digest,* hoping they'd publish them for fifty dollars. Most of them were anecdotes that were best spoken, so we thought they'd stand a chance if I did them on stage.

The first thing I remember about that performance is being scared right before it was my turn. Everyone in the audience seemed so happy with the little songs and poems of the other children and I realized that I was the first one who was going to do something that wasn't even remotely related to Christmas or what it meant to me. The next thing I remember is a bunch of beehive hairdos staring back at me. Since the pageant was during the day, there weren't any fathers there. Just kids and a starter batch of stage mothers. When I got up and started telling the jokes, the only sound I heard was my mother's laughter in the back of the room. It was all the encouragement I needed. I can still see and hear that day. Past the "bits," I recall mixed expressions denoting puzzlement, disdain, or apathy. Some of them had pleasant smiles sort of frozen sweetly on their faces, having had their notions of precious childhood run over badly. When it was over, I sat down and said to my mother, "They didn't understand the jokes!" Thank God I didn't think it was me.

A few minutes later, my friend Harriet, the pharmacist's daughter, was playing "Silent Night" on the piano when a key got stuck. It made everybody really uncomfortable, and she turned toward the room with a look of utter terror on her face. I stood up and yelled, "Harriet, just play the one next to it!" Everyone turned around and laughed uproariously. It was a fine moment even though I didn't see what was funny. I was just trying to help.

୬

Mom says that when she was pregnant with me I'd go nuts when she and Andy played Frank Sinatra songs. She and my father tried with different singers and music, but only Ol' Blue Eyes made me kick and roll. From the time I was very small, I loved show business and felt like I was organically connected to the television set. (Someone recently asked me if I ever thought any of "this," meaning fame, would happen to me. I said yes. If none of it had happened, I guess the same thoughts could've been dismissed as delusions of grandeur. As it is, perhaps the hunches were tiny revelations. Who knows? I've known lots of people who could've been in show business. They have talent, depth, and personality. I usually attribute their reasons for not pursuing it to a form of sanity which I do not possess.)

I loved variety television when I was a kid. It used to be good. It used to exist. I watched Jackie Gleason every week when he had his variety show. I would try in vain to pick out June Taylor from the crowd of dancers that bore her name. The camera was overhead and they looked like a kaleidoscope—if kaleidoscopes had thighs and high heels. I remember Sammy Spear and his orchestra, too, less from the music than from the smiling face of Mr. Spear, arms folded, head bowed at Gleason's intro.

Red Skelton and Andy Williams had shows, too, and I probably knew every singer there was. Judy Garland also had a variety show and I loved her as much as Gleason. When I was five, the year her show was on, someone gave me a huge doll that was built like Barbie, only well over two feet tall. I promptly named her Judy Garland. I never called her Judy, either, or allowed anyone else to. Her name was a run-on version of my idol's name and had to be spoken that way: Judygarland. The dress she came in was so glamorous that I didn't want to take her outside in it. I kept the dress in a box, and I took the big naked doll everywhere with me. There must have been something daunting about a nude doll who was huge and anatomically correct, lacking only orifices. Of course, the only hair she had was on her head, and that was a blond bubble that resembled Jayne Mansfield more than anyone else. By the time she was an "outdoors" doll for a while, Judy-garland was too dirty to put back in that nice glittery dress, so I would try and dress her in a toga of sorts, from a torn sheet.

Once, after my mother began dating my stepfather, we went to visit him at the golf course. My stepdad said he had a surprise for us. Jackie Gleason had a house on the green, and as we pulled up in the first golf cart I was ever in, there he was. I was astonished to see him so close. His show came from New York, which was Very Far Away. To see him right there with a golf club, grinning and joking, was like seeing Jesus or someone that famous. He asked us if we wanted to see some magic. We said yes and he motioned over to the garage door and said, "Open Sesame!" Well, the damn garage door opened and I would have fallen to my knees and prayed to him right then and there if any-one else had. From then on I would tell new pals, whenever the man's name was mentioned, "Oh, I know him!" When I realized that hardly any of them believed me, I would tell real lies just to see if I could have any effect on them at all.

Memaw took us to see the Lone Ranger when I was five. This was a very big deal. The voice of Clay-ton Moore—still the only Lone Ranger as far as I'm concerned—used to mesmerize me. (I also loved Aldo Ray because of his voice and didn't believe it when my mother told me he wasn't one of the biggest stars in the world.) When we drove up to the place where the Lone Ranger was supposed to be, I was dismayed to see virtually the entire population of Cobb County there. How could they love the Lone Ranger as much as I did? How could all of these adults just crowd around and not let the little kids see? Even my grandmother, a well of patience, finally said, "Okay, y'all. There are too many people here. Let's go see a movie and then we'll go get some ice cream." I was hot and sad as we started wordlessly back to the car. Then, appearing out of thin air was Jay Silverheels, who played Tonto, walking alone on the sidewalk. We were the first to see him before he got to the larger gathering. He smiled and spoke to us for a minute. I'm pretty sure he signed something for us, but I don't know what on earth I did with it.

Around my eleventh year, a lesser version of show business was furnished in the form of a show at the Elks Club. My girlfriend's father was a member and they used to take me to some of the soirées. That night I got to sit in the front row and saw a sketch, which I'll describe here: A long white blanket was strung across the stage and lit brightly with a spot from the rear of the room. The crackling of a record player could be heard and the theme of some very syrupy music was playing. Then, on the same record, these words were spoken with increasing fervor and bliss, over and over until the idea of some sort of climax was anticipated: John, Marsha, John, Marsha, and so forth. With each exclaimed greeting, an item of clothing was tossed over the line, as if two excited lovers were undressing to the syncopated sounds of one another's name. At the end of the sketch, the curtain was pulled down to reveal two people washing their clothes in a tub. The room went wild with laughter. Except for me. I wanted to be in show business, but held a large measure of disdain for anyone who thought this was funny, much less those who went to the trouble of staging it. I remembered thinking I could easily do that at home. This was right around the time Peggy Lee released "Is That All There Is?" and I completely understood the song.

I guess it was inevitable that we "put on a show" of our own. This was accomplished largely at my instigation, and I considered planning and rehearsal to be unnecessary. I pretty much just made either my sisters or girlfriends participate. We threw together curtains made out of blankets and learned to lip-sync or memorize the words to popular songs we played on the record player. I remember thinking that popping our heads up, one on top of the other, to say, "Hello!" three times, in different tones, was amazingly original. My nerves were at the breaking point as we summoned game adults to see what we'd practiced for perhaps thirty minutes. We put on a record and we got everyone to sit down and watch us. A giant smile stretched across my face while my stomach and heart flipped around inside me. Our "little shows," as my grandmother called them, were a mélange of just about every form of music available, from the Lennon Sisters to Billy Joe Royal to really bad barbershop quartets. Despite my quaking nerves, I wanted to make the grownups laugh, and to be in the spotlight. I wanted to feel like I did when I saw Judy Garland sing or when I heard Jackie Gleason say, "Open Sesame!" I just wanted to play the one next to it.

Roland Decatur Anderson, Jr.
senior class portrait
University of Alabama, '56

6.

Years before reading what Tolstoy said about happy families being alike and unhappy ones being unique, I felt hemmed in by our strange brand of discontentment. Combined with a Southerner's need for propriety, our misery became a secret. I thought we were a complete aberration. Until our mother got divorced for the first time, I didn't know of anyone in the entire family, on either side, who'd ever been divorced. I walked into other people's houses and watched for things we were missing—besides fathers—and tried to remember what they were. I memorized the rules: (1) Daddies drove when the whole family went someplace. The longer the trip, the more dictatorial the father in terms of time out of the car, stopping for things, and the decibel level of everyone everywhere. (Conversely, our mother was eager to be democratic, to please everyone, and it might have given her just as many headaches as the perpetually irritated daddies.) (2) Daddies rarely went to church, and when they did, everyone got home much sooner. Also, daddies usually let the mothers take care of the family's salvation. (Our mother felt like we were already taken care of.) (3) Daddies seemed more uncomfortable with me, the Daughter of Divorce, than the mothers were. However, as I got older, none of the adults really knew what to do about me, including my own mother. I looked much older than I was, and that flipped everyone out.

Some of these references are very general, therefore unfair. We knew some pretty wonderful parents who were kind and fair and funny. Father envy, a thing I still possess in small degrees, tormented me on the occasions when I met a good one. The assortment of families on our street was my first social study. One night, right after we'd moved into the house on Sunny Lane, Tana and I lay in our bunk beds talking before going to sleep. I said, "Do you think we'll ever be normal?" The haste of her reply amazed me. She said, "No. It's too late for that." I might have already known that, but the fact that my younger sister was so in touch with it was unnerving. After a moment she added, "You mean normal as in having a father and all?" I said yes. She thought about it and said, "Probably not . . . Good night." I tried to think what life would be like if we were suddenly cast into a home with a father who loved us and a house that no one had to buy for us, and I didn't think I could make that adjustment. It was one thing to know that "normal" had passed us by. It was quite another not to even want it. I felt wise and uneasy at once.

Our little nuclear family kept short-circuiting no matter what we did. There was no strength at our center: the more we pulled at our mother, the less capable she felt. Mom started going to group therapy, an inexpensive version of curing what ailed her. Sometimes we would take the evening ride to the building where her group met, and we'd play in the waiting room until the group finished. My sisters and I would walk around the halls pretending we were speaking in a different language for the benefit of the people who cleaned the building at night. At times we heard tears and shouts coming from the room, but Mom always seemed to feel better once she got out of there, and the other people in the group were nice to us.

It seemed that I went a long stretch—from the age of nine to fifteen or so—feeling quite pitiful. (Sometimes I miss the bouts of self-pity I had as a child. They were undiluted and remorseless. I had them as an adult, too, but drinking raised these feelings to a whole new level. Merely calling it self-pity seems inadequate.) My school absences no longer bothered me. They felt like tiny buds in the bouquet of my growing dysfunction. External symptoms of familial breakdown—the kind that an adolescent notices first—began to manifest. Our house was messier than any of us could believe. I remember going to my grandmother's house and being amazed at the little way she took care of a mess the minute it happened. If something spilled on the carpet, she got out this little bottle with a sponge on the tip, rubbed it in the rug, and waited for it to dry, then vacuumed it up. This sounds ridiculous, I know, but I was almost paralyzed at the thought of daily chores, and watching her do it would help me in twenty years when I decided to be "functional," too.

One day Memaw came over to the house, tsked (not for the first time) at the slovenliness she beheld, and announced that she was getting us a maid. I think Mom was relieved in some ways because it took some of the pressure off of her. First we had a maid named January. She was my mother's age, and instead of five children, she had ten, including three sets of twins. When people heard that, sometimes they'd have to sit down. January was calm and sweet and kept whatever blues she had on the inside. Her husband was in prison and would get out long enough to give her another baby and then he'd go right back in. She cared about my mother. When she first started coming, I was angry with my mom for not being able to at least keep up the house, thereby preventing the indignity of someone, especially someone black, having to come over and clean up for us. I think it bothered Mom, too, at first, until she realized that January just wanted to work and didn't judge her at all.

Sometimes during the summer, January would bring one or two of her children over while she worked, sometimes getting the younger girls to help. Once, after they had gone home, I saw a note on my dresser written by one of January's daughters. The dresser was very special to me and the message was written right on it—not on paper, but on the yellow, antiqued wood. I was distraught. The dresser had been given to me by my grandparents and I'd had it less than a year. When they gave it to me, my mother had said, "This is your first piece of furniture." I had not known that the presentation of furniture was a ritual of importance, so I was impressed. The dresser was simply the prettiest thing I'd ever had.

January's daughter Cincy had written: "I wish I had pretty things like you. You're so lucky. Love, Cincy." I was outraged because the message was in ink and the dresser would have to be repainted, but my fury was easier to bear than the agony, which lasts even now. I was eleven and hated to think that whatever amount of self-pity I possessed wasn't justified. It was a note from a girl my age, a girl whose father was gone, too. She thought of us as rich, and she just wrote in this secret, sweet, feathery writing what was in her heart, and when she did, mine was broken. Of course, I was too big a brat to say that out loud to my mother. Besides, I loved the excuse to be angry. And, like a true bully, I didn't say anything to Cincy or January, relying instead on my mother to deal with it.

About a week later, I asked Mom what she'd said to January about it. She looked at me and spoke in a calm, deliberate voice. "Well, Brett, I asked her to be careful about mixing ink and furniture." I started to blurt out that that wasn't enough, but something in my mother's expression wouldn't allow it. She seemed to know that everything I felt was misplaced sadness and I loved her so much for doing that, for not yelling at me or Cincy for anything, but just for knowing.

One day soon after that, my sisters were outside playing. January's children were scattered much farther than we would ever be and my mother was taking one of her innumerable naps. No one ever talked about Mom's naps. We'd heard of other women who napped and knew that a couple of them lived at the other end of our street. One was crippled and none of us ever saw her, and the other one was sad because her baby had died five years before and her husband was out of town a lot. Not only was our mother the only single mother at our end of the street, she was the only one who slept a lot and couldn't clean her house. January was one of the few people who saw all of the symptoms, and I had mixed feelings about her acceptance of it. We never spoke of it before and I believed it to be a form of complicity. So that day I was slamming around the kitchen for something. January was ironing, humming to herself as she sprinkled water from a Coke bottle onto the clothes. I liked being around her. She was strong and loving in a silent way and abided my temper better than anyone else I knew. Just as I was going into my room with food and a bitter grimace, January stopped and called my name. I don't think she'd ever said it before. I was afraid she was going to fuss at me for scowling or, worse, ask me how I did in school that day. She used to tell me what a "gift from the Lord" it was to be smart and get good grades. (Sometimes she and my mother would sit right in front of me and talk about how I was going to make something of myself—if I put my mind to it. I would pretend to be irritated, but I liked believing that I had one thing going for me.)

I stood by the hallway and asked her what she wanted. I realized that I might have sounded gruff toward her when I answered, so I apologized, adding, "Maybe I just need a nap." My scorn, always needing a bull's-eye, reached all the way down the hall to my mother. January put the Coke bottle down slowly and firmly and in such a way that made you wish she'd just slammed the thing down like you would if you were mad. "Come over here, Brett." Jesus, this was too much to take. She was saying my name for the second time in a minute, maybe for the second time since I'd known her. I was uneasy and wished my mother would come down the hall and take the chill out of the room.

January stopped ironing and said, "What you so mad about?" I said, "Mom. She's always sleeping and there's nothing wrong with her. And she never cleans up and she used to cook and she doesn't anymore." Tears were pushing hot in my cheeks, either trying to come out or trying not to. "She cries at night and says nothing's the matter when we ask her and I wish she'd just get out and be like other mothers."

January was almost smiling. "You want your mama to be like other mamas." She said it as a statement, not a question. I said, "You know what I mean. It's so hard here, and I don't know why, and she won't do anything about it." "What you want her to do?" January really wondered. I wouldn't reply. This woman was defending my mother and doing her work. I couldn't understand it. I would have hated anyone else for agreeing with what I just said, but January seemed safe. I wanted her to stay here and just let me breathe in whatever she was exuding. She began ironing again before she spoke.

"My mama's dead. Your mama's bound to lay down when she thinks things is too hard. We all has mamas and it's good to have one. You mad too much. Make a wrinkle 'tween your eyes as big as them dimples." She grinned at me. I sort of had to smile back even though the poison of unspilled tears was almost making me sick. I began to walk down the hall with my sandwich. She said one other thing as I was leaving. "Your mama may never get outta that bed, but she still your mama."

Then January went to work full time for another household and we didn't have anyone else for a while until she called up one day to ask us if we'd found another housekeeper. My mother told her no. January wanted to know if we could please hire a friend of hers. I never quite knew what she said to Mom to get her to relent on the subject of another maid, but the day we first saw Fennie was unforgettable.

I came home from school and saw this slip of a figure hunched over the kitchen sink. I said, "Hey," and when she turned around I beheld possibly the oldest person I'd ever seen standing up. She smiled and I don't think there was a tooth in it. She got busy asking if I was hungry and taking out the milk and saying how glad she was to be working for my beautiful mother. I introduced myself and went to the back to find my beautiful mother and ask her what the hell was going on. I found Mom sitting there wearing a caftan and a very concentrated expression. "Mama, she's older than Torrie" (our great-grandmother). "I know, honey." "Well, you can't let her clean the house." "I know, honey. But January said Fennie's very poor and a fine cook and can do this. Of course, I won't let her do anything heavy. She really wants this job." I was too young to figure out a world in which some poor, ancient woman could possibly be considered fortunate spending her twilight years cleaning up after six healthy females.

Fennie worked for us around the holidays that year. My sisters and I were complaining about how rotten our Thanksgiving was and Mom said, "I have an idea. We'll go out and eat. But first, we have to go somewhere." We got dressed up and went to the car. Mom came out carrying the turkey. Once in the car, she wouldn't tell us where she was driving. Pretty soon, we realized that we were getting close to Lemon Street, which was the poorest part of town and, not coincidentally, where blacks were, economically and socially, if not legally, segregated. It was behind the square, beyond everything. Busing might have forced educational integration on our town, but no laws had been passed to prevent anyone from living in the squalor we were seeing for the first time. None of us were talking as Mom pulled onto the roughest unpaved street of all. Hell, we were poor, but this place was ungodly.

Mom stopped on a little patch of dirt in front of a shack. It wasn't a yard and it wasn't the road. I said, "No one lives there. What are you doing?" Without answering, Mom got out and went to knock at the door. Fennie came out. We could see that she had a fire going and a couple of stove burners on to keep the place heated. I squirmed. I was angry at Mom for doing whatever the hell she was doing. Fennie looked embarrassed for us to see her house. I could see Mom saying something to her and then Fennie came over to the car, with tears in her rheumy old eyes. She leaned in and said, "Yo' mama said you girls wanted me to have this turkey from y'all. Ah tol' huh you all were sweet gals, but I didn't know this. Thank you. Thank you. Thank God." Then that little old woman and my mother carried the turkey inside.

When Mom got back in the car, I said something feeble like, "I didn't know you knew where she lived." Mom was silent. One of the little ones said, "Oh, Mama, that was so sweet. How did you know Fennie didn't have Thanksgiving?" Then she gave Mom a kiss. I wanted to crawl under the floorboard. My mom was cheerful and never said anything else about it. That Thanksgiving, we ate at Shoney's and we bloody liked it.

Fennie didn't work for us much longer. One of her eyes started bothering her, and the trip to get her clear across town whenever her ride didn't pan out was too much trouble for all concerned. As it turned out, I think having Fennie around finally broke something in Mom. A few months after that, I came home and

beheld a different sort of domestic apparition altogether. A tall redheaded woman chain-smoking Pall
Malls was sitting in some ersatz maid outfit grinning
at me through a cloud of smoke. One of my sisters
passed me by and rolled her eyes way back in her
head—the double whammy of disgust and disbelief.
"So I was tellin' yer momma about so-and-so," spake
the new nanny, referring to an oft-wed film star, "and
the reason that gal's been married so many [pro-
nounced 'minnie'] times is that she really likes other
gals, if y'all know what I'm talking about."

Mama had gone out and gotten a white maid. "Miz
Church," as we were asked to call her, lived in the same
projects where we had once lived and was a daily reminder of what would happen if we believed everything we read and didn't floss regularly. She used to
scratch so hard through the fabric of her outfit that her
dirty fingernails left marks on the cloth. She was vulgar without ever uttering a profanity and constantly
speculated on the sexual mores of utter strangers. Her
countenance and demeanor blended together in a hor-
rifying road map of her life. My sisters and I were too
stunned to say much about her, except to ask about the
date of her departure. By then we wanted to have our
home to ourselves, to see whatever was going to happen without witnesses.

School was getting more boring by the day. Every
now and then I would get a teacher who was so excited

about a subject that it made learning a pleasure, but that was rare. I never could figure out why some people taught at all. We had one teacher who would wear a pint of Shalimar, an entire box of blush, and swish her ass all over the room while talking about fractions. I thought, "We're eleven! Who are you trying to impress?"

Until I was in sixth grade, all of my teachers had been women. I'd known about Mr. Carter for years, and he was not only the first man who'd ever taught me, he was also the oldest teacher I'd ever had. He had lost one of his arms in a washing machine, he said, when he was in the sixth grade. I used to wonder why he taught sixth grade, too. Maybe that's when his life stopped being normal and he wanted to remember it. He had quite a temper and used to wave his arm and a half while he yelled, and I would look into the place where it stopped and try to wish it back for him.

School only occasionally forced me into something better than what I read on my own. I did have some teachers who brought me my only connection to sanity, which would have to last until I grew up. They brought me hope and books, but mostly they brought their faith in me that I would not remember until much later.

By the time I got into college and could avail myself of all the quality reading I wanted, I was too long gone with debauchery and fantasy born of alcohol to really care. I could have been writing. I should have been writing. The times I was forced to write excited and challenged me like nothing before or since.

The first time it happened, I was nine and had to write a short story for English class. The teacher's name was Mrs. Sims and she was a serious woman. She asked us to write a story and I had an idea for it right away. The inspiration for it came from reading the short fiction I saw from time to time in women's magazines. All of those stories were short versions of romance novels, with predictable plots and dialogue. This was my first parody, and I wish someone had scooped me up and made me write all the time after that.

I began with the description of a girl named Ivy, who worked at a nondescript job at some office and kept plants around her all the time. Throughout the story I kept mentioning Ivy's red hair, her life at home with a cat, hundreds of plants, and her loneliness. Finally, through a series of meaningless coincidences, a man asked Ivy out. She went on her date. They laughed at dinner and they seemed to be falling in love. The man, looking "deep in Ivy's green eyes," puts his hand on hers and asks the question she knew was unavoidable. "How did you lose your arm?"

I had found a place for Mr. Carter's missing arm! I was so happy writing about it. I deliberately used silly devices to hide the punch line, and turned it in proudly.

Mrs. Lee asked me outside of class if I'd read the story somewhere else. I was shocked. God, I lied all the time, but I wanted her to know how I had come up with it, so I told her about the awful stories that all ended the same in the magazines that I'd read when I went with my grandmother to get her hair done. I could tell she believed me. She was quiet for a long time, then said, "So you think this is funny?" "Yes!" I blurted out. "It is funny! You don't know about Ivy's arm until the very end and you don't expect it!" Mrs. Lee said, "Okay, I believe you."

By the time I was in the fourth grade, I began reading Anne Frank and other writers who were black or Jewish or otherwise screwed because they didn't fit in anywhere, it seemed, in our great country. No matter how far down I felt our family was, I realized that we had emotional baggage and none of it imposed on us because of our color or beliefs.

When I was in elementary school, a Jewish girl named Naomi enrolled in our school. One of the teachers was amazingly condescending toward her. Naomi knew it, too. Perhaps the teacher harbored a genuine desire to make Naomi feel welcome, but her attempts were awkward and shrill. Naomi bore up under the cloying remarks the teacher made about Hanukkah, which she miserably mispronounced. The teacher announced to the class, "Naomi and her family believe in something different than Jesus at Christmas. Hon, do you want to come up here and talk about it?" Naomi made the long walk up to the front of the class and stood right next to the sparkling Christmas tree.

She started to talk, her little voice trembling, as she described what she knew about her own—in the words of the teacher—"very special holiday." Just watching her from my desk, I wanted to die. It was embarrassing enough to be shy and have to speak extemporaneously, but she was being forced to carry the weight of an entire creed upon her shoulders. The teacher gave her a big hug before she went back to her seat. I tried to catch her eye during and after her speech, but she just sat back down and didn't face any of us for the rest of the day.

When I was in the sixth grade, I made a project for the social studies fair. I drew a poster of tiny college students holding protest signs and being stepped on by a giant Uncle Sam. The students were holding up signs that said BERKELEY and COLUMBIA. Next to the demonstrators, I made a chart of casualty statistics of soldiers who had fought in Vietnam. I guess I was so imbued with watching continuous televised coverage of the war that it had to come out somewhere. But I won a third-place ribbon in the state fair.

When I was in seventh grade, a couple of my teachers did something wonderful for me that I'll never forget. There was a federally funded program called Bridges designed to promote racial cooperation in the schools. (Try to imagine such a thing today.) Dennis Folsom and Anne Ruffin, who were married to one another, asked me to participate in the program. I was thrilled. At thirteen, I was chubby and not brilliant. Because the Folsoms thought of me for this program, the sting of not being pretty or popular was not as intense. Entering the program felt like a huge responsibility as well as an honor.

Despite my excitement, at my first workshop I realized the irony of my situation. I was chosen to be a leader for better racial relations in my school. My school only had two black students out of a student body of nearly a thousand. What was I supposed to do about that? Like my mother said when I told her of my plight, "Well, honey, it's the thought that counts." I still had fun while I was there, though. And the kids who were part of the program were paid a stipend just for participating. Apart from occasional baby-sitting, I think this was my first paid gig. Of course, an additional benefit was helping to change the world, although I can't quite remember how I did it.

Politics in Georgia and Alabama were interesting and infuriating. The racist antics of Lester Maddox and George Wallace might have made the South a laughingstock but created a base of popularity for segregationists. Nearly every elected official was a Democrat, owing to the fact that Abraham Lincoln had been a Republican and we'd lost the Civil War. Really.

This warped sense of fealty kept Democrats in power, no matter how crazy they were. It didn't change until Nixon and Reagan made the Republican party appealing to the lower and middle classes.

I learned to be a lefty at my mother's knee. Nothing my Republican stepfather said or did changed me from siding with her. He called her a "bleeding heart," and I was proud that he was right. I watched Mom cry during the carnage of Vietnam and when Martin Luther King, Jr., and RFK were shot. She would also clench her teeth at the slightest negative variation of the word "Negro," glaring at the speaker before she'd walk away. One day, in a grocery store, my mother heard a young black boy call a friend of his "nigger." My mother said to him, "Honey, I would spank one of my children for saying that. Please be careful about using that word. It means more than you think." The little kid looked at me like my mama was crazy, and I just shrugged, trying to see if anyone else had heard her.

Similarly, when I was twelve I called a girl down the street a slut, in an offhand way. My mother jumped all over me. I was startled. I thought she only reacted that way about race or creed. I couldn't understand it. Thinking it would abet my cause, I mentioned, truthfully, that the girl had also spoken the horrid *N* word, and I was surprised at my mother's answer: "That child is still young. She hears that sort of talk at home. If she lives around ignorant, mean people, it's going to be hard for her to be different. But you know better. You might try walking a mile in someone else's shoes, young lady, before throwing around judgment." I then confessed that the girl in question had hit me. To my amazement, she said, "Is she bigger than you?" I said no, and my dear, sweet, fair mother said, "Well, then let her have it." There's no one like our mother.

There was a lighter side to my awakening, too. When shows like *Laugh-In* and *The Smothers Brothers* appeared on the scene, it was almost a religious experience in our household. My mother, sisters, and I just about lived for the dark comedy on those shows. We discovered that resistance could be creative, not necessarily forbidden. Suddenly, it was as if our beliefs—or lack thereof—could be a tiny vindication for being bohemian broads in a fatherless, liberal home.

But I could go next door and see young Republicans being born the same way. My friends' parents had different takes on the Watts riots, Vietnam, etc. Once when I went to dinner at my girlfriend's wearing a peace sign, her father asked me to take it off. I asked why and he told me that it was the symbol of Satan, the broken cross or something like that. I was embarrassed and politely told him that it only meant that I was for peace in Vietnam. My friend and her mother just looked down at their plates while this was happening.

He said that if I didn't take it off, I'd have to leave their house. The next thing I remember was walking home after dark and wondering why I wasn't like other people. But thanks to my mother, I didn't really want to be.

My parents' wedding day
Feb. '57, Atlanta

7.

When I was still in elementary school, they built a fancy new subdivision near our house and called it Indian Hills. They had their own country club, exclusive to the residents, and everyone there had to get approval before even choosing exterior paint color for their homes. We spoke of the place with awe. Before Indian Hills, our only identifying geographical markers were where one street ended and another began. The overt delineation of class lines had never been drawn before, so close to home, and no one really knew how they felt about it. Before, when some streets were nice and some not, we pretended that we didn't care. The locals would sometimes say that only "Yankees" lived there, strangers from far away, and that "they" had the money and their kids had the swell clothes. It was only the beginning. Imitation developments, subdivisions "lite," sprang up, too, with other unlikely names. My mother said only that the "finest residential communities" were the ones that cut down the most trees.

By the time I turned fourteen, I was gravitating toward richer friends for reasons that had less to do with class warfare than permissiveness. It was just that the kids from Indian Hills had the best pot, the best parties, and the most indulgent parents. Sometimes the parents would be in the house during the party, and they knew damn well that pot was floating around. One of the smartest girls I ever met lived there. Her name was Elaine and she'd made an almost perfect score on her SAT. She dressed like something from Haight-Ashbury and showed no remorse over her sexual escapades. I idolized her. She managed to take stronger drugs than I ever wanted to—right there in school—and she could converse with the teachers and function normally in altered states or not. At the time I was still scared of getting high and would do it only on weekends for fear of losing control. Even when pot was already a part of my escapist regime, I shunned hallucinogens. I took them perhaps five times in my life, from the ages of fifteen to twenty-one and, except for an hour or so on mushrooms, I hated them.

I didn't get stoned on pot until I'd been smoking it for a while, and then only socially. A boyfriend I had would give me some to keep. "Here," he'd say, smiling, as if to make up for not seeing me for a week or so, "take this with you. Enjoy." So I would take it home, savoring the mystery of it, the hipness, but I really didn't get it at all. I'd go in the bathroom, stand on the toilet, and blow the smoke up the exhaust fan. My sister Tana would come in and talk to me, kidding me about acting different after I'd smoked it, even though I felt no effects from it. I'm one of the only people I know who believed President Clinton when he said he didn't inhale. I didn't know how. I'd watch everyone else getting red eyes, leaning farther back in their chairs, and I would try to mimic them. I thought I was immune to pot. It didn't occur to me that I wasn't doing something wrong . . . wrong. Then one night, an older pal who knew that I hadn't been getting high was with me as we sat up and watched the moon over the Chattahoochee River. After passing the joint back and forth for a few minutes, I cried, "The van's moving down the hill!" I scrambled to safety and he started laughing. "You just got stoned for the first time." I liked it, but God, I wish I hadn't done it again. It would be another seventeen years—three years more than I was old at the time—before I stopped.

Other than that, the only thing I liked was boys. They fascinated me. There were none in our house, and I was able to obsess on them for intervals that were not healthy by any standard. The advent of males in my life was sweeping and urgent. One boy lived right down the street and got the first kisses from nearly every girl on the street. He was a year or two older and we ran through him, or he through us, like a lit match in a dry Christmas tree.

The yearning for whatever was going to happen, the unknown, was immense and pointed and would not end for years and years. I wish I could bottle that feeling and give it a name, but I think it's a relative of what made me a drunk, what made me think wherever I was for so long was always the wrong place. It was what made me dash out to buy mascara, and fall in love with older men on TV, and have a woman's heart in a child's breast. It was what made me try too hard to rhyme in my diary (even then I thought I had an audience). It meant so much to me that someone see and understand who I was. Whatever that feeling was like, it was with me all the time and, except for having too much of it, it's the greatest feeling in the world while it lasts.

I hate to think how early I would have chased boys if we'd had dances in elementary school. I was so excited about going to my first sockhop that I was almost sick. We assembled in the darkened cafeteria of East

Cobb Junior High and the air reeked of thirty-five-cent lunches, Stridex, and Windsong cologne. I suppose young women do not have to be Southern to think dances are life-changing events, but it sure helps. Any of us who had seen *Gone With the Wind* before our political awakenings—which was all of us—knew that we did not want the barbecue at the Wilkeses' to end the way it did, with a bunch of silly men riding up on their fresh horses to cheer, "We're at war!" We knew we'd lose, and not just because we'd seen the movie. We lived with the images of Vietnam every night on the news until it became numbing, but not as numbing as the excuses for why it wouldn't stop. Our dresses ran the gamut between Grace Slick's maids-in-waiting and Scarlett O'Hara's festive virgin wear. We loved the boys and thought that they needed to be rescued from their violence, beer, and cries for the thighs of girls who liked to do it not for love. It was sad to see the parodies of antebellum skirts beneath the teased hair of the redneck girls, especially amid the contemporary fashions of the rich ones.

Passion marks appeared on the necks of all the kids, but mostly the lower classes and the females, at that. From time to time, a cheerleader or some other good girl with a fine reputation would stumble and get one, too. Instead of being like the rest of us, she metamorphosed into a prematurely married young matron just because her daddy saw vampire marks on her throat.

It was safer to the father to end a wild young love with a cheap fast wedding than to send his trampled beauty forth used in any form. When we were young, we envied such unimpeded infatuation. We were jealous of the premature weddings, thinking that a marriage license gave them all the sex they wanted. We did not know that without rules, without boundaries, such love often died with a puzzled expression on its face.

At the school dances, bands with weird names played loudly. The cafeteria was dark and my incomplete lust burst from the seams of my homemade dress. I pretended not to watch the kissing couples, but couldn't help myself from staring. What they did to each other I did, too, in the cave of my own emotions. The same people did not matter to me in the light, walking down the halls to class, in the daylight of our boring lives. But when they clutched in the glow of black lights, they illustrated what it might be like to be wanted. Boys were mythical lights that sparkled across the waters of loneliness. Boys were the promised land.

When I was in the ninth grade, I asked a terribly handsome boy in the seventh grade to a dance. Our neighbor Carole Williford helped me sew the dress I wore. At the dance I looked deeply into that boy's eyes, loaned him a mind, and sent him thoughts that he did not possess because I had imagination enough for us both. I could not want someone empty, and it was easier for me to create someone who was full. I leaned in to kiss his perfect and surprised mouth, for I was not how he thought nice girls would be, should be. He was confused. I was a girl who made good grades, who never talked in class, and I threw myself upon him like the neck-sucking girls who got into fights at skating rinks.

The first time I went "steady" was accidental, unlike so many of the mini-marriages at school. I was in homeroom and the guy was swinging around his ID bracelet and I asked, "What's that?" He said, "My ID bracelet. Wanna wear it?" It was that eventful and proved to discourage a formality with me I would have done well to feign as the years passed.

ॐ

My mother got a job with *The Atlanta Journal,* first delivering papers and then as a circulation district manager. The same year, when I was thirteen, I got my first job at the Dairy Queen. The white uniform I had to wear never seemed to wash clean. A hairnet and paper hat covered my only attribute, which was my hair halfway down my back. I looked like a polyester cotton ball with large thighs.

My boss used to get mad at me for taking liberties with the little curly thing on top of the ice creams. You were supposed to twist it a certain way when it came out of the machine, but that bored me so I started to twist it my own way. He'd say, "When people order from here, they want [pronounced 'won't'] their cones like this!" He would then demonstrate the correct way and send me off to clean the fry vat. Thus began my association with fine restaurants.

Then, thankfully, when I was fourteen, I got a job at the same newspaper as my mother. My position was called "circulation draw clerk." I was the one who took the calls from the downtown office when people didn't get their papers. I routed the nondeliveries and referred other errors to the carriers. It wasn't a sophisticated job, by any means, but it broadened my world to the point where school began to feel like day care. This was my first real job and I worked seven days a week. I was no longer the baby-sitter or the fry cook, and I fairly tingled to meet men who liked me and thought I was funny. Until then, I hadn't known that a man existed who didn't prize cheerleaders above God Almighty. I loved going to work just to see who I could meet.

After I'd worked at the paper for a whole month I met "My First." He was eighteen and played guitar, even writing his own songs. He wrote one called "Horny Bullfighter." I thought he was brilliant. He also turned me on to John McLaughlin and jazz. I started writing poems for him, and he would try to set them to music. Although I was five months short of being fifteen, and could not think of one wise woman who had given herself at such a young age, I wasn't long for the world of chastity.

My grandfather used to say, "Never do anything you wouldn't want to see on the front page of a newspaper." Well, how the hell was I supposed to know I was going to be famous? He also used to say, "When in doubt, don't," which fell, once again, on deaf ears. I don't remember my first home run or first drunk or first anything as well or as vividly as the permanent surrender of that one thing that is valued above all else in a Southern woman. It was also the first time I experienced massive regret. Because it was boys who turned into men, beer that turned into tequila, and pot into speed ... and then they all turned on me. It was too late for Jesus and too soon for rehab, so I turned inward and waited for life to catch up.

Apart from tender young loves, which sometimes work out, I believe that it is impossible to have sex as young as I did and realize the loss you are incurring, especially at the moment you are doing it. Then you go out and start trying to get it right or find religion, which is what happened to a dear friend of mine when she fell into the abyss of her own sexuality. Her first choice in men had been so upsetting and the encounter so awkward, that she bounced in the completely opposite direction, adhering to her Savior, and eschewing all secular boys no matter how splendid they were. "Catting around," the lovely phrase given such activity by those too pure to indulge, gave me some time out from pain and boredom, but it also gave me much to repent.

The diligence I showed toward men and contraband was impressive when compared to my attendance at school or any other discipline. For some time I smoked pot and didn't get stoned, and had sex without orgasms. However, I don't think the deep breathing that accompanied either activity hurt me, and I continued both until my brain and body finally cried, "Eureka." But boys at school weren't on my menu. They didn't like me, either. Maybe a couple of them did, but I preferred older men who didn't run away when they read my poems and who at least pretended to enjoy talks about books and life.

From the seventh grade on they showed us films at school that warned us about the dangers of drugs. Those films helped me because without them I might have used needles. "Shooting up" so frightened me, with its perils of inevitable addiction, that I never touched a needle or any kind of "works." Once, attending a party when I was seventeen, my date suddenly started heating a spoon to shoot cocaine. I thought snorting, the way I took it, relatively innocuous. But seeing him with that flame beneath a spoon caused me to panic. I was too high on pot and liquor to leave, so I waited until one of those sunrises appeared that happen after a night of failed escapes. Then I got in my car and went home, feeling sick all the way.

ॐ

Most Southerners tend to look askance at the jokes that we all marry when we are fourteen and, when we do, we usually pick our cousins. Thanks to the advent of state-of-the-art interstate highways and a belated eagerness to dispel such mythology, most of us now wait to wed and then choose virtual strangers from surrounding counties. I have no doubt that I would have been married off or sent packing as incorrigible at that age in any other period in history: when I was fourteen, I looked twenty and had my eye on men who were either thirty or so damned handsome that they functioned as time-release headaches.

Much is made of the lasciviousness of people who live east of Dallas and south of Washington, D.C. I suppose the farther down you go geographically, the farther down go the ages and panties of consenting females. I know Southerners who don't care much for sex, per se, but if you watch them at a stock-car race or when a chamber orchestra plays on a Sunday afternoon, you can see ecstasy on their faces. Fiery grips of lust jump up in odd places, and those who have watched people lick their fingers after eating ribs or suck the peanuts out of a Coke bottle know bliss lives in the South. . . .

I blame the weather, too. Heat lends itself to scantiness of speech, fabric, and motion. Glowing skin on even the most powdery ladies creates a cosmic upset. And when it's not hot, you're waiting for it to get that way again. Winters in the South always seem temporary. . . . But I was trying to talk about sex. It is difficult to mention that without reference to profanity. I read a book once that tried to suggest that the South specialized in promiscuity, profanity, and indolence because of the heavy influx of Celts in its early history. I just think it's sweltering and the rivers move slower, and there are shorter jeans and soft, curving hills with surprises on the other side, and I am glad I had my coming of age before there was a sixteen-lane highway running right through the middle of my hometown like there is now.

The summer I was fourteen conspired against morality in several ways, from the sweltering weather to the fact that I had a job and money and met boys in abundance. The songs on the radio were very good that summer, my diary entries were becoming repetitive, and right around the beginning of my sophomore year I threw my virginity out of the speeding car that was my life.

My maternal grandmother,
Jewel Elizabeth, AKA Memaw,
checking out her first
granddaughter's dimples—
my best inheritance.

Marietta, '58

A STONE, A LEAF, AN UNFOUND DOOR.

—Thomas Wolfe

8.

I turned sixteen and hoped the "sweet" part would hit soon. I lazed away the summer when I wasn't at work, a stoned audience to the dissolution of our home. One day my mother came into my room wearing the same expression she had the day she had left my father. Even though I had not seen that look in a dozen years, or maybe because of it, I paid attention. "We are going to Alabama to get some of the money in the trust fund," she said sternly. "I'm sick and tired of never getting a dime from your father, and we can at least ask if any of that money is available."

I did not ask why it was so important all of a sudden. I'd known about the trust fund all of my life. Big Dad, Julia's father, had set it up, and the amount of money in it varied wildly according to the source of the information. All we knew was that he left the money to his great-grandchildren, providing enough to sustain his daughter through her life. Right before he died, Big Dad was already on to my father, doubting that he was capable of not abusing funds he did not earn. Years before there had been talk of trying to get something from the fund when it became apparent that child support would not be forthcoming, but that boiled down to nothing. I don't know how or if we would have managed without my Granddaddy and Memaw.

I'd never allowed myself to think about the money very often or for very long. It seemed like something my father would have done. I felt bad that I'd skipped a grade, showed subsequent academic promise, and was now getting into college earlier than any of us bargained for. Every now and then Julia would say something about the fund in one of her greeting cards, saying that it was "such a pity" that she could not get into the account and "buy us pretty things." That seemed to be her obsession, by the way. Whenever she sent her annual five-dollar birthday check, she would write, "Buy yourself something pretty with this." I usually bought birth-control pills—to prevent something pretty from happening.

So my mother and I got in the car and went to see about getting some money for college. I did not realize until years later that this trip would be our undoing—mine and my mother's. Not our relationship, but as individuals. It took a long time to recover from that day and figure out what happened to each of us when we went back to Alabama.

Our first stop was at the bank in Montgomery where the loan officers worked. Smug men wearing dark suits grinned uneasily at us. They seemed innoculated against sweat—their own and especially that of other people—and they told us that there was nothing they could do, that the trust fund was "airtight." I took this to mean that the combined forces of me and my mother could not overwhelm the strength of mere oxygen. When we left their paneled enclave, I worried that if I ever did go to college I would turn out like them. We decided to drive on and see Julia on the off chance that she had something hoarded away with which to help.

It was strange to be back in Tuskegee. I had not seen it for so many years and it was perfect to be there in the hottest part of the summer. I remember knowing where each turn was right before my mother would make it. When we finally arrived on Maple Street, baby memories began to wake up as if after a long nap. The houses all reminded me of the street where Atticus Finch lived in *To Kill a Mockingbird*—prosaic on the outside, oozing with sadness and boredom from within.

When we pulled into the driveway, Mom sat and waited for a minute with her eyes closed. Then we walked up to the front porch and knocked on the door. We could see Julia's car parked in the garage on the side of the house and knew that she was home. We waited and then my mother began to knock more loudly. It was really hot, although we were in the shade, and I was a little surprised to see my mother so worked up. You'd have to know my mother to realize how long it takes her to get really mad. Now that I think about it, her rage did not come from being left outside on a hot Southern day. It had been simmering for years.

Her knocks turned into pounding and her voice became furious. Then my often sweet-to-the-point-of-weak mother actually yelled. "Come out here, god-dammit, Julia! I know you're in there!" I was embarrassed. Neighbors had started to peek out of lace curtains and a few of the bold ones had even stepped out on their porches to see what was the matter. I wanted a beer, a joint, anything to make the moment pass. I asked my mother to cool it. I was afraid Julia would have a heart attack or something and thought that was too high a price to pay even for college tuition. After almost a half hour, and after my mother had gone around the entire house banging on the windows, Julia finally came to the door.

It was an awkward reunion, to say the least. Julia pretended she hadn't heard us because she had been listening to some ballgame on the radio. Only in Dixie can such brazen bullshit be bandied about in between sugar-coated hellos and invitations to sit down. We went into the parlor, the same one where my father had arrived forty years earlier in an ether cloud. Even if I had not remembered some of the furniture, anyone could have seen that Hoover was president or perhaps Roosevelt was in his first term when the newest piece of anything was bought. So there we were, three generations of Southern women doing what we did best: ignoring an incontinent elephant in the middle of the living room. But Julia, despite our tense arrival, seemed glad to see me. We passed pleasantries in the hot, dark house until my mother, who had regained her composure quite heroically, I thought, started to get to the subject of the trust fund.

I began to squirm when Mother mentioned my upcoming stab at college. She told Julia I made good grades, but not good enough for a scholarship, etc. (I hardly expected one. Hell, on a good week, I might have hit class three times. What did my mother think? That I took field trips the rest of the week?)

I told Julia that I was thirsty and started toward the

kitchen. She became disturbed and said that she would get me something to drink. This was unheard of, even in a family as screwed up as ours was. I was the youngest person there and, as such, I would fetch beverages for my elders. She fairly trembled as I went to the back of the house. I stood over the huge porcelain sink guzzling glasses of water, postponing my return to the room with the honey-dripping warrior women. I took a paper towel from the roll to wipe my sweaty face. As I tossed it into the trash, I saw something shiny in the bottom of the bin. Since that day I have wondered how not doing that one small thing would have made a difference to my life.

I moved some papers and saw some empty beer cans and a subscription card to *Penthouse* underneath. My head reeled. I realized that my father was in the house with his mother and that, for all intents and purposes, she had been hiding him all these years.

I affected calmness as I brought the ladies drinks. Then I asked Julia if I could look at the rest of the house. She started to sputter some more and said, "Sugah, ah had it closed off a long time ago. Since ah'm just heah by myself, ah don't need all that floor to clean." She laughed tensely. At that moment, I'm sorry to say, I reconsidered how I felt about her having a heart attack. I ignored her statement with a cool smile and left them to talk. My mother kept her there as I walked toward the back of the house, sometimes remembering and sometimes not what used to be behind some of the doors. It's not like the place was huge, but it did have turns and twists that they don't build into houses anymore. There were three doors facing the hallway from one side. I stopped in front of one of them. Even now I am not sure of the exact sound I heard. It could have been a little cough, a movement, a squeak. It was very small and I am surprised I heard it past my beating heart. I knew my father was in that room on the other side of the door.

"Daddy?" the word sounded so peculiar coming out of my mouth. I'd called my stepfather that, even though I'd suspected the impermanence of our relationship. To actually say and mean the word "Daddy" after more than ten years was tormenting. I cannot begin to imagine how he must have felt hearing it.

I started talking to the door. Within seconds I knew that he would not come out, but I had to tell him about myself. I could almost see myself outside my own body, confiding my dreams to a wooden door. I already had a taste for the dramatic, and the vision of me speaking to a father who had been gone for so long and getting nothing in response was almost too much to bear. I finally started to cry, saying some very unoriginal things like, "I can't believe you won't come out and see me. I am your oldest daughter. I'm almost all grown up now. Don't you ever want to see me?"

I heard my mother and Julia approach. Mom was

saying, "Come on, honey. Let's get out of here." I told her, "He's in there! And he won't come out." Then we left. We just left. We said goodbye and keep in touch and all that custom-in-the-face-of-calamity crap that characterizes mentally ill societies the world over. I have cursed myself a thousand times for just walking away. My mother says she feels the same. But it is too late for blame.

I felt drunk. I would get drunk. I watched the house get smaller as my mother drove down the street. For the first time in my life, I wished I could drive. The next thing I remember is being at the sheriff's office. Mother was saying something about getting some information there. I didn't see how, but was in no shape to resist. I'd had enough of men who hid behind things—whether it was doors or bank vaults or fifty-year-old wills.

I do not remember the sheriff's name, but he looked like Jim Brown. He was the color of strong coffee, and his khaki uniform seemed like it had been sewn and ironed while on his body. He looked tight and crisp. He seemed to borrow characteristics of all Southern sheriffs: He wore sunglasses and spoke in a sedate monotone. He seemed to like his job, and the degrees covering the walls of the office indicated that he was perhaps a bit overqualified for it.

My mother came to the point. She told him who we were and asked him what he could tell us about Roland

Decatur Anderson, Jr. I almost laughed when he said, "We have reason to believe that he resides with his mother at . . ." and then he stated my grandmother's address. I know that Tuskegee is a small town, but he knew the place without having to look it up. I said, "So do we." I watched him trying to figure us out, too. Here he was, a black man in the Deep South, sitting in his office with two white women who were treating him like a sheriff. I appreciated that my mother never stooped to that obnoxious noblesse oblige or semihysterical condescension prevalent among whites who wanted to appear unprejudiced. She neither laughed maniacally at his jests nor called him sir an unnecessary number of times. I listened as my mother filled in the blanks about Andy. As we cooled off in his office, my unspent tears faded away.

When she was finished, the sheriff said, "That's a pretty weird story, ladies." Mom and I looked at each other. She had only told him bare facts, leaving anything that could be construed as strange out of the information. We wanted to know what he knew. He began to tell us. I'm not sure if the actual noises outside grew smaller or what he said was that much of a shock. All I knew was that, after he was through, the three of us were more intrigued with the man we had in common.

He said, "A few years ago, we had a stabbing in that neighborhood. It was mostly white back then. White man was the victim. Didn't look good for the town. Most of us get along pretty good these days. This kind of thing makes people uptight. Anyway, I started to hear rumors about your daddy." He was looking right at me, perhaps gauging my maturity. I pretended to be tough, to let him know that I could take whatever he was going to say. I wanted to tell him that nothing he could say was worse than I had thought about in the years since I'd last seen my father.

He continued. "It turns out that a few people were afraid of your daddy. I heard the stories about how he lived there with his mama and only went out at night and drove to places in her car. They said that Mrs. Anderson keeps the curtains drawn and never entertains. When she leaves to go to her ladies' group, she always goes to someone else's house. They never meet at hers. When a repairman comes, she always stands right beside him until he fixes what he came to fix and then shows him out the door when it's time to go. They say she looks out the curtains to make sure he's gone.

"As a matter of fact, I already got a couple of calls today from people to tell me that y'all went by the house. News travels fast. They wondered if you knew he was probably there.

"Now, I am not telling you I think your daddy killed that man. I'm sure he didn't. The strange thing was that almost everyone I talked to seemed glad for the chance just to tell somebody about him. But gossip happens, and even in a town where everybody knows everybody else's business, your daddy's something else. I went by there once, but your grandmother wasn't in. I didn't go by again because I didn't want to bother her and, like I said, your daddy's not a suspect. But it's odd, no matter which way you look at it."

It was odd and I had looked at it from every angle, but it was less upsetting than I thought it would be. And at least it was interesting. If you're going to have disappointments in life, it's better to hope for mildly entertaining ones.

Then the three of us were quiet. The street noises filtered back in. I thought of *To Kill a Mockingbird* again. I couldn't help but think of my father as the Tuskegee equivalent of Boo Radley. Whatever naïve hope I had of my father turning out to be someone like Atticus was ashes by then. I think it hurt my mother to see me at that moment. She looked at me almost apologetically for having married him—a crazy man, both remorseless and absent. Hell, I was just glad the sheriff didn't tell us he thought my father was a murderer. Finally, my mother got up and we said our thank-yous. Before we left, I remembered to ask him one more thing. "Did you ever find out who killed that man?" I could see myself in his sunglasses as he shook his head no.

Mom and I went to a motel in Auburn for the night. The rest of the trip is a convenient fog to me. I remember sneaking down to the hotel bar, getting really drunk, and going to the rodeo with a man I met there, a man I was sure my snobby father would have hated, and then going back to his room and riding away the only way I knew how. I fucked him darkly and forever just to drown the images of that afternoon in the deep sea of forgetting where I would live for the next ten years.

Jana and me...
a long time ago.
Montgomery, '59

Apparently I believed Jana's
glee was contained in her
precious little paws.

9.

About a week after we got home from Tuskegee, I received a letter from Julia. She said that if I wanted to
write to my father I could do it in her care. She instructed me to address it to her, but for me to write an
"A" in the upper-left corner of the envelope so that she
would know to forward it to him. I showed the letter
to my mother and we agreed that Andy was probably
behind the request. I was just glad that he wanted to
hear from me.

I wrote to my father. I tried to let him know as

much about me as I could, sparing us both the intimate details. I didn't ask the questions that were screaming to be answered, either. I wanted to choose my words carefully. He wrote me back. His letter was filled with his rambling thoughts on art, politics, books, and a particularly vicious diatribe on the state of popular American music. I was offended. It seemed like he went out of his way to denounce the things a teenage girl would be interested in.

My next letter wasn't as obliging. I asked him where in the hell he'd been all that time, and told him that the business of Julia forwarding his letters wasn't fooling me. I said, "I know you are hiding in that house." Surprisingly, he wrote back. But I didn't want to hear his excuses. He mentioned something about the statute of limitations and said that he "couldn't help what had happened." Except for the mysterious reference to the law, it was an echo of Julia's letters over the years. But then I realized that was as close to an apology as I could expect. I wrote to him a few more times and then stopped. Almost a year later, during a move, a box of my personal letters was stolen. At the time, I was sorry for the love letters and poems that were missing, and the crazy things my father had written were the things I missed the least.

A couple of months after our visit, around the time of my last letter to Andy, I came home to a telephone call. It was a nurse from the local hospital. She said,

"Your mother has admitted herself for depression." I thought, How odd. We have so much of it at home, why would she send out for it? That was the beginning of our family's final mutation. We were closing up, as if for a long winter that we sensed and did not speak of. We were bundling up, shutting down, falling slowly.

That was the first of my mother's intermittent stays at hospitals—one state-run—for depression. Although it was still summer, I felt like the boy in the Aiken story who saw the snow falling and falling until it surrounded him in a concussion of silence. My life started to become a slow-motion secret, too. It was all any of us could do to land in the softest places, and wish the same for the ones after us. My sisters were farmed out to relatives, and I was left on my own. It wasn't that no one wanted me. I insisted that I would be all right on my own. When a family is falling apart, the impulse is to save the weak and the young and perhaps not the one swearing self-sufficiency. I hoped the screams of incorrigibility weren't coming from anyone I'd disappoint too greatly in days ahead.

When my mother became ill, school was the last thing on my mind. Actually, school was the last thing on my mind when I was there, but now I had an excuse. I just knew that my reward for suffering through it was not having to go to school in the fall. At sixteen, I had the right to stop going, so I did. If it hadn't been for a friend of mine down the street, I don't know how I would have made it out of there. I met her while I was baby-sitting. She had two little boys and was married to a minister who was also very supportive of me in those crazy years. My friend had things I'd never seen before—*Whole Earth Catalogs,* eucalyptus, and Leonard Cohen and Josh White albums. Listening to Taj Mahal, we talked about philosophy and history, and I got older and smarter just being around her. Then her husband divorced her and she was alone with her children.

Although she was fifteen years older than I was, we became best friends. She had no regard for judgment or salvation in conventional terms. When she fell in love again, with the man who is now her husband, she still found time for me. She's the closest thing to a big sister I ever had and was my first best friend in adulthood. When my family broke up, she let me stay with her until I found a place to live. She gave support without pity, friendship without condescension, and she had faith in me. I met people through her, directly or indirectly, who would change my life. And although we are now far apart, I still remember something she wrote in a book she once gave me when things were very hard: "My wish for you is that you never cease the search for peace within yourself."

After the drive from Alabama.
Jana won the coin-toss
for Mama's lap.

Marietta, Summer, '61?

SHE COMMENCED DRINKING ALONE,
LITTLE, SHORT DRINKS ALL THROUGH
THE DAY. . . . ALONE, IT BLURRED
SHARP THINGS FOR HER. SHE LIVED IN
A HAZE OF IT. HER LIFE TOOK ON A
DREAM-LIKE QUALITY. NOTHING WAS
ASTONISHING.

—*Dorothy Parker*

10.

My life at sixteen was strange and drunk. My new
roommate was a twenty-three-year-old girl who
seemed to live on cola, potato chips, and cigarettes.
Since I wasn't yet smoking cigarettes, and had orange
juice every morning or with my vodka at night, I imagined I was healthier than she. I also read more difficult books than she did, ones devoid of romantic
themes, and, since I wrote every day, I believed that I
was making some kind of headway. The two of us
lived as if we'd been freed from the most pedestrian of

parental rules: things like eating our vegetables, going to bed at a decent hour, and not running with scissors. Although I'd always been careful with sharp objects, I started having blackouts and began waking up with veritable strangers.

That's when I started to use a kind of code in my diary. I thought that if anything happened to me, I wanted to thank people for loving me, but I didn't want them to know about the rest of my life. When my best friend moved to Macon, I began going there to see her, and I met a man. He was more than ten years older than I and wilder by far. But he was nice. We ended up doing very little besides going from one bar or party to another to drink, dance, and smoke pot. He was married, rode a Harley, and listened to Marshall Tucker and the Allman Brothers. He also liked little pink barbiturates, which knocked him out. I could never understand how unconsciousness was anyone's preferred high.

Mom was still in the hospital, and my sisters were living with relatives in and out of town. I missed them and, although we tried to see each other as much as possible, we all knew our family was never going to be the same. I felt bad especially for my two sisters who were Andy's children, like me. Although they weren't much younger than I, they had begun to think of our stepfather as their dad. After he left and only paid attention to his "real" children, it left scars inside of

Tana and Toren. His new wife even asked us not to call him Daddy anymore. I wanted to be strong for them, but it was impossible. I was weaker than any of us and hated myself for it.

I got another job at a fast-food joint, this time at a mall near Atlanta. The menial, boring work involved the preparation of chicken carcasses for their new roles as sandwiches. Sometimes I got to make twenty gallons of coleslaw at a time. I spent every day from nine to five in a place with no windows, only fluorescent lights, and I was making minimum wage. My life was in suspended animation. No one could reach me, and no one tried. But I was hanging out with people who did not lose sleep pondering their lack of accomplishment, so I was hidden well.

I am lucky that the men I knew before my first marriage were nice. Some women/girls I knew weren't so lucky. Most of the men were easygoing and fun, not in a hurry to find out what they wanted to do in life. In spite of my recklessness, I was riding on some rather large ambition, so I was surprised that I sought the aimless sort. Every now and then I would fall in with a comparatively well-adjusted fellow who'd say things like, "Boy, you really drank a lot last night!" But they never complained about the wanton side effects.

One night I even scared myself. I was at a nightclub down in Macon. Although I was only sixteen at the time, I was able to get in without being carded. The club was a Georgia version of Gilley's, and all the good Southern rock bands would showcase there. We sat down with our drinks—mine was a Cuba Libre, which was only a Coke with rum and lime, but I thought it quite exotic—and someone at the table said, "Hey, you wanna do a hit of acid?" I only thought about it for a second before I said yes. I knew that pot and booze were all we had and was getting bored with their effects. Getting high used to be like opening a safe. I was already starting to forget the combination.

When the acid hit, I wasn't ready for any of it. I asked someone to take me home. Everyone thought it was funny. "It's her first time," they said, smiling to one another. I went into the bathroom to talk to God and make some sort of deal. This would be different, I sensed, than the deals I used to make in the middle of throwing up during a drinking spree.

I've heard about "guided trips" during the consumption of psychedelic drugs, when someone is there to "lead" the tripper through the intense journey. I was largely unescorted that night. About the most holistic thing that anyone brought me was a drink. The first side effect was unexpected and surreal, and I attributed it to my recent intake of bad literature. I started to remember the entire film script for *Gone With the Wind*. There is a place in the brain that does not want this to be possible and I found that place and bribed it with wine. But it did not stop. At the same moment, I was faced with my mind's potential and the fact that it was empty. It's one thing to abruptly realize things that Scarlett O'Hara could have said or done differently, and quite another to become Medea in the middle of acting that out. I thought of the drug films I'd seen at school, the ones I laughed at, and cursed myself for breaking one of the few promises I meant to keep.

Before long, I found speed, too. I started with prescription amphetamines that I got from a friend, but I mostly ended up with the rotten little trucker pills that were just like having twenty cups of coffee at once. They called them "white crosses," because they had little white crosses etched on the front of them. I don't think they were pharmaceutically manufactured at all—just cooked up in someone's basement and appliquéd with something that looked medical. The "black beauties" I sometimes got were often the same, but running into the real version left little doubt of their purpose. I liked cocaine, but it was rare, expensive, and not as powerful as snorting Methedrine. Being on Methedrine—and I "only" snorted it—is like putting a high-performance jet engine inside a hedge clipper. You become extremely powerful and completely senseless. Crystal meth highs were the worst ones, and that includes drinking straight gin on a hot day with the spiritually disadvantaged.

The time it took to get drugs, hide them, and

arrange my life so that I could take them and not be responsible for the duration of the high was phenomenal. I could drink longer when I took things and never had drugs around without booze. Drinking always took the edge off speed and provided anesthesia against the interior bruising that happened when I went fast for long periods of time. For me, the main difference between drinking and drugs is that I can actually come close to guessing the number of times I took speed and coke. I missed out completely on needles, heroin, crack, free-basing, and Ecstasy. But I have no idea how often I got drunk. If I guess that I had at least three drinks a day from the age of sixteen to twenty-six, when I had my last one, that's almost eleven thousand drinks. When I surmise that I was very drunk over half of those days, I can't believe I have enough brain cells left to perform simple addition.

(I rarely enjoy anyone's account of chemical and alcohol abuse. I certainly don't relish remembering my own. Blaming nurture or nature doesn't make a difference. I was born to patterns of excess. Hell, I almost named this book *Patterns of Excess*. I'm just glad that I lived long enough to see these patterns surface in different ways, like art, work, correspondence, whatever. Only now I can accomplish things from these excesses—at least, most of them. I still smoke cigarettes and drink coffee, and the only reason I exercise at all is that I feel like hell if I don't. But I hate it. I have actually meditated and lit up a cigarette fifteen minutes later. Maybe my death wish isn't as pronounced, but it's still here in its own way.)

When my mother was released from the monthlong stay in the hospital, she and I got our own apartment. She said she felt better, but I saw no signs of it. If anything, with her children scattered about and our house now being rented to another family, she seemed worse. She was seeing a psychiatrist who was later politely discouraged from practicing his profession, owing to either incompetency, bad judgment, or both.

I was sixteen, still frying chicken for minimum wage and wailing the nights away in very loose form. Somehow I thought that holding a job made me capable and worthy of finally letting my mother have it about just sitting around all day and crying. Depression wasn't a good enough excuse, in my mind—not that she ever offered one. She would say, in response to any snide remarks I happened to make, "Yes, you're right. I'm a weak person." Since I believed myself to be in direct contrast to her, I thought this made me a strong person. After all, didn't it take strength to drink as much as I did every night and still show up at work the next day?

But it finally became too much for both of us. One night I saw her sitting on the sofa, sighing and looking at nothing while I was getting ready to go out to the movies. I screamed, "Jesus, you can't keep doing this!

You have to go out there and live a life!" My tirade continued and a while later I noticed that she was writing intently on a legal pad. The thought flitted through my head that she was writing a suicide note. I might have even said something to that effect, and if I did, I am sure it wasn't spoken with concern.

Later that night I came home to find a note on the door telling me to go to the emergency room of the hospital. The note said that my mother was all right, but to hurry. I looked at the signature and saw that it was Alice, a friend of my mother's, whom she'd met while the two of them were at the hospital for depression. I found out later that, as she started to lose consciousness, Mom had gotten scared and called her friend for help.

Mom had tried to kill herself before, but I had only heard about it in oblique, secondhand ways—it was in Miami after she'd given birth to her fourth child. As I drove to the hospital, I was trying to remember how and when the other time happened. When I got there, the doctor, who was a friend of our family, told me that this time she'd come close to dying. She'd taken a bunch of pills prescribed by her psychiatrist. I said, "If you were a shrink and your patient had a history of depression, overdosing, and was currently drinking heavily, would you prescribe horse-strength barbs?" The doctor, noticing the looks we were getting from the people in the emergency room, quietly took me outside and lit up a cigarette. He asked if I was okay. I said,

"I need a joint." He shook his head and said, "As luck would have it, I'm not carrying any. Have a cigarette." I took it. It was mentholated. I breathed it in, having learned to inhale and then some. I liked it. It seemed acutely ironic for a doctor to give me my first cigarette.

We stood there for a minute and I said, "What do we do now? I can't just take her home, right?" He told me that according to law she must be committed. He continued, "All the papers are in order, and in a few hours, after she's had some time to rest, you can drive her there and sign her in." I said, "You're kidding, I'm sixteen. There's no way they'll let me do that." But they did. It was like being on the other side of the door from my father after not seeing him for so long. You think it isn't happening, that someone should prevent this, but no one does and you just go on with life.

Mom stayed in the state hospital for a few months. It was about thirty miles away and we saw her on weekends. I had a car and would gather up as many of my sisters as I could for the trip. Tana was staying with our aunt, Toren was with Memaw and Graddaddy, and Kristen and Katy were with their father. I'd scramble home from wherever I'd been, pick everyone up, and we'd drive to the other side of Atlanta to see Mom. She was feeling bad enough, and seeing us made her sadder, because she wasn't there for us. Plus, she was in a mental institution and there were bonafide crazy people running around. On good days we had some laughs and I am sure much of it came from relief that things weren't worse.

If my academic precocity had been on a par with the ways I was becoming a reprobate, I might have been a nuclear physicist. As it was, with Mom far away and ill, I was becoming totally untethered. Sometime that year, I read something one of Erica Jong's characters said in a book that basically expressed her fear that she'd be too happy to write. I didn't exactly share that fear because, for one thing, I was in no danger of being too happy to do anything. When I fell for a guy, I neglected almost everything else in my life. I'd kept an intermittent journal since I was eleven, and entries about boys filled half of it. No one could convince me that finding love was less important than learning, and it was even more useless to get me to think about the future.

One night I went with some friends to hear a fifties band and I became madly infatuated with the bass player. He would get down on one knee and sing some old song to me, and I felt like I was on stage, too. After a few weeks of going to their shows, a bunch of us got together at an apartment and the party continued. Everyone was playing music or laughing except for me. I only wanted to be in love some more.

The whole band was from Boston and they were a little homesick, but they were making so much money they couldn't go back. So the bass player and I started to date. Maybe "date" isn't the right word for it. It generally meant that I would go over to his apartment after one of his gigs, then get up and go home in the morning. One night, after this had been going on for a few months, the two us were in bed and he watched my eyes for a while with a pained expression and sighed. Since this sort of behavior generally fell to me, I asked what was wrong. I was pretty high on Chianti and hoped whatever he had to say wasn't too long-winded, because I was tired. He spoke words to make the recipient jump for joy: "I feel sorry for you, Brett." I didn't mention that that made two of us, but told him to continue.

After hemming and hawing, he explained that he knew my feelings for him were great, but that he had a fiancée back home and that she was coming to spend Christmas with him. I was either still drunk or uncommonly slow and replied, "Where will she stay? Here?" I thought there'd been a mistake. Here we were, practically living together, except that we didn't spend weekends or go anywhere or even buy milk at the same place, and he was dumping me at Christmas. Although dazed at being vanquished, I left after reminding him energetically of what he'd be missing.

The next week was hell. My friends were empathetic and even the other guys in the band were solicitous. I cried and couldn't sleep or listen to any music at all. So I did what any sixteen-year-old with a broken heart would do. I got out my pen and wrote a poem that began like this:

> *your cage is far away tonight*
> *and I am by your side*
> *you cannot give your heart to me*
> *but your body takes the ride. . . .*

I managed to rhyme in the last verse with ". . . to fill your night and leave again like the morning's lonely tide." At the time, I was convinced that this poem could win him back, and that I would probably be asked to be poet laureate of *Cosmopolitan* magazine. I hurried over to his apartment before his betrothed flew in from Boston. Wearing lots of natural-look makeup and a serene expression, I handed him the poem and watched his face light up as he read it. He finished and said, "Wow. Brett. This is great." I tried to look kind instead of saying, "You see? Can *she* do that? Of course not. Yes, my foolish darling, I'll take you back." But I didn't say that. I waited for him to speak. He pulled me close and whispered fervently, "This is gonna be a great song!" I yanked the paper out of his hand and left.

In a few days I thought the whole thing was pretty funny. Then a buddy read it and laughed, too. He started fiddling with his guitar and sang the damn thing to the tune of "I'm So Lonesome I Could Cry."

It fit perfectly. I didn't stop writing poems, it was just a long time before I showed one to anybody again.

When my mother got sick, it gave me a great excuse to drop out of school. I decided to start working full time and go to night school for my diploma. After all, I had to pay rent and figured that a second-rate diploma was more respectable than getting a GED. My sisters were taken care of, and I was already so far gone into a wide world that my relatives didn't know what to do with me. I think everyone was relieved by my independence. What they didn't know was that I probably would have found some other reason to get out of school if life hadn't handed me one.

To my surprise, I liked night school and not just because it was easy. I was allowed to pay for my tuition by tutoring fundamentally illiterate adults. I was touched to sit beside a forty-year-old man who'd decided to humble himself enough to be instructed by a teenager. I was careful to be respectful at all times. He kept apologizing for his "ignorance." He had his own trucking business and told me he'd just gotten sick and tired of pretending to be able to read. He said he had teenage girls who didn't know their daddy had to get someone else to read their birthday cards to him. When he graduated, his wife baked a cake for me.

Being around that man made me remember my own brilliant, absent father with malice. Figuring that

Andy would be proud of his oldest daughter's rebellious mode of matriculation, I sent an overly kind note to Julia asking her to give my father a message. I wrote, "Tell him I was valedictorian at night school and that our class trip was at the monster truck pull." A surly sense of entitlement and self-pity, often the imprimatur of an alcoholic, was beginning to bloom in me.

Jana & I, in a little sketch called,
"A Pensive Alabama Christmas."
We must have been tired out.

Tuskegee, '61?

11.

My stepfather got rich the year after he left us. Later, he told me that it was something he "made up his mind" to do. He said that he wanted to make a million dollars, and he did. He joined the country club of his dreams, the most exclusive in Atlanta. He worked hard and spent almost all his free time at the club golfing and hanging out with other rich people. When I was eleven or so, I got to go there and keep an eye on my little sisters.

Unfortunately, I was already a little liberal in the

making and I didn't like being at a place that wouldn't allow Jews, blacks, or anyone whose name ended in a vowel. Mom never said anything about us going there one way or the other. Actually, I think she was glad we got to swim at a nice pool and had something to make the summer pass faster. So I went and played Marco Polo in the water and silently hated the rich people that were there. The strange thing was that my sisters and I were virtually the only children ever in the pool. Every time I'd been to the Elks Club with my girl-friend, it was as crowded as a public beach. I could never figure out why a pool so grand was vacant until one day I saw some kids leaning over the railing at the clubhouse. One of them watched us for a while and said, "Daddy, is our pool as big as this one?" Good God. I'd been so naïve. *That's* why there were never any other kids at the club. They had their own pools. I suppose to them this was the Elks Club.

I tried to be invisible, ducking down beneath the diving board, until they went away. Besides, the other children intimidated me and I was happy that they didn't see me in my weird bathing suit. Most of the country-club kids were dressed like miniature versions of their parents, right down to the accessories. I saw ten-year-olds with pearls and pocket watches. I was just a dumpy stepdaughter of an upstart—without a tan, a tennis bracelet, or a clue, just watching how the other half lived.

Now years had passed since my pubescent days among the finer people. I rarely saw my stepfather, except for the times I visited whichever sister was at his house. He was more polished, almost elegant in ways, living in a huge house near the governor, and about to be married for the fourth time. We were always cordial to one another, but there was still aloofness between us. I think I was jealous of his father status and knew that I somehow didn't rate in the category of daughter where he was concerned. Since my real father was gone and our letter writing had recently ended, maybe I wanted to take my resentment out on Joe. He got wind of my college plans, or lack of them, and phoned me to say that he wanted to talk to me about my future. Perhaps he was feeling guilty about his providence, his absence, or both. In any case, he asked me to dinner at his country club.

I'd only eaten at the clubhouse before and was taken aback at the elegant surroundings of the formal dining room. Since I was sixteen, I couldn't order a drink, but I was pretty sure Joe knew that I wanted one. He made a show of getting it from the maître d'. I could play grateful little girl if I had to, but I genuinely appreciated his gesture. He began by stating that he knew that I was very smart, but that I was getting off to a bad start. He said that he would help me with financing, but that I'd have to make some changes. I said sure, and meant it. The main reason I dreaded going to college was because of money problems. Joe told me that he wanted me to try and fit in, be like other teenagers, that I'd grown up too fast and it wasn't too late to change. Actually, I thought it was too late, but didn't say so, as I was busy planning how to con someone out of more wine.

Joe was suggesting that I might begin to live in a style more befitting a young woman in search of an education. I couldn't tell what he was leading up to, and at that moment, the maître d' accidentally poured us both more wine and smiled at me. I'd forgotten how old I looked when I was dressed up, and it dawned on me that this clown thought I was my stepfather's date. Suddenly, Joe said, "Maybe you could join a sorority." Seeing my expression, he added, "Or you could try." I think he misread my look. He thought my dismay stemmed from doubts that I'd be accepted in a sorority, not from thinking that it was a nightmare even being in the same room with those girls.

He wasn't going to win. I knew he could easily afford sending me to college. I only wanted him to say, "Whatever it costs, go ahead and learn. Just go to class and don't worry about working and do the best you can." He was generous in his way, trying to do something he didn't have to do because he cared. But the only person who would have said that to me was my mother, and she was in no shape to comply with the financial end of the bargain. I wanted to tell my stepfather what my life was really like, that it was too late for parenting. I just couldn't tell him the truth.

Men were passing by our table and greeting my stepfather with the booming hellos of men with the world by the balls, and then they grinned at me. When I say that Joe introduced me as Brett, without the title of "daughter" or even "stepdaughter," I do not imply impropriety on his part, but from the looks on the faces of his golf pals, I could tell that they surmised a less wholesome relationship than was there. I was furious and flattered at once. It was one thing for the waiters to be hitting on me. I was used to that. But these guys, who looked like the men at the Montgomery bank, made me feel dirty, dirtier than I could make myself feel on my own time. I believe that my stepfather did not know what was going on that night, and I was almost as mad at him as if he did know. I didn't need to strike bargains with pretend daddies, sugar or otherwise. On my way home, I was unhappy and confused, and more drinking didn't help. When my stepfather called a few weeks later to say that he had changed his mind, that he couldn't afford my tuition after all and that he thought it best for me to "do it myself," I was strangely relieved.

After halfheartedly applying to the University of Georgia, I was accepted. I received partial financial aid and was given a job in the work-study program to earn the rest of the tuition. I was surprised that they let me in because I'd finished high school at night. But my SATs were not bad and neither were my grades. They wrote that they were full for the fall quarter, but that I could begin in the winter of 1976. Southern Technical Institute, a branch of UGA, would take me for the fall, and I figured that would be a nice way to start school. I was working right across the street at a restaurant and would stay at the dorm until I left for Athens.

I only signed up for one class. I should have taken more core courses, but I pretended that I wanted to wait for the "real" university. I decided on Comparative Literature 101. The professor was Dr. Roberta Gates. She was magnificent, and I don't know how she stomached teaching a bunch of guys who wanted to be engineers. The male students, with rare exception, wanted to know about classic literature about as much as I wanted to know about quantum physics. Dr. Gates had an ebullient style of teaching that pierced the dullness of the place. I remember her deep, rich Southern accent repeating one of the famous lines from *The Rape of the Lock:* "What dire offense from amorous causes springs." She actually made that slide-rule set want to know what happened next. Pope would have been proud.

Dr. Gates saved me that quarter, at least as much as anyone could have. She drove to Athens once a week or so for a class she was taking and once she took me with her. We spoke of books and writing along the way, and I felt at home discussing those subjects with her. Toward the end of that quarter, she gave us a list of books on one of which to do a report, and I chose one of Henry Miller's saucier tomes. I remember hesitating when offering my explanation of the "land of cunt," and how Dr. Gates laughed when she said it in class, not noticing in the least the red faces of the boys who were listening. She gave me an A and exempted me from finals. Dr. Gates was the first person to convince me that looking at the world darkly—and writing it down—might eventually be what would make my writing different. And, like my own mother, she used the word "different" in a captivating way, not as if it were a sin.

While I was at Southern Tech, a guy started to follow me around campus. There were over a thousand men at school and less than twenty women. Most of the students commuted, so that left about ten women actually living there at the dorms. Every so often I would be out and turn around and see him staring at me. He would be everywhere I turned, and it was beginning to unnerve me. One day, right as classes were changing and the little grassy area between buildings was filled with passing people, I decided I'd had enough. I turned and yelled, "Quit following me!"

His expression was mortified, and he quickly changed it to one of amusement. He said, "I'm not!" I screamed back at him, "Yes, you are! And you are stopping right now!" I looked at the people watching us and said, "His name is so-and-so and he is always there, every time I turn around. And if anything happens to me, go and find him!" He slunk off. One of the sophomore girls came up to me and said he had done the same thing to her the year before. I still kept an eye out, and he stayed away from me the rest of the time I was there.

But the feeling of being unsafe was upon me. At night, when I came in from work, I had to park a long way off from the dorm and walk back. A friend got me a can of Mace, which I carried in my hand until I got to my room. After work one evening, I'd stopped off for my usual five or six beers at a bar down the street. Carrying my books, waitress uniform, and Mace from the car to the dorm while looped was challenging. By the time I got upstairs, the effects of the beer were making much ado, and I fairly swam into one of the bathroom stalls. Somehow I managed to Mace myself. The Mace was bad enough—painful and immobilizing—but the fact that it was self-inflicted gave me a feeling of shame and stupidity unknown even to a wrestling fan.

The Christmas between my quarters at Southern Tech and UGA was dismal. The dorms emptied out, except for me and maybe a couple of other students who didn't have anywhere to go, either, and I waited around until it was time to go to Athens. My mother had been released from the state mental hospital and moved down to Florida. She really didn't know what she wanted to do, but I guess she thought she could do it better down there. My sisters and I went to Me-maw and Granddaddy's for the holiday and tried to pretend that things were all right. I thought my rage toward my mother was entirely on behalf of my sisters, but I just wasn't ready to own my anger toward her. Although we were all living with people who loved us—except for me, and at least I was a phone call away—we felt further apart than ever. To top it off, I got a call from Mom on Christmas Eve. She was crying, saying that she missed us. I told her that she wasn't exactly forced to leave. She said that she felt my sisters were being taken better care of where they were. I said, "What about me?"

Christmas morning I was driving somewhere with my sister Toren, who was fourteen at the time. It was cold and gray. We stopped at a traffic light and saw a homeless man shivering at the corner. My sister and I really didn't have much to say to each other back then. All it seemed we had in common was blood and being bystanders to the same familial distress. For some, it might have been a binding experience. But we had chosen the path of detachment. Toren looked at the man and said, "I wonder where he's going to spend today." I said, "What?" She continued, "I wonder if anyone will hug him and just give him something hot to eat." I looked at Toren and knew she felt what I did: we might have been miserable, but we had food and clothes and knew that someone cared where we spent that day. I watched my sister gaze at the man and wished she didn't see him at all. Her anguish intruded on my solitary ordeal. By witnessing it, I shared it. It was the most jaded Christmas I'd had since I was six and tiptoed down the stairs in our Miami house only to see my stepfather eating the cookies I'd left out the night before as he assembled our toys and our mother writing "Love, Santa" on the gift cards.

ॐ

So I went to the big school in Athens and my college career was a series of feeble attempts at being normal, coupled with a few mind-expanding moments that didn't involve drugs. Academia blew refreshing breezes up my skirt and I didn't even mind that I was also confronting my intellectual inferiority in vast new ways. I was reading more than I ever had in my life and I was almost trying. Of course, the fact that most of the reading was forced on me was irrelevant. I neglected some assignments in order to read literature not on any required reading lists, though, and I later found out how like my father's my attitudes were—and how my self-destruction was to parallel his.

My mother had returned to Atlanta and was trying to get her life back together. She was renting an apartment and had gotten a job. Since my trusty car had died, I was glad when she offered to drive me and my stuff to school. We went down the hall in the dorm and I tried to open the door to the room to which I'd been assigned. It was locked. We heard a muffled "Be right there." We waited. A very flustered girl with a sweet face came to the door as her sheepish boyfriend adjusted himself on her bed. I thought it was cute. They had been making out and seemed as embarrassed as if they had been caught screwing on their parents' bed. "Sorry," I said. "I'm your roommate, Brett. This is my mom, Carol." We both smiled in a way to let them know they shouldn't worry. I said we'd come back in a bit. "No." She was quick to answer. "Donnie, go now." The fellow got right up, bid a fast hello and goodbye to me and Mom, and headed right out. "I'll call you later," he almost whined through the door. The girl said, "Go." Mom and I looked at each other.

Before coming to campus, I had filled out a questionnaire in which I was asked whether I preferred a roommate who smoked, drank, or dated frequently. I checked yes, yes, and yes. And here I was faced with my new roommate—Amy Lee Appleby. She didn't smoke, she sighed, as my mother lit up. My mother quickly put it out and said, "Well, honey. Let's get the rest of your things and we'll go get some lunch." Just then, Donnie came back to the door and asked if we needed any help with my things. My mother loves it when men do gentlemanly things, and considering his inglorious exit, she was impressed that he returned.

Amy explained that she was a music major and had to get up very early to practice piano on one of the few instruments at the college. I said fine. "I mean five A.M." I said, "Oh." She told us she was from an even smaller place than I was, much farther from Atlanta, and that her plants were very important to her. After about an hour talking to her, I knew we were very different. We didn't really like each other, but it was not because either of us was particularly beastly. She was uptight and bullied the hell out of "her little boyfriend," as my mother called him, but he adored her. It was obvious to me that Amy loved her father very much, but was purse-lipped when conversations about mothers came up.

I also noticed, almost immediately, that she kept her vodka and gin on the lower shelf of her metal desk. During the semester that we shared a room, I stole so many drinks from her that she began to write nasty little notes on the bottles. When I found the first one, I was hurt and offended. But I took the booze, anyway.

I'd been given some swell going-to-college presents when I left. Memaw bought me a big orange robe, made out of thick terrycloth, which zipped down the front. She said, "That'll last you until menopause."

Granddaddy gave me a red leather briefcase. When I wore the one really fine dress I had, which was gray wool and fit like a dream, I could pass for a Junior Career Woman. Although college was only sixty miles away from home, I was unprepared for the horrible homesickness I felt. I couldn't believe it. When I was little, I got sick at school and it was only a block away from my house, but this was incredible. I thought I was an adult, for God's sake, and this was college. I called my mother about a week after I started and told her I was coming home. She sounded disappointed, but said "Fine." My grandmother called back about a half hour later and said it wasn't "fine." "You have two quarters paid for with loans and what-not, and you are going to stay there and try to do this." I kept looking down at my arms for signs of lifesaving, pity-garnering hives. But none appeared. I resigned myself to staying in school.

The magnitude of the college experience did not occur to me until I registered for classes. If it hadn't been for a ragged copy of *Catch-22* and a hangover, I am not sure I would have lasted the day. The idea of paying attention to any of it was dreadful. I walked up to a table with a sign saying POLITICAL SCIENCE. I said, "I'll take it." "You'll take what?" "I have to have this. It says so on my sheet." "Well, we're out of 101." "That's okay. I like this one—Politics of Violence 427." It looked interesting.

The professor was Dr. Hendrick Van Dallen. He came to class the first day wearing an SS helmet. After assigning us fourteen books to read—and none of them with pictures—he laid out the game plan for the quarter. Dr. Van Dallen was very political. I was too green to know exactly where he stood, but since I liked him, he must have been on the left. I was the only freshman in the class. An inordinate number of ROTC guys were in it and the discussions were fiery. Forty percent of our grade would come from a paper in which we were asked to "structurally analyze and compare Diana Oughton and Adolf Hitler." I looked forward to it, for I preferred the Herculean and complex to the ordinary, even though the failure rate was higher.

The time came for the paper to be due. Predictably, I waited until the last minute to work on it. Then I wrote the damn thing in three days. I drove back to Marietta in the car I'd borrowed from my mother and asked her to type it. She did, and damned if I didn't get a B– on it. I contented myself with imagining what I could do if I actually ever applied myself to something. Dr. Van Dallen mentioned as much to me after I'd turned it in. "That paper saved you from a D for the quarter." Sadly, I took it as a compliment.

The campus work-study program promised to be no different from the fried-chicken adventures I'd had in the mall back home. The choices boiled down to dishing out food at the school cafeteria or dishing food for the athletes at the big boys' dorm. I got there and the job-giver asked me what I wanted to do. I said, "Something interesting." She looked through her stack of papers and said, "I have one thing. You'd assist a professor of psychology in administering an experiment based on her dissertation. I know the professor and she is interesting." Images of me wearing a hairnet and ladling out creamed corn to jocks propelled me faster than I thought I could run.

Arriving out of breath, I met Dr. Mann. She was from Australia and had a great accent. She spoke with me for a minute then said, "This job is sort of for a senior or graduate student." I told her I could do it. She was unmoved. "You'll have to read and understand my dissertation," she said. I told her, "No problem," and she gave me the job. If all I'd had to do that quarter was to work for her and go to Dr. Van Dallen's class, I would have been happy. The rest of my classes were dreary and made my mind numb. I wondered how anyone could take a full load in college.

Dr. Mann's experiment was in something called "strategy modeling" and was on the cutting edge of experimental psychology. I read and reread her dissertation and began to make the stimuli needed for the experiment, still not really understanding what it was about. I tried for a couple of days and worked until my slothful brain was almost injured. But then the work gradually began to make sense. Right before we were to start administering the experiments, I was sitting in my dorm surrounded by her dissertation, when it came to me. I understood what she had been writing about. I gathered up the papers, ran to her office, and charged through the door, grinning. "I know what you're doing!" She said, "I'm reading some stuff from my *Star Trek* fan club." "No, no, not that! The experiment! I figured out how it works." She grinned back at me. I was gleeful during the administering of the tests. I felt like I'd accomplished something important, however vague and unattached to my chosen field.

Dr. Mann and I hung out together. We attended colloquiums and parties with other professors and graduate students. I was starting to understand ideas and people that were brand new to me. Freedom of speech and thought became a form of oxygen to me. I started to get hooked on more complex issues. Since I was still lonesome and spent a lot of time searching for romance, these ideas ran circles in my head, like a rested dog with no place to run.

Pretty soon, in addition to my campus job, I started baby-sitting for the children of professors and teaching assistants. I liked sitting because I got to be around kids, and being in "real" houses was a nice change from dorm life. Although I needed the money for life and not the beer I spent it on, I rarely made a distinction between the two things, and managed to think of myself as a hard worker all the same.

After I finished sitting, the parent would drop me off at the bar and I'd come back to my dorm room drunk and late. Even though I'd try to be quiet, Amy would turn on the little lamp by her bed, glare at the clock, sigh, and roll back over. It was like rooming with a maiden aunt. She continued her mannerly abuse of Donnie—whose whine could reach octaves I'd never heard from a girl—and she became colder to me.

Sometimes, because I sort of cared, I would talk to her about her family. Her curtness and severity in deportment and dress intrigued me. She was mixed up about sex, and about the boy who worshiped her. Something else was hurting her, too. Amy thought her father had been wronged when her mother divorced him. When her mother would call, Amy's voice was stuffy and cold, like it was when she spoke to me. But sometimes when she talked about the breaking up of her home, she would cry. We were both young and didn't really know what the hell we were doing. We just went about it in different ways.

Once, when I'd spent two days away without telling her where I'd been, she really let me have it when I came through the door. "It's bad enough that you drink your life away, but I didn't know what had happened to you or anything. I asked the registrar's office to move you out of here."

"Gee, Amy. You were worried about me?" I said it partly out of being touched and partly to annoy her. I almost had her. She was just so damn uptight. She could stay out with Donnie and not tell me where she was, but she somehow viewed my case as being different.

Then, for the first time since I'd known her, she said some really mean things. I didn't defend myself. I knew that I was crazy and it scared her. Hell, I scared myself. It might have been easier if I'd been either a bitch or a degenerate all the time. But, apart from stealing her booze, I was nice. She ended with some very personal attacks for which I had no defense. Then, since it was Friday, she was off with Donnie.

The next morning, the phone rang before eight o'clock. I looked at the clock and wondered what branch of hell was open at that hour. I picked up the phone. "Hello, Brett? Good morning, dear. May I speak with Amy?" I was still pretty sleepy, and the last words her daughter and I had had still rubbed me the wrong way. I was so upset, incidentally, that I had not taken any of her clear sustenance the night before, even though she was gone and had left plenty in the cabinet.

Joy rose in my breast, and I rose to the occasion. "Gee, Mrs. Appleby, Amy's not here." "Oh, I see. Is she practicing her piano?" I was as innocent as a lamb, replying, "I don't think so. She wasn't here all night. I thought she went home for the weekend." There was a telling silence on the other end of the phone. "Uh, no, honey. She's not here. Oh, my." The woman's voice was so sweet. She lived in fear of Amy's wrath, too, and she didn't even steal her liquor like I did.

"Hey, I know. I'll bet she's with Donnie. She stays with him sometimes." Her mother paused a moment before saying quietly, "You mean she stays at night?" "Sure," I breezily replied, "He's a great guy, isn't he? Just loves her to death." At least I hadn't lied to the woman. "I'll tell her to call you as soon as I see her, all right? I'm sorry I don't know his number or I'd give it to you." I could tell Mrs. Appleby was trying to sound as carefree as I did. "Yes, would you do that, dear? And you say she's probably with Donnie?" "Oh, yes, ma'am. You know Amy. She works so hard at her music. She's either studying or over at Donnie's." "Well. Thank you so much, dear. You can tell her I only phoned to say hello. Nothing important." Right before I put down the phone, I reckoned Amy's mom finally had something on her.

Amy came sniffing in around noon. She wasn't speaking and I had cleaned the room and replenished a small part of her booze and bought some snacks for us. I think she was impressed with my momentary ability to function, but I had an evil plan in mind. Absent-mindedly, she asked, "Did anyone call?" It was odd, because she never got any calls that weren't from her parents or the Whining Boy Who Loved Her So. I casually said, "Your mom."

Her reaction was immediate and panicked. "What?

My mom?" She couldn't even pretend to be cool. "What time?" "Early this morning. Well, early for a Saturday. You know me." I smiled. Amy tried to smile back. "Oh, sorry if she woke you. What did you tell her?"

I furrowed my brow as if trying to remember, when I was actually enjoying this moment of sadism as fully as any I'd ever had. "Let's see. She wondered if you were practicing and I said I didn't think so. I told her that I thought you went home for the weekend and she said not, so I said you might be at Donnie's. I figured she'd have his number."

There were some disadvantages to being a Good Girl, and Amy was finding out about one of them. Good Girls hate getting caught. Especially if it means getting caught in a trap you use for getting others in a world of shit. I might have deserved condemnation, but not from her, and not the moral variety. As the color drained from her face, I said, "Your mom sounds like a doll." I wasn't lying, either.

The recent divorce of her parents, at her mother's instigation, was the most painful thing in Amy's life. I'd met her pop, too, and he adored Amy in a way that was quite touching to see. I think he delivered mail, and his little girl being in college made him feel wonderful. But Amy's pain had to come out somewhere, so mama got the knife. "You didn't tell her that I was out all night?" "Uh, yeah. I said since you weren't here last night, that's what made me think you went home for the weekend." I knew what was racing through her head. Donnie always begged her to spend the night, and on one of the few occasions she acquiesced, she was found out. I knew Amy would take it out on him. I looked at her wide-eyed, and said, "Did I do something wrong?" She said no and was nice to me for the rest of the time we roomed together. Yet something tells me that she thanked her lucky stars when we parted ways.

A few years ago I was doing a show in Atlanta when someone came backstage and gave me an empty vodka bottle with a note in it. I was pissed. I was just about to go on stage, and I hate performing back home, anyway—but I read the note. It was from Amy. She was just trying to say "Hi" and I couldn't take the joke. I wish I'd written her a check with interest for the booze I stole. And I wish I'd laughed and hugged her when it happened, instead of reawakening that old self-loathing and storming off.

༄

I left college more inauspiciously than I arrived, if that's possible. Maybe, if I'd known that I got my last A at Southern Tech, I wouldn't have bothered going to Athens at all. Also, my mother was doing well at her new job and happily dating the first guy any of us ever liked. My friends were back in Atlanta, too, and it wasn't like I was availing myself of what college had to offer.

Two weeks before spring finals, an old pal of mine, Larry, came into town and called me. He said he was at The Dog House, a local bar, and did I want to come and have a beer with him? I asked my friend Daniel, a teaching assistant in the Psychology Department, to drop me off. This was one of the first instances of my worlds colliding. It was so funny that I wish I could have watched it without feeling guilty. Daniel was called Moses by people in the department because of his resemblance to Charlton Heston playing the character, and his own ascetic life. He was environmentally conscious, among other things, so for him to pull up just in time to see my good ol' buddy miss tossing a beer can into the bed of his truck and it landing on the pavement instead, was both amusing and embarrassing. Daniel shuddered and said, "My God!" I felt sorry for him and hated to say the next thing that came out of my mouth, which was, "There he is. That's my friend." After his initial shock, I thought Moses was going to throw up. I jumped out, thanked him, and ran off to get drunk in Athens for the last time.

I was looking for excuses to pull myself back down into the familiar without the constant reminders that there were people in the world trying to realize dreams of substance. I just wanted to have fun and forget. Seeing Larry made me even more homesick. We drank beer after beer, and then he took me back to my dorm to wait while I threw my stuff into bags. My friend Kate stopped me in the hall and I told her what I was doing. I seemed so happy that she withheld in her words the doubt that I so plainly saw in her eyes. She hugged me, saying, "You'll be all right. You better keep in touch." Kate was one of my dear, smart friends and among the ones who've treated me the same in the twenty years it's been since I ran out of the dorm scattering "incompletes" behind me. I didn't even have the guts to fail outright.

As if leaving college a few weeks before final exams wasn't degrading enough, I got a job as a cocktail waitress the day after I got back to Marietta. It was at a hotel lounge and restaurant, and the uniform I had to wear was unforgettable: a red polyester riding jacket with a snap-on faux velvet lapel. It had to be worn with ruffled white panties underneath. The outfit looked as if the Elks Club tried to do their own version of the film *Tom Jones*. Ignoring the sensible footwear of the dining-room waitresses, I went out and bought the highest heels I could find. If I was going to *be* a cocktail waitress, dammit, I was going to *look* like one.

A few nights a week, I served food in the dining room and wore the more conventional garb of black slacks and white blouse. Lounge work was easier, except for the high heels on my feet and the occasional low heel to whom I served liquid sustenance. But being a barmaid meant that I didn't have nasty side work like filling up ketchup bottles and salts and peppers and all those other things you never notice anyone doing until you've worked in a restaurant. It also meant bigger tips. Double shifts were the most lucrative, when I worked from happy hour to close. I came in at 3 in the afternoon and didn't leave until well after 2 A.M. Good nights would send you home with over a hundred dollars after tipping the bartender. Plus—and this bonus, although intangible, was not negligible—I thought that some nice man would probably come in there to have a drink and want to take me away from all of that. It didn't matter. Just get me the hell out.

It was another inglorious summer, and my wretchedness was increasing. I drank so much that, by the time I got home, half my tips had been spent at other bars or on tipping other waitresses, trying to prove my largess. Margaritas, hangover cures, and cover bands were bandages to my lackluster education. The big difference now was that I no longer felt the pressure I did while I was at school. There were no earnest acquaintances trying feverishly to amount to something. My new compatriots were surrendering, like me, but in some very colorful ways. The loneliness was still there, but it was getting louder and easier to dance to.

∽

One afternoon, I was trying to figure out how I could be taking home six hundred dollars a week and still not have rent money and decided to ask Julia for some. I told her that I owed college loans, and I am ashamed to say she sent it right away. Of course, I spent it on Other Things, but I figured I had it coming. At the end of the letter I wrote, "If you hear from Andy, tell him I said 'Hey.'"

I left one waitress job after another. I forget which girlfriend told me about this, and even if I remembered, we'd both do well to forget it. She said she knew a man who liked to take pictures of women in peignoirs and paid them fifty dollars for the pleasure of doing it. Somehow, in my little all-of-a-sudden-Southern head, I thought, Well, it isn't screwing and it could be considered art even though the guy wore sunglasses and wouldn't tell me his name and I felt worse than . . . than what? What could be worse than to be so depressed, nonfunctioning, and lazy that I would ever think that this was a good deal? When I got there, the guy who owned the place said the customer with the Polaroid camera was "weird." Although I was standing there ready to pose provocatively for the same amount as a good bag of pot, I remember thinking, Okay, buddy, I give up—if he's weird, what are you? Afterward, the owner said, "Are you sure you don't want to go out with the guy? It pays more." I told him no, went back to Marietta as fast as I could, and bought pot so strong it could have been used as rope on a ship. Mixed with tequila and a couple of hours later, I almost forgot that whole afternoon.

Years later, when I was performing stand-up, I agreed to referee a thing called "Foxy Boxing" up in a place called Rexdale, Ontario. For six hundred dollars a week, I was supposed to do five minutes of comedy and then introduce the strippers, who later donned bikinis, oversized boxing gloves, and giant helmets and pretended to box. I suppose it was more elegant than mud wrestling, in the same way that what I had done with the Polaroid man wasn't screwing for money. Between "rounds," men from the audience would come up on stage and squirt the women with water bottles, ostensibly to cool them off.

I went backstage before the second show, about a minute after I had decided to go back to the airport and fly home, and gave a little speech. It was a brief, impassioned albeit pedantic tirade on the nature of their job, and I ended saying something like, "You are all young! You can *do something* with your lives!" They looked at me like I was crazy and calmly replied that they were making two thousand dollars apiece— American—and for me to shove my female-eunuch stuff right up my. . . . That's when I realized I lacked the fortitude to be a saver of souls and the brains to be a slut.

By the time I turned nineteen, I was more poor than

ever, and getting less and less connected to things that had been important to me. My family was distant. *I* was distant. I was living in an efficiency apartment upstairs from a family in an old part of town. One day I came home to nothing but oatmeal in the pantry. It had been the only food at the house for two weeks. I was sick of oatmeal, but not sick enough of it to stop buying beer with the little money I did have. I decided to do something, anything, to the oatmeal other than put sugar and cinnamon on it. I thought I'd try relish. Yes, relish. That stuff you put on a hot dog if you are out of decent onions. It was the only condiment I had, so I put some in the bowl along with some salt and pepper and the oatmeal. It was as bad as you'd think. It was so bad that I threw the bowl in the trash and threw myself on my old bed and just started sobbing.

It was fall and I hate fall. I hate when people say autumn is their favorite season. It only means that school is starting and there is no money for clothes and books and the green leaves are going away and it will get cold and spring will take forever to come back. Fall is depressing and not a good thing and oatmeal with relish is worse, and being a drunk and not really knowing it is worst of all. The chenille cover on the bed was getting an enormous amount of my tears and snot, and the crying was not ending and my mascara dribbled on the lonesome sheets, and just when I thought things couldn't get any worse, the radio started playing what was then a very popular song: "You Light Up My Life," sung by Debby Boone. Hearing that song at that moment made me want to die. But it was a good sign. Wanting to die at least showed some initiative, but since I sort of wanted to stick around and see how things turned out, I got up and threw the radio out the window. Then, as if God wasn't finished with His comedy routine, I could hear it continue to play from the radio in the house next door. Right before I cried myself to sleep, I knew that it would be a fine day when I could sing to Debby Boone, which was the worst way I could think of to pay her back.

Happy little girls with homemade
haircuts and new pastel dresses.
This was a few months after
we left Texas, seeing our
father for the last time.

Marietta, Summer '62

12.

Just when I think I am getting better, really better, not just chronologically removed from the rich wasteland of my past, I remember when I joined the Army and moved to Macon, Georgia, in the same month. More than anything else in my life except, perhaps, my intake of mood-altering substances, I think this was an indicator of just how heedless I had become.

It was the summer of 1977, and I was recuperating from a tubal pregnancy that had almost killed me. A couple of weeks later, Elvis died. I took both events personally. It was time for redemption, and not the kind they sell at revivals. Except getting out of the Army was harder than backsliding. Macon took even longer to leave.

I let myself get too close to a recruiting station. I was working as a light and water meter reader for the City of Marietta. During the day I drove an orange truck and wore a blue shirt. But my most important accessory was a plastic bottle of watered-down ammonia that made the big dogs leave me alone. During lunch and at night I waitressed at a restaurant next door to City Hall. It was also across the street from the recruiting station. These guys thought I was the hardest-working woman not in show business. I did work hard, both for the sake of the work itself and because it kept my nemesis, loneliness, at bay.

The recruiting sergeant talked me into meeting with them. I asked if I could go to Europe and be in the Army over there. They said sure. (Either *Private Benjamin* hadn't come out yet or I hadn't seen it.)

Due to a varying array of circumstances such as choice and availability, I was signed on to repair and operate bulldozers. It wasn't as romantic a career as I had fantasized about, but I didn't think I'd end up near guns. The next thing I knew I was taking the oath of enlistment and being given orders. Back then—they may still do this—they had a thing called "delayed enlistment." This meant that you signed up and then had ninety days to ship out. Of course, this is ample time to reconsider. Which is exactly what I did.

In the short time I had left, I ended up in Macon for even less stable reasons. I just ran away again, somewhere smaller, which was a big mistake in itself. At first, my friend Larry, who was getting used to seeing me with bags packed, gave me a job on his construction site as a laborer. Then I was hired as a circulation district manager for the *Macon Telegraph and News,* which is a glorious-sounding title, but only meant that I was responsible for several delivery routes in a certain area of town. However, I was the youngest person and first woman they had ever hired for the job.

I pretended that my decision to join the Army would just disappear. I let time slip away and realized that I was supposed to report for duty the next day. I walked into Kaijer Lee's office, who was my boss and the man who hired me, and told him what was happening. I also said that I really liked working for the paper and didn't want to go. I said, "Is there anything I can do to get out of this?" He asked why I had never mentioned it before. "Because," I replied logically, "you wouldn't have hired me."

I will always be grateful to Kaijer for what he did. The next day he borrowed a company car from the paper and drove me up to the recruiting station—over an hour and a half away—to help me abort my fledgling military career. This may not sound like much, but Kaijer was black, and driving that stretch of highway with a teenage white girl garnered some less than friendly looks along the way. You must remember that in 1978 Macon was like 1950 anywhere else. I actually thought we were going to be run off the road a few times.

When we arrived at the office, my recruiting officer seemed most surprised to see me. "Well, Brett, you're supposed to be at Fort McClellan right now, aren't you?" I had wondered what these guys looked like when they weren't smiling and had a feeling that I was about to find out. I said, "Well, sir, I changed my mind." Apparently they needed more of a reason. As sexist as it sounds, you'd think these guys wouldn't have been taken aback by the mere changing of a female mind. After all, they were Southern men, so what was the big deal?

One of the men sneered and said, "You don't seem to understand. You are Army property now." I liked neither the term nor his tone. He continued, "You took an oath and you must be where your military contract requires you to be." "No." One of them said, "Beg your pardon?" I said, "No. I got a great new job and I do not want to go into the Army." The men excused themselves for a moment and then, as if they had departed to multiply, came back with more of themselves, other men in uniform.

I was sitting and they were standing, and I was encircled by their khaki regulation-issue crotches. In a semifriendly way, they began to speak to me in a combination of threats and cajoling whines, designed to get me not to "let down Uncle Sam." If Starsky and Hutch had been recruiters, they couldn't have done it as well. I was listening and listening and could see the worried look on Kaijer's face as they drove home their main point, which was basically that unless I got on a bus to Alabama that day, I was going to be in a hell of a lot of trouble. It was at that moment that I made one of the riskiest jokes of my comedy career. If I had waited until I was a comedian to make it, then perhaps one of them might have laughed. As it was, I can only attribute what I said next to the bravado of youth, a sudden dislike of bulldozers, and an utter loathing of authority: "Look. If I have to fly a hammer-and-sickle flag, stick a needle in my arm, and start eating pussy, I will. You have the wrong girl."

I sort of laughed to show there were no hard feelings and to let them know that I was kidding, but there was a complete silence in the room. I looked over at Kaijer and, to this day, think I saw him stifling a chuckle. One of the men quickly went into the next room, brought out a piece of paper, and told me to put what I had just said on it. I said, "I hardly think so." So he told me to write the reasons that I didn't want to go in the United States Armed Forces after I had sworn to do so, and then I got mad and told them to just deal with it. I said, "You act like I broke a covenant with God, for Christ's sake. Now I am going to just write down that you ought to be glad I recognized my limitations before I turned out to be a whole lot of trouble for everyone."

In ten minutes, I was walking out the door, and Kaijer and I were on our way home. The ride back wasn't eventful, but maybe we were both so relieved that I had gotten out of there without being arrested that we did not notice the rednecks' baleful stares.

ॐ

I was almost twenty. Every day felt like a flying dream—fast, low to the ground, and brakeless. And every night I tried to act out what I had seen in my fitful sleep. An accident was bound to happen. It did. That's the other part of this story.

Once, when I was fourteen and feeling morbidly guilty about losing my virginity, I read an article that seemed to give me permission to be wild. In part, I read that daughters of fathers who were absent due to divorce were prone to promiscuity. I remember reading it and thinking, Oh, now I understand why I am like I am. All of this time I had been making secret deals with my conquests even as I became one. I was trading what I could in order to feel wanted. Nobody got hurt—literally, at least.

In the entire time I chased or missed men, I never came close to being physically or emotionally abused. On the contrary. At worst, there were lies and abdications of agreements that only I had been prepared to make, but I only intensified the search for the One Who Would Rescue Me. But I had never been bullied, threatened, or struck. Nothing untoward had ever happened, verbal or otherwise. So how did I land in that awful place? Did I feel so incomplete that I wanted misery or punishment? Was I running so fast that only being knocked down could stop me? Until I was hurled toward walls, a fist, spaces of utter annihilation that no one needs to experience or provide?

Yet we met, and in the most perfect of ways. I had been twenty for two months, and the sheen of my debutante years was rapidly fading. I was shooting pool with some guys I worked with at the newspaper. We were at a bar that catered to yuppies with a wild streak. I was winning and not yet drunk. Some of the men, except for my coworkers, thought that a girl running the table for a couple of games was cute, but then it began to mildly annoy them.

Then, like the song says, I saw him standing there. He was smiling at me. My triumph did not appear to irritate him at all. I still like that about him. I can remember exactly what I was thinking when I looked at him. Mike is a big man—not tall really, maybe six feet—but broad across the shoulders. He had thick brown hair and the brownest eyes I'd ever seen. In that part of the country a lot of people have visible links to their Cherokee past. I found out later that on his father's side there were several. Anyway, I took one look at him and said to myself, "I'm gonna marry that man." Just like that. After maybe two seconds. He came home with me that night. We moved in together in thirty days, and three months after that we were saying "I do" in a Macon park. His aunt, whom I loved, and who was to be a friend to us both, sang "The Wedding Song." It was beautifully performed, but I still can't listen to that song without blacking out. The only thing worse would be if I heard Debby Boone singing it.

The only wedding picture I have left is of me alone next to the cake. I am smiling and my hands are folded in front of my dress. We went out to eat at a catfish restaurant, and then I changed to my "going away" outfit. We got in the old green Ford van Mike had just bought from a friend, and go away we did.

Our honeymoon was one night spent at the Trade Winds Motel in Forsyth, Georgia, less than an hour away. Forsyth is one of the only places you see on the news that still welcomes the Ku Klux Klan with open arms. We left without a plan, just going north, but when we saw a neon palm tree, we stopped. I had wondered how Mike was so calm at the ceremony while I basically hyperventilated the whole time.

When we got to our room, he told me that he had taken some Valium. Then he took out a bottle of champagne that some friends had given us, and left the room for a minute to go spend our last three dollars buying a corkscrew for it. Jesus help us all.

When we met, Mike told me that he liked to fish and that the season was about to begin. When he spoke of the trips he took with his father, brother, and their friends, his face would light up, his smile reaching far into his eyes. He was strong and his laugh was low and fetching. Even though many miles of bad road came between us in the three years we were together, even after more than a decade has passed with all kinds of defeats and triumphs for us both, I remember his goodness and his crying need to go past what he felt was in the cards for him.

His mother was a pretty woman who spoke her mind. She used to say, "I tell my children that they are as good as the best and damn the rest." She was a fair person and wanted more than anything for her children to be happy. She was like me in some ways. We both read and smoked a lot. When the two of us went out together, people thought we were mother and daughter.

Mike's dad was great. He was a relaxed man and, from time to time, I could see his feelings coursing through his face, beneath what he allowed others to see. He would conduct his life according to his ideals, although, by all accounts, his own mother despised him, never showing him any love in his whole life. It always surprises me when people can manifest love and extend it to others when they had no examples of it at home. Mike's father was someone who didn't come out and say things about his dreams, but I knew what they were, anyway. He had worked most of his life in construction and had also worked around the changes the job entailed, from right-to-work laws to the possibility of union organization. He worked hard, yet could barely keep up with what they needed. Mike's parents married in their teens, and the uncertainty of steady work loomed before them as they approached middle age. I can't be sure, but I think Mike's dad resented me less than his mother did for the way I drank and tried to be one of the boys.

Mike had an older brother and sister, and I liked them both. I believe they thought of me as an extension of the good and bad things about their baby brother. Neither of them drank much and both of them were married to people that they loved. If anything, their lives were so settled as to be beacons of things I was in no hurry to have. Their houses were sweetly fixed up and paid for, and they each had two cars. Mike's sister had a smart, beautiful boy who was the apple of everyone's eye.

People called our courtship "cute." I was amazed. Come to think of it, what happened with Mike was probably the closest thing I'd ever had to a "courtship." Mike knew, because I cleverly confessed, that my past was first come, first served. My predilection for inappropriate honesty was unsurpassed in this instance. I did not yet have comedy to temper it. Mike's recollections of the specifics is surprising. It gave him a savage weapon for the rest of our time together. I had actually volunteered proof of my iniquity and it was never to be forgotten. Funny how easy it is to judge a woman's promiscuity from strictly moral perspectives. If I were a man, I'd be far more concerned about a woman who thought she was in love that many times.

It puzzles me that the sex lives of women are always subject to more scrutiny and speculation than those of men. I'm not naïve, realizing that I have personal grounds for resentment. When Wilt Chamberlain said that he'd slept with twenty thousand women, give or take a few, people merely reached for their calculators, pondering the daily average. But he was never called a tramp. A female who surrenders herself a fraction of that amount raises eyebrows, hackles, and Confederate flags.

I've read that prostitutes supposedly despise men, which relieves them of perilous ethical verdicts. Perhaps what makes me different from them is that I like men and have never charged for sex. However, I cannot say that I haven't felt purchased on occasion or haven't gone to bed with someone when I thought ill will would ensue if I didn't. I've certainly had my share of being cheaply held and soon forgotten. And the low regard in which I held myself is far more tragic, in the recounting, than that of the men who left me in their wake.

I suppose we had warning signs before we actually took our vows, but I can't think of them now. We went so fast. The first time he hit me was the day after we got married. After our one-night honeymoon we went back to our apartment. I cannot remember what the fight was about. In fact, none of the fights seem important now. It's sort of like being asked to describe a ride on a Ferris wheel after stepping out of a crashed car. I just recall the first time I was hit and some other random events that marked the escalation of violence in our relationship. And I remember our last fight because he fired a gun at me.

I've been told that I don't seem like the kind of woman who would tolerate such treatment. Not many of us do. Domestic violence, a cleaner phrase than what it describes, is the leading cause of accidental death for women in this country. Probably the rest of the world, too. But I do not believe anyone—man or woman—walks into a relationship believing such things will happen, or wanting them to.

I understand the syndrome, too. That thing they call "battered-wife syndrome." It's when you think things will change. That he will change. That you will wake up one day and be enough of a woman to bring out the gentle man you fell in love with. And then it gets worse and you wonder what man would ever love you at all. You feel like you were created to give misery. To be beaten is to receive the punishment of hell—cutting out the middleman, in a way.

You learn that cold water will take out most bloodstains—if they're fresh. You watch bruises turn all the colors your skin wasn't ever meant to be. You press your side and hope the rib is just bruised, not broken. You watch the pleading look in the eyes of your friends turn cold before they finally turn away. You tiptoe when you are alone. You learn not to cry because it just makes him madder. And the sickest thing of all is the realization that when he hits you—you win. Because no matter what else happens, you would never sink that low. And you see the agony in his eyes when he figures that out. But what is worse than remembering any of it, is knowing that I allowed it at all.

For years after I left him, I turned away from hearing the statistics about "women like me." I wasn't one of them anymore and I didn't want to know about them. I got out. Let them get out, too. And I hated them for staying. But the truth is that I still get a touch of that syndrome from time to time. Several years ago, when I was starting to write about him and me and going through the filthy attic of our life together, this thought came to me: I'll bet none of this even happened to me at all. I bet I just imagined the whole thing. I still have the scars. What other proof did I need? For the entire three years we were together, there was always at least one bruise somewhere, either turning black or fading into yellow.

Am I fair not to say anything good about him? Obviously there was something there or I wouldn't have loved him at all. And I don't mean that we both drank or played pool or liked the Allman Brothers. There were other things, good things, that I still remember and appreciate. Neither of us was well, to couch it in today's recovery vernacular. We were both young. I was submissive and clinging. He had his own demons, too, and became insolent in the face of mine.

We met in the spring, and the fishing season was beginning. Since I had grown up with no brothers or father, I was captivated by this bunch of earthy men who carried guns and traveled on unpaved roads. But that feeling lasted for only the first couple of months.

I began to hate Mike's constant outdoor life. This was true for different reasons. The first was that I was so emotionally impaired that I felt almost deprived of oxygen when he was away. Since we'd gotten married so fast and the violence began almost immediately, maybe I wanted to punish him. The fact that I'd stopped working right after we moved in together probably scared the hell out of him. He was old-fashioned enough to feel guilty about thinking I should work, and realistic enough to be mad at me for quitting. When I first decided to quit my job, it was ostensibly because of the hours. Our shifts were different and I said that I wanted to spend more time with him at home. But none of the reasons were true. I was starting to build my own prison walls.

Our life was regulated by the seasons and what animal it was permissible to kill. This is not meant as an indictment of sportsmen, even if the line that separates such creatures from bloodthirsty killers is sometimes negligible. My old man was "Iron Johnning" it before the book was written. It was passed down from father to son to the animals that learned to hide after the shock of a season's opening day. I realized that shotguns and pistols and rifles and knives and arrows and bows and lures and sharp and shiny metal things would be a part of every corner of our lives together. The sight of blood should have been less shocking to me as time passed.

What I hated was how they sometimes did it. To kill by the rules, I guess, might be different. They often gave the meat to a poor family, and we needed it from time to time when work was scarce. But the sporting part of it ended there. All creatures great and small lay lifeless in their path—wild pigs, deer, ducks, squirrels, doves, rabbits, opossum, bobcats, turkeys, and I cannot remember what else they shot or trapped. I didn't know so many things were edible. They shot sitting ducks, shone lights at deer at night and shot them in the fields where they fed. Once, Mike killed an albino baby doe on opening day. I asked him how he could have done such a thing. He said, with the straightest of faces, "Cause it was one in a million." Then he said he wanted to make a gun rack from the hooves and a vest from the hide. The little thing barely fit in a Crock-Pot.

Another time, our first winter together, my first in the country, we were driving down a dirt road and it was very late at night. Mike suddenly stopped the truck and got out. He told me to hurry and shine the flashlight up in a tree that was next to the road. I did and saw glittering eyes above. He fired his rifle into the branches and a giant raccoon thumped to the ground. He said, "Shine the light!" I did and he fired again. Another raccoon, almost as large, landed at our feet. It was a nursing female. I looked up again and saw more little eyes. They made tiny sounds of agitation that chirped into the night.

Mike busied himself with the dead animals, as I stared up into the tree. Responding to my silence, Mike said that he didn't know there were any little ones up there. He said he was sorry. He put the raccoons in a sack and threw them into the back of the truck. I felt doomed. I was a conspirator for holding the light.

Despite my feelings, I was not anxious to make him mad. Both of us were quiet as we drove away. Only our excited, whimpering dogs in the back of the truck indicated that anything had happened. Mike took the truck down a road I'd never seen, farther into the woods than I'd ever been. We came to a cabin and stopped. Smoke was coming from the chimney. Mike blew the horn and the door opened. Almost a dozen people were inside keeping warm in a single room by a lit fire. An old black man came outside and stood on the porch. He said, "Yes, sir?" Mike hollered, "Y'all eat coon?" I blanched. Even though a lecture on social propriety would have been untimely, my liberal conscience was roughly stirred. But, instead of telling Mike to go to hell, the man quickly stepped outside to tend to the business at hand.

The two men worked together, skinning the pelts in front of the truck lights. They joked about our male dogs breaking loose to find the bitch in heat that was running around the yard. Then the man thanked Mike for the food and the two of them shook hands. Mike tossed the dogs pieces of the meat, got back in the truck, and we started off. On the way home, I tried to explain why I was so upset. Part of the reason was that I *had* to explain. Mike said that we could get forty dollars apiece for the pelts, and unless I wanted to get a job and match that money, I should shut up about things I didn't know about. I did.

In retrospect, I try to realize that these men were from the working class in the South. Their use of deadly force might have abated with the advent of books and culture. But they had long been relegated by choice and economic necessity to the nonacademic, blue-collar world. This only explains part of why they hated weekend hunters who came down from Atlanta with their big cars and thousand-dollar guns to shoot up the woods and drink the best whiskey. Except for the bright orange vest, the clothes required for my husband's job and his leisure did not differ. I think just knowing that these other men had such dramatically different lives back home annoyed them. The fact that they did not hunt well, or quietly, was a secondary resentment, and the only kind they mentioned.

I once asked Mike's mother if this was the way the men had always lived. She replied in the affirmative, adding, "My men are vivid hunters." I had to bite my tongue not to yell out, "You mean 'avid'! 'Avid'!" But then I stopped to think. Maybe she did use the right word. What could be more vivid than blood on the ground?

But it seemed so innocent in the beginning. I remember one of the first times I went fishing with his family. It was a beautiful day and we were on the banks of the Ocmulgee River. I was watching Mike catch fish while standing in the current. He held up the biggest fish of the day, sliced open its belly, grabbed a handful of what fell out, and began to eat it. I didn't know whether to faint or vomit. My soon-to-be mother-in-law asked me if I wanted to know what he was doing. (Testing my love?) She explained that the fish was pregnant and he was eating the roe, which was considered a delicacy. I looked back at him with the yellow junk dribbling out of the corner of his mouth. He smiled at me, explaining, "It's redneck caviar."

My favorite place to daydream:
Granddaddy and Nemaw's
magical hammock.

Marietta, '62?

TWO BY TWO IN THE ARK OF THE ACHE
OF IT.

—*Denise Levertov*

13.

For most of the time Mike and I were married, we
lived out in the country very far away from everything
and everybody. One of our houses was so isolated that
the only other structure we could see was a windmill
off in the hills. Places like that taught me that there can
be mighty fine lines between beauty, boredom, and terror.

There are nights that stand out beyond others. One
of the worst was one of the saddest. Mike came into the
bedroom after the most violent and prolonged beating

of our marriage. He turned on the light and watched me for a moment. I had been lying quietly since he stopped and let me go into the other room. Then I noticed he had a shotgun in his hand. He told me to come into the living room. I followed him and he told me to sit in a chair across from the sofa where he then reclined. He put the barrel of the gun in his mouth and his toe on the trigger. I got the impression that he was unhappy about something. I sat there, barely remembering to breathe, while I told him that I was sorry and begged him not to take his life. In spite of all that he had done to me, I had no desire to see his brains splattered on walls we rented.

Almost as horrible as the thought of his violent death was my belief that if he died I would not be there anymore. He kept telling me that no one who did what he did to me deserved to live.

I wonder if he does that with the woman he's married to now.

I wonder if he pushes her out the front door in the daylight while neighbors watch and then drags her back inside by her hair.

I wonder if he drives her down dark roads at night, telling her that he's going to take her to the swamp and shoot her and leave her there.

I wonder if he comes home from work and says, "Who'd you fuck today?"

I wonder if he chokes her until she passes out and

then watches as she chooses shirts that cover the marks of his fingerprints.

I wonder if he kicks her shin, making it split open, with his steel-toed boot.

I wonder if he holds a gun to her head and makes her flush her wedding ring down the toilet.

I wonder if she tried to braid the clumps of hair he's pulled out so the bald spot doesn't show.

I wonder if all their relatives fail to make the correlation between the number of black eyes she gets and the length of time she's been with him.

I wonder if she wrestles with a policeman's logic as he tries to get her to press charges while her head's being shaved for stitches.

I wonder if his mother tells her what she told me when she said, in a voice calm and ashamed, "Ah told him he ought not to hit you so much."

I wonder if she wonders how much is too much.

The day I left him was not after anything particularly bad had happened, which is astonishing in itself. He had not hit me or anything for at least a few days. I don't even think I had any fresh bruises. Go figure.

He was taking a nap on the couch and I was cleaning up in the kitchen. I was looking under the sink for something and saw a pipe wrench. Pipe wrenches are very big. I never before or since looked at a household object and saw it as a weapon. I picked up the wrench and started to swing it like a bat. I had played all-star softball for ten years before my life had screeched to a halt in this marriage. One of the greatest feelings in the world is to hear the crack of a well-hit ball against a bat. I wanted to feel it again.

It was like being in a trance. I walked into the room where he slept and watched him. I tried to calculate how hard and at what angle I would have to bring down the wrench to part his face in the middle. In that instant, the word "premeditated" came to mind. Since this was years before setting an abusive husband on fire in his bed would land you a movie-of-the-week, I realized that I couldn't get away with it. And, in that same moment, I realized that I didn't want to hurt him, even if I had the stomach for it. Whatever deal we had from some other life would just have to work itself out another way.

I phoned my mother and asked her to come get me. Atlanta was an hour and a half away. She said she'd leave that moment. I put what I wanted in an overnight bag and waited by the side of the road. A little while later he came outside and asked me what I was doing. "I'm leaving you." He said, "Just like that?" Just like that? Hadn't he been watching the same movie I had been watching? I told him what I had almost done when he was taking a nap. He thought for a second, then asked, "You want me to help you with your shit?" I think that's called giving the devil his—or her—due.

It may seem odd that I cannot recall the beginnings of our fights, or the nature of them once they started. Suffice it to say that they did not start when I was pressing the hem into a new pair of curtains or making brownies from scratch. Once I found out that women were beaten during and after such felicitous activities, I was amazed at the dissoluteness of the men who clobbered them.

Our fights were messier when it was dark and we were drinking. Then we were cold and fearful once morning threw herself upon us and we could see the stains that words and blows left. It seemed as if we were always waiting for something and occupied ourselves with rage and self-pity until whatever it was arrived or did not. Paychecks were fine things and omens at once, yet poverty was beguiling in that we clung closer and made promises to one another and let our dreams surface to be touched.

The hardest times were when we were away from his family. It wasn't just because Mike fished and hunted with them, either. They were all each other's best friends, from Mike's siblings to the many cousins who lived nearby and visited frequently. There wasn't physical abuse in Mike's home, but some of it lurked in the family tree. When he and I began to tear out each other's hearts, it was as if we were tearing their hearts, too. But his family treated me as one of their own. I knew that it was hard for them—all of them—to face what Mike and I were becoming. On the worst days, I think that they wished I would just go away, but none of them ever showed anything but kindness toward me.

In another life, long before he was flesh in this one, Mike could have been the one in the tribe who found fire and shared it with the others. Howling winds and growling beasts did nothing to allay his enthusiasm for the hunt. Dirt roads and a creature breathing hard from being chased was ecstasy to him. He used to say that the finest feeling was that of hearing dogs bay as they closed in upon a kill.

Once, when he swore he was taking me to the swamp to shoot me and leave me for dead, I waited for the truck to slow at a curve and jumped out, tumbling into a drainage ditch. It was large enough to hold me, and I waited there, heart pounding, until he drove away. I lay there confused, wondering if I too had not lived some other life of running into caves to escape a man who had found fire. I could almost imagine hearing the dogs baying in the distance.

Almost a year after Mike and I had gotten married, I was staying out in the country with some friends. My mother called to say that she was so sorry to do it over the phone and that she was so sorry to tell me, but that my father was dead. She choked up, saying, "He was buried last week. Julia didn't call and let us know." Mom said that she had found out by accident. I started crying, too, and I let her think it was only because of my father's death. The reason I was with my friends was that I was trying to hide from everyone. I was nursing a matched set of black eyes, and my tears were running into the cut places on my face. It was not a good day for me and men.

꒱

After I quit work at the Macon newspaper, I made a few feeble attempts at getting hired at other "real jobs." Sometimes, when Mike was between construction jobs, he would drive around and look for things that needed painting. And sometimes I worked with him. Actually, by the end of our marriage, I was a pretty good exterior painter which, until now, I've forgotten to put on a résumé.

Mike was not afraid to ask for or to do the hardest jobs. I was scared of heights, so painting the roof of a barn or house, or being on a scaffold was disagreeable to me. But I liked being self-employed. It made up for having to hold my breath when I climbed ladders or pitched forward at an angle to nail roofing tiles.

Once, after we'd been married for a couple of years, one of Mike's relatives told me of a job that was open in a shirt factory. The place was close to our house and I went by to fill out an application. The manager said that I could start immediately and took me to the back of the plant to get my papers in order. As I walked with him through the giant building, I watched the dozens of women slaving over their sewing machines and I shuddered. I stopped by one woman and said, "There aren't any windows in here, are there?" She looked at me like she'd never thought of that before and said, "No, I guess there ain't." I touched the guy on the arm and made up some excuse about finding out about another job and fairly fled the premises. Right after that, I stopped by my in-laws' house and told Mike's mother what had happened. She just sighed and said, "Brett, do you think you'll *ever* get a job?"

Once I realized the violence was permanent, I had stopped working. I dedicated myself to hopelessness and helplessness, and barely had the courage to leave when the time came to do so. It would be tidy if we stopped there, wouldn't it? I left everything we had, which was almost nothing, just feeling lucky to be getting out with a regular pulse and all my memories.

I think the most regrettable times of our marriage happened after we moved away to Mobile and Pensacola. I'd be surprised to hear if Mike felt otherwise. Other periods rivaled it, but this was such a continually low time that I cannot remember the sun shining at all for months. Mike had heard there was plenty of work for steelworkers down there, after Hurricane Frederick. We packed up our two dogs and cat in a 1961 Ford Twin-I-Beam and headed south. After saying goodbye to his aunt and uncle, who were our friends, we went to say goodbye to his parents. His mother was so distraught at our leaving—at her son's leaving—that she was angry. As we were pulling out she said, "Y'all are just white trash. Only white trash gets around like that." I was under no illusions that leaving for Alabama at night in a rusty truck camper without facilities was Amy Vanderbilt's preferred mode of transport, but dammit, we were still family. That poor woman. She had to get that mad so that she wouldn't just break down and cry.

Our memories differ to suit the whims of accusations that may still linger in our souls, and all I can write about is what I felt. We spent awful days and nights without a dollar or a place to stay, one stretch so bad that we ended up living out of that truck camper, taking cold showers in state parks until we could find a vacancy in a town that had been all but obliterated by the hurricane. And there was the time in Mobile when I was working eighty hours a week and having almost that many beers in the same number of days, and I started to lose a baby I didn't even know I was carrying. By the time I finally saw a doctor, he said that I had been a "little bit pregnant," which is like being a "little bit Baptist." Either you are or you ain't.

I think about that sometimes, about how my life would have changed if I'd had that baby. About how I would still be connected to him. It was the second time I'd been pregnant, and whatever was inside me went running again. It appears that my fetuses had more sense than I did.

One night we went out with another couple, our only friends in Pensacola, and found ourselves in a strip club, perhaps because the local library was closed. I got jealous when Mike began to flirt with a pudenda whose hair had been shaved into a lightning bolt, which had managed to find its way too close to his face. I nagged him about it all the way home and all the way inside. His response, other than to deny incorrect marital behavior, was to pick up a big glass hurricane lamp and throw it at me. I saw it just in time to duck. Scalp wounds bleed a lot. He took me to the hospital and waited in the truck while I went into the emergency room. On the way there, he kept telling me that it looked worse than it was.

As a nurse shaved a three-inch-wide strip of hair from my forehead to my crown, the police arrived. I was listening to the reasons I should press charges while having fifteen stitches put in my head. The nurse kept poking around for glass shards they might have missed as she informed me that I couldn't have anything for the pain because it wouldn't mix with the booze. I refused to have Mike arrested, but I couldn't look at the officer or the nurse when I said it.

One of the cops was quite earnest in his pleas. He said, "This is going to happen again." I said, "I know.

But I don't have anyplace to go." Then I left. When I got back to the truck, Mike was furious. The police had gone outside while I was being sewn up and cited him for just about everything they could, including having an out-of-state license. They'd given him several tickets. I know they were trying to help, trying to punish him and relieve their frustration at my not having pressed charges, but I was scared all over again as we neared our house. Mike thought, perhaps rightfully, that I had participated in the fight as much as he had. "Damn you, bitch. You know how I get when you won't shut up, so why don't you shut up?" It was a good question.

We got inside the house, and by then the effects of the liquor were wearing off. I looked in the mirror at my brand-new inverted Mohawk hairstyle. I felt sick, tired, and ashamed, but he wouldn't let up. Mike wanted to know if I was aware of my own responsibility in these "situations," as he kept calling them, but it came out like "sit-shay-shuns." He was raising his voice and I'd already backed into a corner when the doorbell rang. It was the police. They came right in. One of them went over to Mike, standing so close I thought one of them was going to hit the other, and the cop said, "Don't even think about it."

Not long after that, I had to go to the doctor because of stomach aches, which were probably related to drinking, diet pills, being beaten, or all of the above. I was lying on the table and the doctor came in. I started to tell him my symptoms, looking up at the ceiling as I spoke, and then, hearing nothing in response, I faced him. He was staring at my legs. I looked down to see what was the matter. My calves were black and blue. I stopped talking. He pushed up my gown, examining the rest of my leg, and then he held up my arms so that he could see them, too. I could see the color drain from his face. "What happened to you?" He was almost out of breath. I remember feeling kind of surprised. After all, he was a physician, and wasn't he used to seeing the human form in all of its frailty? I didn't answer him at once, hoping that he was being rhetorical. He repeated the question and looked as if he were going to cry. I remember feeling worse for him than I did for myself. Then I looked down at my own body, and it was like seeing it for the first time. My skin was not unmarked on any limb. Then, after never saying it to anyone, I said, "My husband beats me." It was as if I had come out of a dark closet. Once out, however, I saw the light, blinked at its brightness, and went right back in.

❧

Something very strange happened once, about a year after we were married. Something neither of us expected or understood later. It happened as we were driving back from a weekend in the woods. We'd had a fight a half hour before. He'd hit me once, and if I'd been crying, I'd stopped by the time he said, "Look!" He sounded so excited. I hoped it was a deer. Sometimes an animal would distract him from his anger.

He was watching the sky. Over on the driver's side of the truck, up high, maybe a few hundred feet in the air, over a field, was an enormous cylindrical object moving parallel to us on the highway. It crossed ahead of us and seemed to hover for the merest instant. It was completely silent. There were lights on it, reddish-orange and white, very small, and they moved fast in a counterclockwise direction. Then it disappeared.

I looked at Mike and realized that he was scared. I was surprised. It never occurred to me that being a visitor to fear could be worse than living there. I started to joke about it, about the fact that we'd be added to the statistics of open-mouthed rednecks who'd seen a UFO in a country night sky. (I think it's funny— now—that he honestly didn't know what I meant by that.) But then I experienced a brief and definite sense of melancholy when whatever it was flew out of sight. Years later, I figured out why. I actually hoped that they might take me with them. You know you're in a bad marriage when you think a flying saucer can save you.

Yet, after all of these things happened, there were other memories, good ones, that I keep. One episode happened right at the end, and both my family and I recall it with fondness. We speak of it every now and then for reasons that we need separately and together. It occurred on one of the weekends that Mike would come up to visit me, after I left him in Macon. I was staying with my mother and two youngest sisters back in Atlanta. Mike and I never stayed with my family, but at one of the lesser motels that littered Highway 41.

That weekend, my youngest sister, Katy, who was only twelve, was very sick with the flu. For almost two straight days, Mike was there for her, talking to her, bringing her things she needed, and even wiping her brow with a cool cloth. Katy says she will never forget him for that. It was not an aberrant act, either. He was capable of the deepest kindness and loyalty. I would love to have only selected thoughts of him, leaving out the ones that make me flinch. So sometimes I search for those gentler ones, so I will know there was a reason for us to be. I think we both knew it was over, but had to scramble for some ending that suited us both. The one that happened will have to do. . . .

On our last night together, we were staying at The Georgian Oaks Motor Lodge, an idea whose time had passed. On the other hand, our marriage had begun beneath the glow of a neon tree, and there were some on the sign of this place, too. It was late. I told him that we had to stop "meeting like this," that we had to stop meeting at all. I know that he agreed with me, but hated that we never changed enough to make it work.

Saying goodbye and meaning it are two different things, and we did not let go soon enough.

That night we were both lucid and regretful. We knew there was no turning back. I know that he hated what we'd become and all the things he had done to me. We cried for ourselves and for each other. But then we stayed too long and too many words happened and he went out to his truck to get one of the guns that lived there. He had waved guns around before, but I still couldn't shake the fear of seeing one in his hand while indoors. It was the .22 rifle, a friendly little thing, as weapons go. In between my tears and his ranting discourse on the nature of failed relationships, he took off the safety. Then he aimed it at my head and I thought—Hey! No fair!

He fired it at my head. It happened quickly, which might be the best thing to be said for guns. I heard the bullet whiz by my ear. There is nothing, to my knowledge, quite like that sound, or feeling. I think we were both surprised. I said to him, "Hey! I heard it go by my ear!" My tone indicated that he had broken some unspoken rule.

Then he was gone. Just like that. I looked for the place in the paneling where the bullet had gone. There was just a crease in the wood. The wall was dark and kept the prize for itself. "And, if God choose, I shall but love thee better after death."

I've thought about what happened between us for

years. We both drank and took drugs, and our behavior changed for the worse more often than not. I am sorry that I sometimes knew when I was making him mad and I wish that I had not. But I would like to refute a version of our time together that he has recently offered. A reporter found Mike in the embryonic stage of my fame. (Most of my close friends had never even heard his last name.) I should have realized how easy such things are to find, and I regret not being more circumspect when all of it started. When first interviewed by a reporter from *The Macon Telegraph and News,* he was forthright, telling him, "Yeah, I hit her a few times. But that was a long time ago. There's nothing she could say about me that she hasn't said to my face." There was no mention of the claims he would invent later, charges that cause me to be more specific in the chronicling of our life in these pages.

As time passed and he was repeatedly approached, he tried not to comment at all. But then he became sick of the vilification and began changing his version to the point where he eventually denied everything. Currently, he insists that he was not a "wife beater," but that I was guilty of assault, as well. I might have stood for it when we were together, but I am not going to be battered again, physically or otherwise. I have nothing to gain from making a sideshow out of my past unless it is to help free another, male or female, from similar circumstances. I can tolerate tirades about my morality because we've all lived in glass houses at one time or another. And to refute is to dignify where such matters are concerned. Besides, I am in the belly of a big beast, one who will be fed with or without the crumbs of my past. It is a price of fame. But I will not sit still for revisionism about what I endured, what I survived, and what I know to be true.

The truth is this: I never hit him or physically accosted him in any way. Period. Ever. Nor do I hold myself up as a paragon of virtue because of it. For me to hit back would have broken the rules. Being passive was a way I could punish both of us. Of course, I wasn't aware of such intricate psychology as the marriage played itself out. But I suppose saying otherwise might make it easier for him to spread the real memories thinner and thinner until he believes, like I did when trying to recount this—I'll bet none of this ever happened at all.

As incredible as it may seem, there are also things that I left out because they are too horrible and would cause harm to those who are close to him.

Years later, after I'd moved to New York and was inexplicably happy in a life of my own choosing, I was visiting home and some old friends mentioned that Mike had not only remarried but had fathered a little boy. I was so far away from where and who I'd been that I was surprised that I felt anything at all. My emotions were mixed. My first thought was—happy at last, eh, you Bambi-blaster? But then, a few minutes later, I thought about how happy he would be, his family would be, that he had a son.

A few months after that, I was in Atlanta for a gig and decided to take a drive up Highway 41—all the way to Kennesaw Mountain, which is an old Civil War battleground, one of the few Georgia battles that the South won, I might add. Once a year they even stage mock skirmishes and reenact the whole damn battle. Just another reminder that we often have a hard time letting go of things and even create rituals of them. (They have Easter-egg hunts there, too, so I guess no dark day is too far in the past to commemorate.)

I went there to rent a metal detector. Visitors to the area often look for war relics around the mountain and sometimes unearth arrowheads in the process. But I had different intentions. I wanted to go back to The Georgian Oaks Motor Lodge and dig that bullet out of the wall. I even remembered the room number, so I guess I shouldn't be so hard on the pretend Confederate soldiers for holding grudges. The man at the rental place said that they were all out and for me to try again the next morning. I left and went to the motor lodge just to have a look around.

I couldn't find the place. It was weird. I'd lived in Marietta most of my life, and The Georgian Oaks had been there for as long as I could remember. I could see not being able to find a bullet in a wall, but losing an entire building was a different matter. I stopped at a nearby bar to ask where the place was. "Didn't it used to be right next to Adrian's Motor Court?" I asked. The bartender told me it had been torn down about a month before.

As hard as it might be to believe, that was the first time in my life that I thought Someone was trying to tell me something. I drove past the rubble of the place, knowing that the bullet lay in the heap of crumbled drywall, wondering if, in a hundred years, some new native American would dig it up and think there had been some epic battle on that site—one that involved more than two people.

Finding that bullet wouldn't have done anything good for anyone anyway. Where was the sense in visiting a place I'd worked so hard to leave? It wasn't worth the fight I had been having with myself for wanting it in the first place. From the moment I looked up the place that rented metal detectors, I had imagined sending the bullet to my former husband's new wife. I knew that was a childish, horrid act to consider, much less actually execute, but I was moving along the little drama just the same. I thought wryly of its unique properties as a wedding gift. Every bride gets eight deviled-egg dishes; who registers used bullets?

I had spoken to Mike's wife once, right after I appeared on *The Tonight Show*. During my set that night, I said the lines "I was married to a redneck from Macon

for three years. . . . I *deserve* to do comedy." There was
a laugh and that was the clip the local affiliate used to
advertise my concert. Despite the "if they could see me
now" mentality of many insecure performers, I was
worried about actually doing a show in Macon. The
promoter hired a couple of big off-duty police officers
to hang out with me.

After the first show of the evening, I was in the lobby
and a little guy came up to me and said, "You ought to
lay off Mike." I looked down at him, in more ways
than one, feeling a surge of adrenaline. There was a
part of me that thought I should stop doing jokes about
him anyway, but I didn't like getting called on it by a
tiny redneck after a good show. I said, "Why?" The
man bristled and said, "He's a pretty good ol' boy." I
got closer to him and said, "You don't think I know
that? You think I'd let a complete bastard beat the hell
out of me for three years?" I noticed that the woman
with the little guy looked like she wanted to be anywhere else, and I couldn't blame her. Her boyfriend
squinted his eyes and growled, "You just better watch
yourself." Then he started walking off. I ran after him.
"Did he tell you to come here and say that to me?!" My
heart was pounding. The guy started muttering that I
was going to be in plenty of trouble.

When I had gotten into town, the police told me
that they were there to keep an eye out for Mike and
had his address "just in case." I told them that it wasn't

necessary. After witnessing the hassle with Mike's pal, one of the policemen asked me if I wanted Mike's number. It was like we were all in a bad play and none of us could stop the performance. I took the number and went back to my room and dialed it. His wife answered. Mike wouldn't come to the phone, she said. Her voice was cracking and nervous. So was mine. I told her to tell him not to send any of his "little redneck friends" after me, that if he had a message for me for him to give it in person. Mike's wife asked me how I got their number, and I replied meanly, "I'll always know where you are." Although I felt besieged, I knew that I was doing the wrong thing. For all the time Mike and I had been together, I had never had any power. Now that I did, I was abusing it.

Later, I found myself wondering what their marriage was like, if Mike was any happier, if he'd found someone who didn't locate and exacerbate his darkness as I had. But there was no way of telling. Maybe Mike's mother was looking at his new wife with the most somber of expressions and saying, "I told him he ought not to shoot you so much."

Jana, me & Joren in Florida, '64
Joren's asthma was terrible and
she was so sweet all the time.
Now I see how close we all were
without actually touching and
wonder if things aren't a bit like
that today.

14.

Some people tell funny stories about their drinking days. I've laughed, but have nothing to match them from my own life. From the very first time I took a sip of beer and didn't like the taste, alcohol was an anesthetic to me. It diminished pain that I wasn't ready to name, much less deal with. Despite the relief it gave, the side effects got worse and worse. Toward the end, I tried to play games with amounts, varieties, and even times of consumption to see if I could recapture the bliss of early highs or at least not get so morose.

In the last year or so of drinking, when blackouts were the norm, I thought I was pregnant because of chronic morning sickness. I would wake up, stumble into the kitchen for coffee, see partially consumed convenience food in the trash, and wonder how it got there. Some people will gauge their own drinking by stories like that. They can say, Hell, I never had that much, so everything must be fine. And there are lists of things people can check off to see whether they are alcoholic or not. The first time I saw one, I checked "yes" on every item. I thought, Oh, well. I probably wouldn't be one if my life wasn't so hard. That excuse turned out to be the most durable one of all for not stopping.

Sometimes a person can have a Magnificent Epiphany, and the idea of not taking another drink as long as they live becomes implanted in their psyches, permanently and irreversibly. But most drunks are like me. They simply have so many rotten things fall on top of them that they realize that alcohol, once a friend, will not stop until it kills them. I am grateful for the mind's ability to diffuse memories of intense physical pain. But the lessening of emotional pain is different. If it weren't I would've stopped drinking hundreds of times. In the end I didn't pay attention to reason.

I have read that alcoholism is a physical addiction combined with a mental obsession. I only knew that my world was becoming smaller and darker. It is strange that, although I was probably close to dying, one of the things that caused me to reconsider my drinking was the frightening thought that, if I continued, I wouldn't be funny anymore. But that was at the very end.

§

After I left Mike and my mother moved to Texas, I was floundering in the heat of my hometown. For a time after my divorce, I was a magnet for people with the best intentions: people who wanted to tell me of their gods, their not-gods, their courses in miracles, their proposals, their steps. Whatever life had shown them was a thing they thought I should get some of right away. Usually, though, the best thing they could do was buy me a drink or six and just take me home for a while.

I'd moved into an apartment and had a great roommate. I thought I was fine, considering that I was right back where I left off, nothing changed, nothing different. I got a job bartending at a neighborhood restaurant directly across the street from where I lived. It was a simple bar, whose clientele was mostly professional people who usually wanted nothing more than scotch on the rocks. They were very nice, as was my boss, and I thought I'd found a little home there.

One night a bunch of us decided to go to an outdoor

concert at a park in Atlanta. I was trying to time my drinks and was doing just fine until someone a few rows ahead of us yelled, "Tequila!" Then I began mixing that with the vodka and the pot already going around. Jerry Jeff Walker was singing, and the rain started to fall, and then we all drove back to Marietta. Since we'd gone in one car, we got dropped off in the same place and began to make our way home in the worsening rain. I had trouble getting the key in the door of my car, but was ready to drive the mile or so back to my place. My friend said, "Hey, maybe you should stay here," but I told him I was fine and headed off. Less than half a mile away, I fell asleep at the wheel. When I felt the car spin, it was too late to do anything and I was hydroplaning.

The next thing is a blur of moving in ways you never want to move in or out of a car. The slowness of the crash is such that you think death itself will be sort of rolling around, then you see pictures of your life—not the one that's been your lot so far, but another one, the one you want so badly to live—and it is spinning and scattering in this messy way all over the road. The quiet after the wreck is as loud as the noise. Then you try to drive away. People come around to see, to help. You can tell from their expressions that you must be an unpleasant sight to behold and that there is no way to put a good face on any of this. When the ambulance arrives, you don't want to leave in it, as if staying where you are will negate the last ten minutes of your life. When a policeman politely informs you that you will either go with him or in the ambulance, it dawns on you that you are in trouble.

So you ride with the paramedics and get your face sewn up, thanking God that the doctor on duty happens to be a plastic surgeon because your lip is hanging funny from the side of your mouth. He sews up your face and the back of your shoulders as you wonder what will happen now. The policeman is there with you, holding your hand, and you want to shake it off because you do not deserve such compassion, but you keep it there because you are afraid. The needle-and-thread is running through your face and you wonder why you can't feel it. You tell the policeman that he's being extraordinarily kind and ask him why. You say, "Aren't you supposed to be really mean? I'm a drunk driver and could've killed someone." He smiles and tells you that he has a degree in psychology and that he is more concerned that this doesn't happen again than anything else. You wonder if you will ever meet a policeman when you are not bleeding.

You are told that you should stay overnight for observation. You say instead, "Take me in." You are adamant, figuring that you may as well go through the worst of it while at least a bit of the tequila courses through your body. Once again, you are denied painkillers because you drank your own hours before. They tell you that your blood alcohol level is .25, and everyone who hears it says, "Wow." So you sit in jail, not letting anyone come and get you out. Part of it is from martyrdom but most of it is from utter shame. Then you sober up.

In the morning it was time to be arraigned, and everything that was happening was no longer happening in a dream. It's like looking at one of those maps that say, "You are here," and the whole map is on fire. Since it was Monday and I had the good fortune to have the wreck on Sunday night, I didn't have to wait around. Being handcuffed to other women who were in for an assortment of festal deeds was interesting. I wondered if this was the lowest thing that would happen to me. After my arraignment someone from county services came in and said that they were releasing me on my own recognizance. I went home, looked at my face in the mirror, and finally cried. A fever, which had been rising since the accident, was now pretty high, so I just went to bed.

While I was getting over the worst of the shock and the bruising, my girlfriends Eileen and Robyn came by with soup and no lectures. Robyn, ever the lover of lost causes, brought me a Bible, too. Once I was back at work, everyone was very nice. I think it bothered them that one of their own, a "social" drinker, could lose control and get into trouble. Jokes passed around as I swore off booze—but not pot—for all of four or five days. By the time the weekend rolled around, I was drinking a couple after work and was back in high form. I did get rides or did my drinking at home for a while, so I guess I learned something.

A lawyer friend kindly took my case for free. I went before the judge, who asked me if I was ever going to do it again. I wondered who would answer yes. I was given a $250 fine and two nights in traffic school. I don't know when the courts decided that attempted murder was something they needed to address with sternness, but at the time, punishment for a DUI was barely a slap on the wrist. But then the system turned around and slapped itself when I was actually asked to teach at the traffic school the first night I was there. A woman was in the class who had a scar cutting deeply across her face on one side. I kept staring at it, fingering my own scar and wondering how I'd gotten out alive. The next day I went to see my car at the junkyard. The roof was caved in about an inch from where my head had been, where the car had flipped against the tree. If I hadn't been wearing a seatbelt, the junkyard manager said, and then he trailed off in the wake of my tears. I was relieved and grateful, but not enough to quit drinking or even seriously consider it.

The rest of that summer was roasting and wretched. Prince Charles married Diana on July 29, which was also Mike's and my third anniversary. I got up and watched it on television. The whole thing resembled an outlandish fairy tale. As it turns out, it was. Charles and Diana looked so carefree and in love. Isn't it funny how things turn out?

Sometime toward the end of August, I received a letter saying, in part, "This is to notify you that you was divorce [sic] from Charles Michael Wilson on August 17th." From the diction and spelling, I guessed that Mike had gotten one of those fancy lawyers who might have even finished school. If Mike hadn't gone ahead and filed, I'm not sure when I would have gotten around to it. I don't think we ever spoke after that.

That night I called my mother out in Texas and cried. I had never told her how bad things had been, and when she found out, she cried, too. Then I asked her about my father. I told her I remembered her being struck, and wanted to know if it had gotten worse than that. If either of us had made a prior connection about the fact that both of us—mother and daughter—had been beaten by our husbands, neither of us said it aloud until that night on the phone.

In all the years my father had been gone, either by choice or since his death, my mother had never said anything bad about him. Maybe she thought his absence was enough of an indictment. Whatever her reason, I am grateful. All my life I've heard one parent say terrible things about the other parent to the child who belonged to them both. What they said may even have been true, but the child is always harmed, I believe, when this happens. In my case, I felt like I had waited long enough and wanted finally to know the truth.

My mother hesitated as she described episodes of violence that were virtually identical to the ones I'd experienced. First there was the verbal abuse, then the pushing and slapping, which graduated into punching, choking, and kicking. We both discovered that we had gone to marriage counselors alone, our spouses having told us that the problem was ours, not theirs. It never occurred to me that abusive relationships followed a pattern. If it weren't for finding out that the same thing happened to my own mother, I might have been comforted by that knowledge.

My mother told me, "The worst time he ever beat me was when I was pregnant with you. He kicked me in the stomach and then pushed me down a flight of stairs. I thought I was going to lose you." Then, as if getting all the overdue explanations out of the way, she said, "The next month I went to my gynecologist and he told me I was gaining too much weight during the pregnancy. He gave me diet pills." I said, "Jesus. While you were pregnant? How in the hell . . ." Mom said, "I know. I was ignorant. So was he. It was a long time ago and he was almost a backwoods doctor. Sure enough, I lost weight and even felt like cleaning house." I had to laugh. As an afterthought, I asked, "What did he give you?" "Dexedrine." I couldn't help blurting out, "Good God. I was beaten up and taking speed in the womb. No wonder I liked Frank Sinatra music: I probably thought I was already thirty years old!"

My mother had gotten married for the third time and was living out in Houston, where her husband's job was. I was glad she had met someone who cared for her, but he was such a vaporous entity that I called him "daddy in a jar." He was not mean or anything, just one of those relationships you choose when being alone will not do, and someone very present would be too much to cope with. I imagine my mother agrees with my assessment of him because she's made no effort to find or divorce him in the dozen or so years since he left mysteriously. Maybe she feels about husbands the way I do about fathers: once the first one leaves, etc.

Soon after my abbreviated family left for Texas, Mom called and told me that she thought it was a great place to start over. She knew that I was unhappy in Georgia and that my divorce depressed me more than I'd expected. She told me that I was welcome to join them and that they had plenty of room for me. I decided to take her up on the offer. It also gave me a chance to get away from the buckle of the Bible Belt, closer to the zipper, so to speak.

I'm glad I found Texas. I wanted to put distance between me and anyone who had hit me or seen me drunk. I met people and did things there that changed my life. Leaving Georgia was hard but not because I was leaving anything important behind—it was just the only place I'd ever called home. But once I moved away and found myself in Texas, I found something I had put aside sixteen years before—stand-up comedy.

Right after having her fourth child,
Mom still looked pretty spiffy in
her "Mary Tyler Moore" pants.

Miami, '64

I FIND THAT THERE ARE NO
PLACES ONLY MY FUNNYHOUSE.

— *Adrienne Kennedy*

15.

A couple of months after getting settled in Houston, I went out with my mother to see a comedy revue at a place called The Comedy Workshop. The players were talented and funny, and I became intrigued. I didn't go there expecting to laugh. Perhaps the Elks Club soirée of years before had scarred me for local fare. After the show was finished, the management announced that we were all welcome to go next door to their sister club, the Comix Annex, and watch "the funniest comedians in Texas." Already happy with a few drinks inside me, I was delighted to travel a short distance and have a few more.

We walked next door and sat on barstools in the back of a room that was to become one of my favorite places on earth. It was where I fell in love with comedy and got something in return. The Comix Annex was a tiny place, and had an ambience if you like dim, crowded, smoky joints. In the years to come, as I played clubs all across the country, I noticed that they were all gradually decorated to resemble cruise-ship lounges, filled with turquoise and chrome. I'm glad that my first club was dark and grim. Otherwise it might have been too cheery to go back.

That night was only the second time I'd ever seen a comedian in a live performance. The first was a decade before, when I was only fourteen or so. I'd gone to hear John Prine in Atlanta, and the opening act was spellbinding. The comic was from New York, slightly built and breezy. He did a great impression of an old jazz musician. I hardly listened to the music, so impressed was I by what he did on stage. The comedian's name was Billy Crystal.

Now it was ten years later and someone else named Bill—Bill Silva—was telling jokes and killing. He was a fine combination of glib and mean, with just enough glimmer in his eyes so that we knew it was pretend. It was almost too much to take in at once. I was trying to hear everything he did but couldn't take my eyes off a doorway in the back of the room. Comedians were walking in and out, half paying attention to what was happening on stage, but mostly pacing around with their eyes to the ground. I noticed that they were all men. One of them was black, a couple of them wore boots, and a few of them were at the bar getting fueled for what they had either finished or were about to do. None of them seemed to be having fun, and damned if I didn't think they were cooler than cowboys. This from a girl who'd been around more than her share of musicians. But this time was different. I didn't want to hang around them or get sung to. I wanted to be one of them.

About a month later, I went there on a weeknight, and this time sat at the bar, closer to that mysterious room in the back. I was with a friend and was minding my own business when the comedian on stage took it upon himself to address me. I had to turn around at first to make sure he was talking to me. I hadn't said a word after ordering my wine and thought I was behaving quite well. I said, "Who me?" He went off.

I wish I could remember what he said, but I know what I felt like. I was thrilled. He was the same guy, Bill Silva, whom I'd seen the month before. He was funny. I figured that if I couldn't say something witty by way of a retort, then I wasn't worth my salt. I responded and the crowd laughed. Bill flashed me a good-natured look before ripping into me again. I riposted and the crowd laughed harder. By then, some of the audience had turned around and were watching me. The comedian and I shared their gazes. It ended well, and as the comic came off the stage, he walked by, raising his glass to me. I raised mine right back, and my heart beat just like I'd hit a home run. Then I got drunk and went home.

I've often wondered if I would have started doing stand-up comedy if I hadn't been drinking. Perhaps that does an injustice to my talented colleagues who have never sought to orchestrate reality by way of mind-changing solutions. All I know is that for me, and at least a few others, the combination of looking for something and running away from other things seemed to require assistance. It was as if my gene pool was crawling with critters who wanted to run when they barely had gills. I had tried every escape imaginable except those that could be considered healthy. Of course, I was a Southern woman and knew the magic of bubble baths, good cries, and napping, but even those innocent diversions were ways of avoiding reality when done to excess. I guess you could say that, for me, finding comedy was seeing light at the end of the bottomless pit.

Just as I was settling in in Houston, my new stepfather got a job back in Atlanta and they all moved back there, leaving me to saturate alone. I found others like me. I kept waiting tables and wondering what would happen next. One night, after a few of us had been drinking all day, all week, all month, we were quaffing big, dark, foaming beers and sucking the smoke from hash cubes, which we'd ingeniously placed on pins atop a matchbook, which, in turn, lay beneath a jelly glass. You light the hash, let the glass fill with smoke, and then inhale the opiate as you suck the smoke from the raised glass. I share this not to instruct but to illustrate the inventive desperation of a life ill spent. The dry-ice appearance of the hash and the empty bottles of beer were starting to sedate me. I wanted to stop for sleep or hot food and probably a big hug, but I settled gratefully for a sofa to sleep on with no strings attached.

My mother, her husband, and my sister Katy had gone, leaving me their rented house. I had bedroom furniture, kitchen things, and enough to live with, but had not exactly gone out of the way to spruce things up since their departure. Although I wasn't homeless, I felt that way, so getting to "sleep over" at my friends' apartment felt like spending the night at my grand-mother's. And that night, not being alone was my only goal.

The people who lived there went to bed and I was left dizzily watching television in the dark, with the volume turned down so as not to disturb anyone. Johnny Carson announced a comedian. Suddenly I felt sober enough to pay attention. His name was Blake Clark. He was from Macon, Georgia, but I forgave him because he was smart and really funny. I tried to remember when the next auditions were down at the Annex, and realized they were the next night.

A few months before, while I was still waiting tables at the Lone Star Café, I'd been approached by a customer who had a comedy night at a disco. I'd gone up there and done well. At first, I took a waitress tray on stage with me, thinking I'd be "The Funny Waitress." After two seconds with that thing in my hand, I put it down and it was just me and the microphone. I remember the crowd laughing and some of the comedians asking if that was really my first time on stage. I told them that it was in my current lifetime.

The next week I tried it again, and the results were so dreadful that I couldn't speak for a week. I went to the doctor, who told me that I had "trauma-based laryngitis." So much for the healing effects of comedy. Since I'd been busy drowning older sorrows than that, I'd all but forgotten the incident. But now, thanks to my bent for late-night television, I was reminded of it again.

I went to the Annex the day after I saw Blake on *The Tonight Show*. There were about ten other wannabe comedians in line and I signed up with them. They gave me my stage time and I went out for a drink until it was time for the club to open. Once there, I worried about what jokes I was going to tell on stage, but that anxiety paled beside my psychological state. I don't know how else to describe it, except to say that I was trying to make a very wide U-turn in the road of self-esteem. They finally called my name. I went on stage and I don't remember much besides the audience laughing much more than not.

Right after I said thank you to the audience and walked off the stage, I went outside, looked up at the stars, and said, "God. One year from tonight, *The Tonight Show*." I will never forget that it was October 17—I think—and that the sky was clear and sparkling, filled with Texas stars. I also thought that God probably wouldn't mind such an insistent tone coming from someone who hardly ever spoke to Him at all. I'd never before felt so much hope unattached to another person.

Steven J. Moore, the artistic director who emceed on audition nights, came outside and said, "I want you to be a regular here." I almost cried. That meant that I could sign up for spots during the week and could work out of the club. And it was my first time there. My gratitude and ego practically canceled each other out. Then he kindly added, "You're really not good enough to be a regular yet, but these guys will eat you alive if you only come here on amateur nights." I shook his hand then went in to have five or six drinks.

Sometimes I felt like the only girl player on a baseball team. Even though I believed my act no worse and no better than any of the newer comedians, there was always the implied "girl on the show" attitude to deal with. Black and Hispanic comics probably felt the same way, and I think that's why they were nicer to me, collectively, than the White Boy Club.

This isn't to say that I had no allies. On the contrary. A bunch of them were just plain terrific. Steve Epstein, Dante Garza, William Melvin Hicks (aka Bill), Cheryl Holliday, Andy Huggins, Conrad Lawrence, Rushion McDonald, Dan Merriman, Steven J. Moore, Nat Perkins, Ken Polk, Gary Richardson, Bill Silva, and especially my dear friend Ron Shock, all treated me as an equal, and with kindness and respect. (If I have omitted anyone's name, it's only because a long time has passed and I might have forgotten.) I used to catch Ron looking at me with a grin and I'd ask him what the hell he was thinking. He used to laugh his one-of-a-kind laugh and say, "You're gonna make it, Butler." Ever defensive, I usually just said, "Right," rolled my eyes, and left the green room.

The camaraderie made me happy, even when it was the tense variety. The ones with whom I had discord were probably more like me than any of us would have cared to admit. We were just drinking and scared, and they viewed anyone new as competition. I think we needed targets for our fear and rage and, since we ranted in the same bottleneck, it became each other. If you'd taken away the booze, the problems might have stopped, but then I don't know how many of us would have been performing.

Some of the improvisation players from next door, many of whom were talented actors, came to do stand-up, too. It was disconcerting to see them excel in another arena and still be—collectively, anyway—more balanced people than we were.

After I was there for a while, a few of the headliners would start to throw some advice my way, like they did with any new comic. I'd been asking them things all along, but not a lot at once. I noticed that the better they were, the more secure they seemed to be with sharing "trade secrets." For example, Dan Merriman would tell me to work—or at least focus—on one thing at a time—facial expressions, writing, posture, ad libbing. It helped me concentrate better, and I was glad for the tips.

When one of us was doing well on stage, it was common to see the other comics sitting in the back row staring intently without laughing. I think this was less of an intimidation tactic than a form of study. All of us had miles to go, with the possible exception of Bill Hicks, whom we knew to be divine.

I can't really talk about my first years in comedy without mentioning Hicks. At twenty-one, and younger than almost all of the others, Hicks was the "baby." The oldest baby in the world, we guessed. His ancient qualities were apparent to all of us. It was as if something magical was happening right there at the Comix Annex at San Felipe and Shepherd in Houston, Texas.

We'd go in to watch Hicks every time he was on, laughing at the same stuff over and over, just to be there when he'd come up with new stuff. I never saw another comedian like him. Even when the subject of a bit was something as mundane as cats and dogs, one of my least favorite topics because of its pedestrian nature, Hicks could come up with a cosmic take on it. He would flow from the lurid to the sweet in a matter of seconds and then right back again. He had the ranting energy of the devil on her period, flowing smoothly back to the boy you'd take home to meet your grandmother—knowing full well when he got there he'd find a way to scald every tenet she held dear. Hicks was a beacon for a lot of us. Today, a few years after his untimely death from cancer, there are some who would say that his impact was overrated. But I don't think there's one of us who wouldn't have traded our entire acts for five minutes of what Bill could do on stage.

Houston was a passing-through sort of town. In between comedy and trying to survive, I met some fine friends. Reuben was among the best people I got to know while I was there. He lived across the street from me and had a hairdressing salon in the living room of his house. I saw lots of things for the first time at his house: *Interview* magazine, New York art, and all-black outfits. He used to say that his reason for living was to help me acquire a "fashion sense." His pals were skinny, hip people wearing black clothes. I would come by in my cowboy boots and denim skirts, wearing T-shirts with the names of auto-parts stores on them, or else frilly shirts that were a Texas woman's idea of dressing up. Reuben and his friends gave me make-overs a little bit at a time.

Reuben and I talked about art, music, and politics. He said my drinking was something I'd grow out of. I hadn't mentioned it. He just brought it up one day. He knew I'd already crashed a car and could've been killed, and that I still drove around that way late at night. He would smile and tell me, "Your brain is too busy to be sober," and he said, "When you do quit drinking, you better call me and tell me how much fun you're having."

One day after coming home from a gig in Louisiana, I saw a wreath on his door. Friends told me that he had been shot and that his body had lain there for a week. If it hadn't been for the heat, there's no telling when they would have found him. The police came by to ask all of us if we'd seen anything at all. Because Reuben was Hispanic, the case had been turned over to the Mexican Murders Division or something like that, and you could tell the officers knew the case would remain unsolved. We all knew it. Reuben just took the wrong person home on the wrong night. They said he'd been shot while on his knees, his hands tied behind him.

Reuben took me to see Tina Turner when she was starting to tour on her own, after breaking up with Ike. She was so strong and wild and great. Reuben said, "I thought this would be good for you. Look how far she's come." Reuben was the first person to tell me that I should try being a blonde.

⁓

A bunch of us went to a music club after our sets at the Annex one night. It was a Monday and we were listening to a piano player in the bar downstairs from the big room, which was closed during the early part of the week. The manager was emceeing the show and he began to speak with us from the stage as we drank, focusing on me. We got off a few good ones, and since I was in rare form, most of the laughs were mine. During his break, the manager came over and asked me if I wanted to host the Monday shows for the next month. It took me a minute to realize that I'd just gotten my first paying gig. The next time the club sent out its flier, my name was on it in big letters. (I still have the thing.) The pay was paltry, but included drinks, and I couldn't think of a better job for a two-month-old comedian to have.

Since that happened so quickly and by "accident," I thought I'd try my luck at other clubs. If I didn't have an early spot at the Annex to bolster my confidence, I'd just get dressed up at home, drinking wine and putting on mascara while memorizing my set. I'd get in my car, drive around, and look for bars advertising bands. After pulling into the parking lot, I'd sit there, trying to work up the nerve to go in. Pretty girls would be walking by with their dates, men who looked so strong and protective. I think I just saw them that way because I was afraid. It was hard not to feel so damn different from them as I sat there in a limbo of purpose and anxiety. Half of the time I would have pushed my car and my act over a cliff just to have a date myself, or at least someone to be with.

Pot made me forget my material, so I braced myself with wine. When that wore off and I got thirsty enough, I'd go inside, order a drink at the bar, and look for the manager. I'd shake his hand and then offer a run-on introduction: "Hi, I'm Brett Butler and I work over at the Comix Annex and have my own show at Fitzgerald's on Mondays and I was wondering whether you'd let me go on and do about ten or fifteen minutes of my set when the band's on its break and you don't have to pay me." I could tell from their expressions that they weren't used to hearing that, much less from a woman. I truly believe that I got much of my early stage time because of the curiosity of bored men. One of the first managers I asked said, "Damn. I was hoping you were here for the waitress job. I just had one call in sick." I was so desperate that I said I'd even sling hash if he'd give me stage time. He laughed and said that I should just "get up there and get it over with." Another manager said, "Okay. That's the stage right there." It was about five feet away from us. I guess he thought I wouldn't be able to find it without directions.

One night I had to speak directly to the lead guitarist in the band, who said, "Hell, yeah. I'd like to see a gal try to be funny on purpose." He led me to the bandstand with the admonition not to "touch shit." I didn't. During my set, I saw him laughing and wondered if he knew I was being funny on purpose.

Getting on stage under such circumstances was nerve-racking. Most of the time, I'd have to introduce myself. I guess no one wanted to accept responsibility if I wasn't funny, so I'd climb up and just start talking. At first, everyone would pay attention. Once they figured out that I wasn't giving away free drinks or a T-shirt, many of them would go back to whatever they'd been doing, which was usually talking. Loudly. It wasn't like I was playing places where they listened to the bands, either, so I didn't feel completely diminished by an audience's inattention. But when the band laughed at my jokes, I knew I had a fighting chance.

It was scary, but doing comedy this way taught me that there was much more to it than just being able to write and remember the jokes.

I thought I was on to something, with this new rendering of "Avon-calling" comedy. One good set led to another and, fortified by laughter and more drinks, I'd get in my car and hit another club. I did this for months. Along the way, I'd get a puff of someone's joint or a bump of blow or just enough gas money to get out the door and do it again. One night I did eight shows at eight different clubs and taped them all. The sound of my voice on the last show of the night was liquid and garbled. At first, I thought the battery on the recorder was dying, but it was just me. I think I even finished the last set sitting on top of a piano at a gay bar. It's hard enough to remember what jokes you tell when you're sober and you have to do two or three sets in a night. I've no idea how I didn't repeat myself when I was sloshed and had to perform the same material eight times.

One night the agent for the Annex called and said that he had a one-nighter for me. It was a comedy club in Lafayette, Louisiana. It was for two shows on Friday night and the pay was seventy-five dollars. I took it, even though the round-trip bus ticket there was fifty-six dollars. Once I got there and finished the show, the manager of the club couldn't believe that

I'd traveled that far for that tiny a profit. She let me stay the next night for free and even go on stage. It was my first out-of-state gig. The audience was a bunch of flannel-shirted men who were drinking heavily. I mentioned as much to the bartender before I went on. He told me that the men had been working on offshore oil tankers and that they had to come in due to high seas in the area. Then he added, "You ought to do pretty good—most of 'em haven't even seen a woman for at least a month." Great, I thought. And I bet the first thing they want to see one do is tell jokes.

The stage was so high up and close to the audience seats that the only way for them not to see up my skirt was for me to get far back, near the curtain. Finally, I just walked close to them and joked about it, telling them that if they'd be kind enough to listen, I'd toss my room key on the floor when I was done. They were great. The novelty of being a female comedian was almost more entertaining to them than any jokes I thought of. When they laughed at me, I think both of us were surprised.

Around the time I was running amok at bars, whether working or carousing in them, I got my first full week on the road. It was the "big room" in Austin. Other comics would return from the club saying the crowds were the greatest and that they were hungrier for comedy than any other place they'd ever worked. Headliners of national importance liked working there, too. This was the beginning of the comedy craze, and we all felt like we were part of it.

When the agent called to ask me to emcee the Austin room, I was so excited that I quit my job. At this point, I was barely hanging on by a thread and figured that the added desperation of being unemployed would give me the impetus to go out and try hard at booking myself. Just going to new cities excited me, and the chance to perform in them, too, was downright thrilling. The fact that I was getting paid to do what I would have done for free seemed criminal. Most comedians, I think, just to ply their craft will seek stages and crowds that are close to being battlefields. I honestly don't think I am exaggerating. I'd worked some of the worst rooms already: Austin was a reward.

I packed for the trip like I was making my damn debut on Broadway. Since Reuben was dead, I had to do it alone, and I didn't know anyone who could help me make the wardrobe transition from barmaid to comic. The only two women I'd even seen working the "big room" were Judy Tenuta and Marsha Warfield. Somewhere between the gauze fantasy of Judy and the tough darkness of Marsha was where I would find sartorial peace.

I had been trying out not drinking, and I think I was in the middle of two weeks or so of not having a single drop, so the way I got to Austin is actually very clear to me. Since I was responsible for getting myself the few hours across Texas—and just about anywhere in Texas is hours from another place—a sober friend said he had to go there on a business trip and that he'd give me a ride. About halfway there, he cried, "Oh, look! Female cedar trees!" I couldn't recall ever hearing that phrase before, much less in an excited tone, so I just replied, "Really? Great!"

He pulled over to the side of the road, got out of the car, and ran toward the aforementioned flora. He started grabbing branches as if they were made of gold. When he got back in the car, he began waving around the greenery. After a minute of this I asked what the hell he was doing. "The female of the species exudes negative ions and we need some" was his reply. When he dropped me off at my hotel, he said, "Here. Take one. You'll need to purify your room once you get there." He was serious, and even if I thought he was crazy, I was jealous. He might have been nuts, but I had a hunch that he'd be sober longer than I.

Meanwhile, I was as unsuspecting as that poor dismembered cedar tree en route to Austin. After telling some of the other comedians that I was going to be working with someone named Lenny Schultz, they told me to "dress dry." I found out that they were speaking literally. For all my care in packing and all my excitement about working my first "real" comedy club, I would be opening for one of the most notorious, messy, and funny prop comics of all time. You might remember Lenny from an old NBC show called *The Bionic Chicken*. Bionic was big then, and chickens— well, chickens are just funny all the time. I'd worked with impressionists, jugglers, ventriloquists, and the "guitar guys," which means guys who knew just enough chords to write some parodies. These latter acts used to drive the crowds wild. Audiences loved them and we hated them. But none of them prepared me for Lenny.

When I walked into the club before the audience was seated, I saw someone stapling plastic sheets to the stage and covering the floor beneath the tables in front of the room. "What's that for?" I asked. The guy replied, "Oh. You never saw Lenny, did you?" I was beginning to wonder about the negative-ion conspiracy and whether I'd make it through the week without a drink. That night I closed the show, standing on the floor of the club, well away from the stage, where Lenny, in theatrically spent tears, was taking his bow. He was dressed in a rubber swimcap, wearing a Speedo bathing suit, covered in spaghetti, yogurt, and peas, and crying as the song "Send in the Clowns" played loudly. I spoke this phrase reverently over and over again: "Ladies and gentlemen, Lenny Schultz. Lenny Schultz." When I got back to my room, I opened the window, threw out the cedar branch, and went out to get a beer. When you want a drink, you can use anything as an excuse.

❧

All at once, strip clubs started hiring comedians. By that time there were about twenty of us in town who were at least making a partial living from comedy, so we gave it a try. The bar owners must have decided that naked women and liquor were not enough, so they just threw us out there, too. Since there weren't really any other women in town who scrambled like I did for gigs, I said what the hell. It was easy money and it was right down the street. I guess I thought I'd be tough if I did it.

My expectations were genteel compared to the reality of a Houston strip club in the early eighties. Every place was trying to "out-sex" the next. Until then, I'd always thought of strippers as rather innocuous, but my only points of reference were the "exotic dancers" who worked at country fairs before yelping, hungry men who were enthralled at the sight of so much flesh before them. Instead, I walked into dark rooms where neither dancer nor lap seemed to be thrilled to be anywhere. Wild as I was, I was amazed at the graphic performances. Mutually participatory excursions that resembled more a gynecological examination than sensual undulating were the norm. I blushed in the darkness.

Even though some of the clubs were "elegant" and some of the women as beautiful as I'd ever seen, something seemed very wrong. The dancers aimed inert gazes and smiling lips at the darkly devoted men at their feet. The music was pounding and the drinks were watery, and in the worst rooms, it was the other way around. And for some damn reason, I thought it might be a place to try and be funny.

Since I was a new stand-up and didn't have much material, I worked the less lucrative lunch shift along with the dancers deemed too chubby to work the night shift. I went on only moments after a dancer had finished, stepping onto the place where she had been sweating and grinding, leaving with money tucked where she could. A few times, after the men had gotten over the initial shock of seeing a clothed woman with a microphone, they would assail me with eloquent arguments about why I should either stop talking or do as my sisters before me had done. I usually replied that if all other methods of getting them to laugh failed, then I would follow suit. So to speak.

Since the men never spoke to the dancers, when they got over the physical effects of whatever performance they'd been watching, and the blood had returned to their heads, I was "it." Things rarely became mean, but there were times I was offended at the sheerly uter-ine level of their remarks. I'm sorry to say that I was not principled enough to just leave. It seemed more im-portant to keep working, learn whatever it was I was supposed to, and take the money. I'd heard about pay-ing dues, and I wanted to be able to say I'd done it. If you're a woman doing stand-up in a strip club—and I don't care how nice a joint it is—honey, you're paying dues.

I became seasoned out of self-defense. Responding to the charming, if occasionally monosyllabic, remarks from the customers sharpened my ability to think on my feet. But I paid a price. I was a witness to murkier sides of hell than even my own. Things that go on in such places are consensual and, for the most part, harm-less. A lot of the women were just regular people, who were skilled, possessing the looks to render such skills palatable, and when they went home, they led regular lives. But a lot of them were damaged, lonely, and ad-dicted just like me. I could write my jokes and stories and at least work at a job I loved, one that didn't re-quire strangers touching me. Perhaps these women were just better at saving time. I waited until I wasn't working to let strangers in my life.

By three or four in the morning, I'd end up at some all-night restaurant eating eggs, just tables away from the girls on their dates who were within minutes of being held tightly. They sat with their men, a little worse from the wear of a Houston night, and I stirred my coffee and stared at them. Drunk as we all were, fired up as I was about working tough rooms and doing well, and as obvious as this sounds now, I was lonely beyond belief.

Two months after I began doing stand-up I met a brilliant, kind, and interesting man. He was funny, too, and delighted in my work. Playing the first Lenny Bruce records I'd ever heard, we'd talk for hours about comedy, analyzing my jokes. He was the first man I'd known who wanted to hear about my dreams. It was as if my aspirations took form as I told him about them, naming them as I went. I told him what I wanted from comedy and what I was prepared to give in return.

He was a musician, a raconteur, a patron of the arts. During the time we were together . . . if anything, he made me feel as if I were teaching him. He was also a highly political man, an essayist with revolutionary themes, existing for activism and theorizing about his leftist beliefs. (This was ironic if only because he was very rich.) His life was a mix of underground radicals, artists, and writers, and he was lonely, too. We fell desperately in love.

He was twenty years older than I, and the difference in our ages did not escape either of us. I tried to keep my musings on my own lost father to myself, but there it was, lurking everywhere. Sometimes we spoke of it, but mostly we fled from those places of sentient doubt where new lovers are loath to tread. We slept with each other and illusion crawled in between our sheets. For as long as we could, we hid. He was the first man I knew who would discuss, not argue; weep, and not ebb. He met my mind and ambition with rare joy. Our stories wove my days together, and I began to land in that dangerous place where I did not exist apart from him. But love that was not agony at some level was foreign to me, and this one was no exception. Beyond the barriers of money and my drinking and my crazy life, we met one another in the shadow of a person I would never meet. That person was his wife.

I'd been with married men before, but never one who loved me back and stood on the edge of Leaving Her for me. Now, I know that I was seeing a mirage. Our want was real, but it existed in the hunger and the ache of our separateness. We cried at fate and wished for freedom, but never hard enough to break the pattern of deceit and surreptitiousness. I had a dream once that we finally went away together, and in that dream I lost him, only to find him crying about his distant children. Our hearts were broken but mine was worse and I went away. Eventually.

Easter morning. We would have
grinned like that all day if
they would've let us stay
home from church and just
eat candy eggs.

Memaw and Granddaddy's
house, around '65

16.

Someone said that the definition of insanity is doing the same thing over and over again expecting different results. Tennyson was more succinct when he said, "The woman is so hard upon the woman." In any case, for about a dozen years I thought doing the same thing over and over again expecting different results constituted hope.

It's Friday or Saturday night and bars are the only places loud and dark and throbbing enough to meet those places in yourself. You ask your boss for one of those nights off, even though the tips are better on weekends, but the feel of bars on weeknights is depressing somehow, not as alive or forgiving. Your desperation is a secret, more easily lost in large rooms full of people who can become someone else for two full days. When you get there, the slowness is only because you are earlier than most. If you haven't had too much to drink before you arrive, you notice that some of them nurse drinks or stop at one or two. You move away from them right away so you can find the ones who do not stop, the ones who make sure that the liquid of the night flows ceaselessly.

Providing that vomiting has not been a large part of your day, wine goes in before the makeup goes on. If there are any diet pills, those must be saved until actually getting in the car to leave. If they are in short supply, then save what you have for the fourth drink at the bar. Chemical consumption while getting dressed and putting on the face and hair is the only method by which to separate oneself from the glaring futility of the night ahead.

I remember bottles of Liebfraumilch, a cheap white wine with pictures of buxom German nuns on the front. The ice cracked as it was poured, and sipping it quickly steadied shaking hands and created glee where shadows once chuckled. It was all to prepare for Happy Hour, an insane phrase by which other people's shadows could also be brought forth and publicly executed.

The men were dressed from office jobs and, provided all you had clean wasn't the trampier fare of the dance club you closed the night before, it was a good time to try on more conventional clothes. It was odd. The women who worked in offices longed to don short skirts and low-cut blouses and maybe eyeshadow that sparkled. Those of us who more closely resembled the girl-behind-the-girl-next door yearned for suits and seamed hose. We were all trying to be different from the outside in. The rich girls had their own bars altogether, and sometimes I stole into those places, sure that my conversational ability was marked enough to make up for my rougher edges.

The most ridiculous rituals were trivial in their rashness or vice versa. Entering the bar, allowing the eyes to adjust to the darkness, repudiating the healthier game of outdoor drinking so fetching to others were important beginnings. Casually finding a stool, looking around with an unhungry gaze, were magic and necessary maneuvers designed to fool yourself as much as anyone. The best part about getting there early was that you could stake out your territory. The only way I'd sit on a barstool late into a shift was if I was so high on things that made me go fast I was certain to bring energy to that spot. It was only a few drinks before my congenital shyness diminished enough to let me breathe.

The bartender comes by and you pretend to think about what to have. On awful nights, the clink of change in your purse makes the choice much smaller than he would believe, looking at your perfectly made-up face, still young, still containing the veil of hope that isn't entirely selfish. (If I had ever won an award for acting, it would have been in those days. But then I'd have had to share it with a million other people who know what I'm talking about.) You ask, with a voice that says you have time on your hands, "What's your house white wine?" He would name it and you would pretend to think about it. Mistaking your hesitation for a challenge, he would list the other availabilities, so you choose the one you pronounce the best and say you'd like to "try" a glass.

When he puts down the napkin, setting the glass down gently, you fight the urge to grab it at once. Instead, you smile, thanking him, and wait for him to walk away. Not sipping it immediately isn't just for his benefit. Certainly it does not look good to appear desperate, but there is another reason. If he is the chatty sort, you'd make the talk, for it is nice to have an ally so close to the elixir. Once he leaves to tend to something else, you find a cigarette, take it out, have it ready to light, and then reach for the glass when no one is looking. It is terrifying enough to watch your hand

shake as it reaches for the glass without having someone else witness it, too.

Once the glass is nearly empty, you try to get the bartender's attention, making sure he is far away and not
facing you. As a matter of fact, you wait until the bartender's the only man *not* looking at you. Suddenly, a
stranger is peering your way. You greet him with your
best casual smile and, using only motions, let him
know you are trying to get the bartender. "Would you
please . . . I need a check. . . ." Your purse is over your
shoulder and you are half off the stool, pretending to
go. When the drinkmaster finally comes over to you,
a sweet "How much do I owe you, hon?" pours from
your still-parched lips. Before you can make the move
a real one, the one to give him some money and go, he
informs you that the "gentleman across the bar" would
like to buy you a drink. Well, if that isn't the sweetest
thing you ever heard. Being a Southern woman comes
in handy right about now, as your hand flutters to
your chest and you argue with yourself, with the bar-
man as a witness, about the propriety of such a kindness. Your make-believe exit was not necessary after
all. With a beating heart of relief, disguised as femi-
nine glee, you cross to your benefactor and begin the
night.

As Lady Brett's boyfriend, Jake, would say, "Isn't it
pretty to think so?" These wishful beginnings never
started or never really finished, and yet they continued

for years and years. The relationships were replicas of ones we'd heard about all of our lives, and even posing for them became impossible without alcohol. Drinking acted as part Sodium Pentothal, part obfuscator, so that the game would be louder than the one in your head. If the words kept up with the pheromones, a sadder phenomenon occurred: you thought you were falling in love.

You start to think love is an excess of emotion, a fine thing when borne by poets who died young or actresses who cried well. Yet there you were in a regular world where people got up and drove to work and wanted lives that matched the pictures of their parents at the weddings. You wanted to be part of that circle except for one important thing—you knew that it never worked that way. So the next best thing would be to kiss longer, screw better, and howl back at yourself. You became ensnared in a horizontal Catch-22: the nice men wouldn't have a woman so easy for more than a night and never when they were sober, and the fun ones, the ones with whom you might have had something in common, would flee into the night, running, often, from the same things you were.

Cheap sex was nonexistent, or else a thing that happened among cheap people. How could that be possible, I thought, when I was so clever, when I noticed everything? My existence was proven only when I was not alone. I would notice the way a man performed his

toilet in the same unself-conscious way and realize that
I was ready to alter any part of my life to accommodate
him. The tragic aspect of such dependency was diluted,
for me, because I perceived it. These were mysteries
that I can only fathom now, and the girl who watched
them is distant and glad to have been found out.

3

One day I woke up after a three-day bender, more colorful than most in that I left my car at one bar, my bra
at another, and was lying in bed with a drunk girlfriend
of mine. With this series of firsts behind me, I went to
make coffee and found, in the Yellow Pages, a self-help
group for people who were trying to stop drinking.
The woman who answered the phone said that she
would wait for me to arrive. She was still there, hours
later, when I finally dragged in. She smiled at me,
shook my hand, and all but ignored the fact that I was
the color of concrete and sweating from glandless
places.

The woman's name was Virginia and she was my
age. She asked how I was doing. I told her that it was
one thing to wake up with anonymous men, but that
it was, despite the "unhip" nature of my quandary, upsetting to have slept with one of my best girlfriends. I
was saying, "I'm not gay. What was that about?"

I looked up on the wall and read some of the things

about what they did in those places and what they hoped to accomplish by being there. I decided right then that I belonged with them. There weren't any magic cures, no membership fees, no judgments. In short, there weren't any of the things that were in my life before I walked in that door. After Virginia spoke to me for a while, I was surprised that I was really listening to her, believing her with all my heart. I heard about her demons and I could tell that they weren't chasing her anymore like they seemed to be pursuing me. I wanted to be like her. I wanted to be free.

For a long time, I thought I found the number to that recovery place because of some divine miracle that sought only me. After all, I didn't know anyone who was sober, so I believed that my intelligence had finally gathered itself to fight this weakness inside me. Then one day, years later, I remembered that I'd been calling the local Crisis Hotline almost every night around 3 A.M. The same guy always answered. He was very kind, calm, and gay, and after listening and listening, he would always say, "Hon, you've got a drinking problem and there are people out there who meet and work on it together. Maybe you could try it." And I would sniffle plaintively, telling him, "Hell, yes, I drink. You would, too, if you had my life." By the time I remembered how he helped me, I'd forgotten his name. I could never call and tell him that his words "took."

No part of my life—no desire, no dream, no behavior—was unaffected by the fact that I have the physical addiction of alcoholism. I've seen "sweet" drunks sober up and find tempers, "mean" ones turn into saints, and have even heard people who have committed violent felonies while under the influence discuss their remorse at having spoken cross words in sobriety. In short, I have witnessed people change for the better and I still wonder that we are not dead.

I danced around these rooms for years before I ever put everything—the drinks, the drugs, the pot—behind me. I'm supposed to say, I prefer to say, that it's just for today. Sometimes the only thing that's kept me from taking a drink, especially in the beginning, was all of the days I had without one. It adds up. Plus I know what would happen if I did it again. I don't know what will happen if I stay sober. I know that alcoholism is progressive: if I pick up a drink right now, it would not be like I'd be picking up where I left off; it would be like I never stopped at all. According to an interior timetable of my own making, I would have died from drinking ten years ago. So there I was. Here I am.

～

Buying something illegal makes you feel dissolute, no matter how provincial you think the laws are that make it so. Pot is one of those things that used to be fashionable, like liquor during prohibition. I suppose it's an apt analogy, but I still hated to buy the stuff and felt free for the first time in my life when I finally stopped.

A year after moving to New York, after I'd quit drinking and doing everything else but pot, I was on my way to Catch a Rising Star for a show. I stopped off in one of the parks where they sell little dime bags of the stuff. Half the time, you didn't know if you were getting oregano, tea, or actual cannabis sativa. I was usually so nervous about "scoring" that I couldn't even look in the bag until I was well away from the place. That night, right after the buy, just as I neared the entrance to the club, an NYPD squad car pulled up and the officers politely asked me to get inside the car. Two of New York's finest seemed friendly enough, and bored with the small-time aspects of giving tickets to pasty-faced WASPs who needed hemp to make it through the night. The cop who was driving asked me what I got. I gave him the bag, and he asked if I'd gotten anything else. I just sank back in the seat, embarrassed at being nearly thirty years old and still doing this, and said, "Yeah. A kilo of smack. Good stuff. I'll take you to the docks tonight for the big shipment." The driver sighed and the officer next to him laughed and turned around and looked at me. "Say. Were you just in Atlantic City? Jeez, my wife and I saw your show. She's . . ." The look from his partner stopped his sentence. They looked at each other for what seemed like forever, and then they wrote out a ticket. They didn't even ask me for identification, but like the polite girl who fears authority, I told them who I was.

Six weeks later, when I answered the summons, I went to court and watched my fellow reprobates get fined and/or sentenced. I noticed that the judge's attitude was similar to that of the police who had caught me. He even made a few jokes as he passed sentence, and sometimes the defendants laughed. This is not to say that I enjoyed any of it. I did not. I felt ashamed, miserable, and too old to be having these things happen.

They called my name, the judge made a joke about it, and I laughed like it was the first time I'd ever heard it. He looked at the ticket and said, "This summons is filled out improperly. Case dismissed." Just like that. I wondered if the police had done it on purpose. Despite my relief, I also thought it wasn't fair. I was the only one that walked out under those circumstances.

My addiction to anything but booze never lasted long enough for me to get "strung out," but my periodic escapades with speed are among my most frightening memories. The obsession with getting high was more disconcerting than the effects of the drugs. Once, during my first marriage, my husband bought some crystal Methedrine and hid it in our house. I literally tore up the place looking for it and consumed a gram of the stuff in an afternoon. Now, as I sit here writing for hours on end, when I have to be up taping an episode of the series tomorrow, I can see where I switched tracks, but I still think of my life, and my impulses toward it, as a pretty fast train.

I was scared of hard drugs, just the same, and afraid of the people who took them. The police could show up at any moment, I knew, and I hated myself for being near any of it. But not being high was worse than such fears, so I stayed to score. Sobriety was uncomfortable. I didn't care whether I was alone or not, just so long as I twisted reality. The peak of hypocrisy occurred when I thought I was better than the people I was with, even though I was doing the same thing they were.

When most people I knew took diet pills or cocaine, they became very extroverted. The opposite happened to me. I would get a quart of cranberry juice (establishing the fantasy of health during addiction, I suppose), and sit in a corner writing and smoking. I'd write until knots appeared on the joints of my fingers. Talking to people was a last resort. Of course, if the only way I could get drugs was to be in a social situation, I would make the best of it.

Sometimes—and I know I can't be the only person who's ever thought about doing this—I just wanted to stop the loud music and say, "Am I the only one who feels horrible right now?" But we were enamored of our ornaments, cushioned by denial. An entire generation built itself around the idea that we were free and that anyone who pointed out the chains would not be asked back to the party. Self-respect was like the emperor's new clothes. And, since people who are using tend to associate with one another, there we were: whole rooms of people who didn't like ourselves, desperately needing the company of those who felt the same. We were there to be fooled. We shared the smiles of false belonging and nonaction. We dreamed fearlessly and lived the exact opposite.

When I quit drinking, almost everything got better right away, but I knew I wasn't sober as long as I smoked pot. I liked pot, I discovered, best of all. But the same process of chemical betrayal that had happened with alcohol happened with pot, and finally, at the end of 1989, I quit that, too. Dreams returned with a vengeance. For so long my brain had been opiated and deprived of these insistent visions, so all I could do was wait them out. When I got completely straight for the first time, I added up how long I'd been high and it came to seventeen years. I was amazed that I'd accomplished anything at all.

I hardly ever want to pick up. But sometimes, because poisonous memories are easy to forget, I am tempted to stray from this constant sense of self. I will pass the smell of a joint on the streets of New York, and I just hold my breath until the smoke goes away. Red wine still bothers me if I'm sitting near someone who is drinking it. So I move away from that, too. It must still look like communion to me. Blood of Christ, indeed.

Feeling good may not be permanent, but it's portable and legal. I have a good imagination and I could not and did not imagine what my life would be like without drinking. Fortunately, I met enough people who'd sobered up and gone down rougher roads than I—before and after. They were happy and were never evangelical, unrealistic, or judgmental about it. And when they talked about "miracles" they did it in nonexclusive ways. I began to think of God in whole new ways that let me in.

This is my favorite picture of me.
Mom says it reminds her of Scout,
in "To Kill A Mockingbird".

Marietta, '65

THIS IS WHERE I ALONE FINISH
FINALLY FAIRLY WELL,
I EXCHANGE IT HAS NOT HAPPENED
FOR IT HAS NOT HAPPENED AND IT
GIVES ME PEACE OF MIND.
LIKE THAT.

—*Gertrude Stein*

17.

Despite famous advice to the contrary, I decided to go home again. I thought Atlanta was better for work and an easier place to be than Houston, so I left. I felt like a little kid again, leaving Texas, chasing my mother, trying to be babied—finally and again. Except that I was twenty-five years old. A friend of mine who was also a comic drove with me all the way from Houston to Atlanta. I cannot think of anyone I'd rather have been with less than me for that long at that time. I was broken from leaving my married lover, and decidedly off the wagon. Years later, that friend and I spoke of the trip to Atlanta and he said, quite calmly, "All I remember is you crying and screaming the whole way." An apology didn't seem sufficient.

After I'd worked around Atlanta for about a year, dabbling with sobriety as only an addict and a dilettante can, I started feeling better. Comedy was my mission and it gave me someplace to aim. Besides, I was hanging around comedians, and there was always someone more screwed up nearby.

I was beginning to wonder what my next move should be. After talking with my former flame in Houston, I thought about moving to New York. Robert Klein had already suggested it and my ex-boyfriend agreed. "You should go," he said. "You'll learn more there, and getting out of the South will be good for you." Klein said, after we had worked together, that by staying in Georgia I was in danger of becoming too provincial and locked into safe references—and not only on stage. He and my ex were both New Yorkers, both Jews from the Bronx, as a matter of fact, and I thought they were both right.

My old boyfriend said I could stay with some old political friends of his. I told everyone I was going, and the only person who seemed to think I could make a go of it was Mom. She said, "Oh, honey, this is great for you. That's where you need to be for anyone to see you." I worked one last gig in Savannah and drove north from there. I was so thrilled that I kept a camera on my lap the whole time. By the time I saw a sign on the highway that said NEW YORK CITY I took pictures of it. I couldn't believe I was finally going there after a lifetime of imagining it.

I had spent the first twenty-six years of my life in the South, never having been farther north than Washington, D.C. Arriving in Brooklyn after an exhausting two-day trip, only to move in with real live Communists, is a great initiation to the town. I called my roommates the Lenin Sisters, even if one of them was really a liberal Democrat. The Communist was more stern, and reminded me of my old college roommate, Amy. I would be in the bathroom putting on makeup, and she would ask me if being in shows was what I wanted to do with my life. After all, she was a college professor who also marched for the rights of the oppressed, and I was expertly applying mascara for the millionth time, barely able to use the word "dialectic" in a sentence. She fought for social services, tenant rights, and equal pay for equal work. I was worried about getting on stage at a decent hour.

It was late October when I moved to Brooklyn. Late at night, after my roommates were asleep, I would peer at the Manhattan skyline from my pallet on the floor, colder than I had ever been, wishing I could go back to Texas and be the mistress of a married Marxist millionaire again. Anything but this, I thought. I began to realize that the magic of New York was not altogether its greatness, but its darkness, too. Its enormity and frigid temperatures astonished me. I would walk down the streets, smiling at passers-by, not living within a thousand miles, I reckoned, of anyone who would smile back. It took me months to stop saying "Hey" to people I did not know.

I wanted to go home, but I didn't have one. I felt like Sherman and Atlanta at once, burned out and still marauding. But my jokes were starting to get good. . . .

New York itself was like the boot camp I tried to escape years before. It was especially tough, because I didn't bother to familiarize myself with any of the rules. Nearly every time I went out to my car, there were tickets on it, with illegibly scrawled infractions. The notion that you had to go outside every day just to change the side of the street on which you parked struck me as a form of punishment. A couple of months after my arrival, I was driving one night on the Brooklyn-Queens Expressway and saw a wheel roll past me in the next lane. When my car suddenly clunked forward, it dawned on me that it was my wheel. I got out in the freezing December air and saw that the car's axle had broken in two. I removed my license plates, out of affection more than anything else, and hailed a cab to Manhattan. When I arrived at Catch, I had to borrow the eleven-dollar cab fare from the bartender, and I figured that what I owed in tickets would have bought a new car.

Then I learned how to use the subways. Once on the warm cars, facing other people with temporarily visible lives, it was comforting to be among them. I tried to imagine where they'd come from and where they were headed. I also wondered if any of them were as curious as I was about whether or not they were on the right train.

Despite my continual, peripheral search for romance, comedy became the driving force in my life. However, as I first tried to become sober and was told that hanging around clubs, even for the sole purpose of being funny for money, was a way to get into trouble, I almost gave it up. But then a friend of mine who had been sober for forty years said, "Yes, quitting comedy might work for a while, but then you'd just be miserable in some safe little office, filing papers because you never finished college or learned to type, sitting next to a fern, and one day you'd set a match to the place and go out and get a bottle of whiskey." I liked her scenario. Not because I planned to duplicate it, but because I wanted someone to believe in me. But there was something else happening with comedy that had never happened before with any other job. It was the first job that I'd ever had that I didn't savage or ignore for a man.

But, like the old saying goes, "When you're not

lookin' for it, it finds you. . . ." Meeting Ken, three months after I got to town, was the closest thing to a godsend in human form that I'd ever known. When he found out that I was a comedian, he wasn't taken aback at all. Some guys, after hearing that I told jokes for a living, used to get an expression that seemed to say, "Oh, that's cute, but what do you want to be when you grow up?" Ken's kindness and strength were apparent immediately, as well as other traits that I found curious and refreshing. His cleverness stood alone and he never used it to impale nonbelievers. He smiled deeply and generously and did not rush to tell the world his opinions. I was surprised that he liked me, too. (My mother's sister, Ann, was married to a quiet man, given to calmness as well, and years later said, by way of explaining the chemistry of the diametrically opposed, "Honey, if it weren't for us, they wouldn't have a pulse.")

Ken and I met at Catch a Rising Star, where he'd come to see our friend Ariel, who tended bar. We got to know each other in New York time: he worked during the day, after just graduating from college and applying for law school, and was living with his parents. Since my last boyfriend lived with his wife, this was an immense improvement, in my mind, and a wholesome change at that. My schedule was so insane, and I was busy moving in and out of apartments, anywhere I could find an extra room or someone who would take rent for sleeping on sofas, and we more or less kept track of each other, before any actual dating, when he would stop by the club to say hello.

My favorite story of our beginning happened a couple of days after being introduced to each other after my show at Catch. It was about six in the evening and I was hurrying to cash my first paycheck from a dubious day job. I saw him ambling toward me on the street and I did a double take upon noticing his height. He'd been sitting on a barstool when we met, and now I could see that he was almost six and a half feet tall. The brief time I'd been in New York had taught me not to mince words, and I just crammed what I was thinking into that moment. I said, "Hi! Boy, you're really tall. I guess people say that to you all the time. Anyway, do you want to go have some soup in a little while?" He nodded yes and those eyes, the eyes I would fall further and further into and not regret, were smiling at me.

I continued, "I have to get this check cashed first. I don't think they want me working there anymore, but that's fine because it only took about an hour to make this." I showed him a check for two hundred dollars and surged on. "My girlfriend Vivian got a job doing phone sex—oh, not the kind where you talk to the people who call, but the kind where you do the tapes that are one to three minutes long, and she got me a job there, too. They pay you twenty-five bucks a minute and if you write the damn thing, they pay you fifty, but I never did that. You know what's really weird? We made more money than the women who have to talk to the men. That doesn't seem right. Anyway, I went in, but the damn thing's at nine in the morning and you just can't do that stuff with secretaries on the other side of the door, you know, just looking at you when you leave like you've really been in there screwing or something. So I got my check today and, gosh, I hardly make a living at comedy, yet, so I'm really excited about having some bread for a change. I think a club owner down the street will cash it for me, if you can wait until the place opens and I'll meet you back here in a couple of hours. Is that all right?"

About five minutes after I walked away, it dawned on me that I'd never met a man I felt so comfortable around so soon. Part of it was that I was just trying to get by and didn't have time for a bunch of false talk. Then I thought about how he just kept smiling at me when I was blabbing all of those things to him. We caught up later that night and, without fanfare, began to spend time together.

Our winter romance was like one of those corny love songs and I will mercifully spare the reader the lyrics. No matter how late I'd worked the night before, I'd get up early and walk from the Sixtieth Street and Second Avenue studio apartment I shared with a waitress at Catch up to Sixty-ninth and Third, where Ken lived with his folks. He would come down to the lobby, and then we'd walk together to his job at a greenhouse on the East River. It was a snowy winter and, at that hour, the city was still in its pajamas. The usual noises became softened in the white, matching that goofy dream walk of someone in love. Trucks and horns moved like shadows of themselves, because the snow-covered concrete couldn't amplify them.

We'd go get bagels and coffee and walk to the rooftop greenhouse, watching the sun finish rising. Then I'd walk home to go back to sleep. It was so silly and romantic that I didn't feel the winter anymore. Manhattan had changed from a blistering lonely town to one that padded my steps and wrapped around me like a coat.

Ken got a kick out of me being a comedian and encouraged me wholeheartedly. I wonder every day whether I'd be as supportive of an occupation that produces so much angst, disappointment, lack of financial security, ego trips, ego, and trips away from home. After we spent a little time together, I noticed that I was painting again and reading more than I'd ever read before. Some of that was undoubtedly due to my decreased chemical consumption, but for whatever the reason, the lines between art and life were getting harder to see. I was happy for more than a minute at a time. I realized that I was in a relationship that had a chance. Whether I could reconcile it or not, the shaky person I used to be was sliding away and a new, stronger creature was moving in to take her place.

Falling in love caught me by surprise. My history in this activity was suspect even by my standards, and I watched the goings-on carefully, almost like an outsider. I reminded myself that I'd moved to New York to pay my dues, not stumble into some affair that would slow me down and cripple my hunger for "art." And now someone was suddenly there for me and I didn't know what to make of it. I kept waiting for him to change, to begin to worry or try to change me. I kept waiting for him to scowl at adversity instead of calmly walking through it. I kept waiting for him not to smile whenever he saw me, even first thing in the morning. But after a while I got used to the fact that I'd just met a really great guy.

The availability of apartments in New York was so sparse that it forced sudden roommates from more unlikely pairs than us. Louis Faranda, a bartender at Catch who displayed a proprietary attitude toward our courtship, arranged a sublet from a friend who was moving to Fire Island. We paid the rent and moved in together.

Manhattan is an expensive place for poor artists to live, but there are thousands of them, so there must be something to say for it. We saved soda cans for the nickels and rolled pennies. Our supper was almost always from John and Tony's Pizza, which was right downstairs. Every day for almost a year we had one of their slices with a Coke.

Our apartment was a third-floor walk-up. The floors were so crooked that a bookcase could not stand. We put the mattress on the floor and stacked books around the bed. The bathroom was one of the first ever made and leaned in a place right beside the kitchen. The tiny bedroom facing the alley stored our landlord's things, so we slept, ate, and watched the city from the living room. There was a little restaurant called The Blue Danube across the street, and I used to draw pictures of the awning and windows from above. Metal trashcans lay askew in front of the basement apartments. There was some sort of weird bell at one door, and people would be there at all hours, whispering into the intercom and looking around before they went in. Ken used to laugh at me for spying, saying I was like Gladys Kravitz from *Bewitched*.

I somehow began to accomplish more than ever. In addition to trying to keep myself booked on the circuit, I was painting and writing constantly. My favorite picture, which I still have, was one in which I painted all the things in our little apartment floating around me while I slept with a smile. We lived with flowers, books, and an alarm clock to guide our disparate schedules. When we visited Ken's parents at their weekend house upstate, we took home huge plastic bins full of lilacs and scattered the branches throughout the apartment. When the first hot day came to the city, the mix of the usual New York aromas and that of the lilacs was comical in their incongruity.

By then I was going out on the road more. I would throw my entire wardrobe of one pair of shoes, enough shirts for seven shows on stage, and two pairs of jeans in a bag. I had one tube of mascara and knew where it was at all times. Like everyone who's broke, I wanted nicer things and more of them, but for simplicity, you can't beat poverty.

My favorite weekend gig was at a club called Pip's out in Brooklyn right on the water. The owner, Marty Schultz, was always nice to me and would give me good spots. Ken would drive us out in his old Chevrolet and, between shows, we'd eat calamari and linguine with the most amazing sauce at Mama Randazzo's. The first time we were there, I asked the woman who cooked if they sold the sauce by the jar. She said no. I said, "Well, could you tell me what you put in it?" She looked at Ken like I was crazy and walked away. After the late show, we had cannoli at another restaurant, and then we'd walk near the water of Sheepshead Bay, never getting home before 3 A.M.

My contention that Southern summers were the most brutal ended when May and then June came to the city. Manhattan cooked in a concrete skillet. Because our apartment was blocked by buildings on all sides of us, we had no respite from it. We had a fan on the floor of our apartment, but it just moved the heat around. Ken would go running for miles when the sun was directly overhead, and any thoughts I had about his sanity were dark ones indeed. I already wondered why he loved me. This need to move quickly while basting did not help matters.

The nights were loud and not much cooler. We melted beneath sheets as we listened to the prom season get underway. Dangerfield's and Chippendale's were popular with the kiddie crowd, and rocked our corner. The limos with the kids from Long Island were endless. From our window, we could see an ocean of long cars, multicolored taffeta dresses, and lusty boys yelling in their pastel tuxedos. Daddy's money was ill-spent on the vomiting, cursing, and less-than-affectionate sexual overtures made by the children in dress-up duds. We peered down at them like we were watching a movie.

Our first love nest was becoming crowded, and we began the search for suitable quarters. The stories about how hard it is to find a decent place to live in Manhattan are not exaggerated. Finally, through relatives of friends of relatives, we heard of a place that would be available in six months. A doctor had lived and worked in this second-story apartment for twenty years, and it looked as if it hadn't been painted in that long. From time to time, Ken and I would go by to check on the progress of the remodeling. It felt like looking at a sonogram of an unborn child.

We were ecstatic to finally move in. I started hanging things up and nesting like I did back in what seemed to be another lifetime. In a bizarre fit of domesticity, I even sewed our curtains by hand, having found colorful remnants at the fabric shop. Thanks to Ken's parents, we had dishes and basic furniture. In New York, it is not uncommon for perfectly good furniture to be thrown out on trash day. If you knew the right streets and the garbage-pickup days, you could score some things that, once painted, fitted nicely in a first home. We got some chairs, a hutch, and a dresser that way. I bought a gallon of midnight blue paint and slapped it on whatever we found. We spent fifty dollars to frame a Gauguin print from the museum and I figured that *Architectural Digest* would come by any day for a shoot.

Even though our living room and bedroom faced Thirty-fourth Street, it was the best place I'd ever lived in. Street sounds were ungodly, owing to the fact that our building was built virtually on the roof of the Lincoln Tunnel. Honking horns and bus fumes pummeled us through the shaky windows. At night, you could hear people—I am assuming men—urinating against the brick wall below.

The decibel levels were like smog alerts for the ears. Jackhammers, taxi horns, and the random swearing of commuters came through our old windows in stereo. One night, not long after we'd settled in, and as we were sitting down to supper, I walked over to the front window, opened it, and asked politely in a tone designed for polite conversation and not a whit louder, "Excuse me. We are trying to have dinner. Would you please be so kind as to proceed quietly?" I went back to the table, lit the candles, and sat down for the meal. For the next few hours, Ken watched me as if he thought I'd suffered a head injury. The city had begun to work its poetry on me.

When Ken was in law school and I was on the road, it always felt like he was achieving more important goals than I was. My dream was to be a brilliant performer, and I wasn't smart enough or working hard enough to make that happen. Writing at night became a release valve for me, even though I didn't know what I was going to do with it. Still, these were the good old days. We were both struggling and juggling the strange combination of jobs that so many couples have. Ken was studying all the time and not sleeping enough, and I was sleeping too much. We began to have a little money, though, and suddenly being able to give our old soda cans to the bag lady in front of our building made us feel well off. For the first time in my life, I could send money home and, after thirty years, I stopped feeling like the world was going to cave in.

჻

Colin Quinn, a good friend of ours and a fine comedian, introduced me one night as "Flannery O'Connor with a tight five." I was puzzled. I thought he was implying something about my mental state, or that of Southern women in general. I hadn't figured out that such broads were considered different, because I'd grown up around them. I wondered if a richly unstable past was something to be proud of, so I asked him what he meant. He was incredulous. "Haven't you read O'Connor?" he wanted to know. Of course I had. "Well, you remind me of her. She told these great stories about hideous people and was funny while she did it." Oh, hell. I wanted to take Colin to meet all the women in my family.

Ms. O'Connor was "core curriculum," as were many other contemporary Southern writers whom I'd taken for granted. Reading notable Southern writers was frustrating. We'd seen and shared the same world, and they were light years ahead in their understanding and descriptions of it. The best I could do, I thought, was to get some of it across on stage.

But Colin was the first friend who knew that the jokes I told about my ex-husband were patchwork quilts thrown over horrible memories. Before that, people thought I was inventing a character like Phyllis Diller had done with "Fang" as a way to mask my alleged dislike of men in general. But Colin knew that I liked men and that my "Fang" had been one real man and that my jokes were a far, far kinder version of the truth.

For years, I'd let jealousy, pride, and sloth control my allotment of fiction. In a way it was good, because I found out about the rest of the world. Then one day, for a dime at a sidewalk bookshop, I bought a copy of *You Can't Go Home Again*. The next week I said something about it in my act: "They say you can't go home again. You can, but they just don't want you to." Thomas Wolfe spoke of leaving the South and moving to New York, broadening his craft and falling in love with a Jew—all things I had done, too. That was enough to make me go back and look at the paths of other Southerners who wielded pens. When their books weren't enough, I read their biographies. (Odd. I possess the smallest regard for gossip and those who purvey it, but think things written about dead artists are different.)

Within such books and the lives of their authors, I found a link with my own depression, addiction, and the need to run away, sometimes without covering any ground at all. Reading what they wrote and who they were was like being part of an adopted family and accidentally meeting my biological one on a bus. But I was relieved because I would not die of what killed so many of them; my death would not be in the chokehold of alcohol or drugs or with a noose of my own despair around my neck. I wondered what sobriety would have meant to them.

ॐ

After a time, I found the stress of New York less over-whelming. I thought that many of the city's most quin-tessential moments were lost on the natives, and I vowed to relish them in spite of my fright or disap-proval. In one of my first taxi rides, another cabbie de-cided he didn't like something my driver did and gave him the finger as we changed lanes. Without missing a beat, my driver yelled back in his best Brooklynese, "Yeah? Your father shoulda used that!" The other dri-ver just shrugged and sped away to another con-frontation.

Another time, Kenny and I were waiting in stalled traffic while trying to get out of the city for the week-end when we overheard two young men in gentle con-versation. The first exclaimed, "Fuck you, you fuck-ing fuck!" The second gentleman replied, "Okay!" Kenny smiled and said, "Ah, the perfect sentence. Identical subject, predicate, and modifier." Lest its more prurient aspects seem to be what elates me about the city, let me just say that I've never known such a concentration of accessible living, both sublime and triumphant.

The first time I went to the Metropolitan Museum of Art, I ventured into the Asian and African wings before hitting the North American one. After hours of being transfixed by the exotic allure of places and times so far away, I was before paintings of women wearing choking velvet collars and furniture that had arrived a mere few hundred years before. My people. No wonder they got on a boat and came someplace else. England was too exciting for them.

Then I saw one of the giant columns that used to hold up something in Greece thousands of years ago. It seemed perfectly natural to go right up to it and rest my forehead on the marble. I just wanted to feel something that old and belong to time for a moment. Within seconds, I was surrounded by museum guards, who were about to throw me out. I was apologetic and frightened. An amused bystander said that he would "keep a careful eye on me" lest I repeat the transgression. When the guards walked away grumbling, the old man laughed and said, "I always wanted to do that. What did it feel like?"

My favorite trip was to the Museum of Modern Art. For years I had been hooked on Beethoven's Ninth Symphony, shamefully to the exclusion of a lot of other music. I have different versions of it, and that day I was listening to Stokowski's on my headphones as I went in. When I got upstairs and turned the corner, I saw Monet's "Waterlilies" for the first time. I know there are many paintings that he did of this subject, but I had no idea how enormous this one was. The crescendo of "Ode to Joy" caught me as I stood there and realized that I was listening to music a deaf man wrote while looking at a painting a blind man painted. I wondered what either of them would have said to "Yeah? Your father shoulda used that!"

Katy was about a year old and I pretended she was mine... Another eleven-year-old mother in Georgia.

18.

My years of doing stand-up on the road are a fine blur in my mind. In the beginning, all comedians count their series of "firsts"—first standing ovation, first time they have something thrown at them from the audience, first time someone asks for your autograph or recognizes you in public. And I was excited nearly every time I did a show. I really believed that I would be something different to see. I dreaded and tried to ignore jugglers, impressionists, and the like because they were hard to follow. However, I sort of envied those novelty acts for their ability to use often second-rate material and still get huge laughs because they were working with fire, toys, or familiar characters. My favorite shows were ones when I worked with other monologists. In the end, though, we were all trying to do the same thing—be the center of attention and get famous for it.

Now, I try not to be so judgmental. It's too much trouble and people are free to laugh at whatever they want to. There are a few kids out there right now raking in cash for rapidly taking toys out of a trunk, saying something funny about it, and then doing the same thing all over again. Who am I to say that's any less artistic than stand-ups who talk about airplanes and old people driving? Besides, stand-up comedy has largely degenerated into the act of trying to amuse a hyperactive baby. It's no longer proper to blame the messenger. Audiences are spoiled and want fast, easy comedy to go with the food and videos in our lives.

The crowds who once came to hear the comedy of resistance, the most visceral stuff we had to say, just don't come out anymore. Some towns, like New York, San Francisco, Minneapolis, Austin, and Los Angeles (on a good night), still want plain old stand-up. On the other hand, some of the best shows I've ever had were in the most unlikely places, such as Davenport, Winnipeg, Baton Rouge, and Cincinnati.

In 1985, I'd been a "stand-by" act at Catch a Rising

Star for more than a year. This meant that I never got scheduled weekend spots, but got fifty dollars just for showing up in case the "real" comedian didn't. A few times I would be warned that the scheduled comic was nowhere in sight, and I would think at last I was getting to go on for a big crowd. Then whoever it was would arrive, out of breath, and slide past me into the lights. It was frustrating, but I would still get on at "lesser" clubs around town so that the weekend, and my act, would not go stale.

Suddenly, Catch a Rising Star decided to be more than just a club. They went corporate and decided to manage comedians and open clubs nationwide. The only part of this decision that affected me was that they hired a new guy to book the room in Manhattan. Louis Faranda, the bartender who had found Ken and me our first apartment, was hired in the position of talent director. He took his position very seriously, and began putting up the new acts right away. Of course this made the old acts unhappy, but I finally started getting one or two decent times up on stage during the week.

One night in February of '87, Louis gave me my first weekend spot. I showed up at the club in black jeans that had a hole in the hip, a football jersey, and hardly any makeup because this was the beginning of a short-lived phase of trying to be grubby on weekends. I did this because there were a lot of glitzy singers around the place, and it was my way of drawing a distinction between them and the serious comedian I was trying to be. Anyway, as soon as I got in the door, Louis exclaimed, "McCawley's here! He's gonna see you!" Jim McCawley was the guy that booked comedians on *The Tonight Show*. Johnny Carson was still hosting then, and being on his show was just about the only dream my colleagues and I had.

There wasn't time to flip out. I had been working so much that my material was honed and my heart started flipping at the unexpected opportunity. Then I looked down at what I was wearing and despair ripped through me. I had less than ten minutes before I was supposed to go on. A couple of the waitresses, Selma and Cheryl, cornered me and got out their bags. The next thing I knew, I stood back with a cool leather jacket, which covered the ripped jeans and jersey, flashy red lipstick, and hair that had been sprayed and fluffed. They gave me some gold dangling earrings and kisses and I got inside the room.

I'd seen McCawley before. Like all bookers of television shows, he held sway in our little circle. The bevy of fearful sycophants must have made his life wonderful and shallow at once. As I got on stage, I realized he'd never seen me before, and I was glad. I don't think I wanted him to know who I was until that night.

The set was a fine one. Like most young comedians who are up for the game, when I stumbled or the material failed me, I think there was a spark there that said, "Hey, I'm new and I love what I'm doing, so jump right in." I got off the stage just plain happy and proud. McCawley came out right away and introduced himself. Then, like the rest of the dream coming true, he spake: "Johnny's gonna go nuts when he sees you."

Just knowing that I was finally going to get my shot changed everything. It was as if I had more blood inside me. I began to write with a vengeance. But instead of writing jokes, which I desperately needed, I started writing short stories until dawn. It's a pity that I needed external validation, especially from something as ephemeral as show business, but I settled for it wherever I got it. I borrowed the boost and used it to make art someplace new.

The week after McCawley saw me, I went on the road to Cambridge, Massachusetts, where Catch had opened a new club. Excitedly, I told the headliner what McCawley had said to me. I knew the guy pretty well and liked him. Since he'd been on the show with Johnny lots of times, I didn't worry that he'd be jealous. But instead of *kvelling* a bit, he smiled a drop of poison, saying, "Jim says that to everybody." I don't know who was more surprised when I lit into him. I remember saying something about there being more camaraderie among lawyers and couldn't he just say, "That's great," and let it go. After the shock of my speech wore off, he said, "Brett, I was just kidding!" I forgot we were comedians sometimes.

The guys from Letterman had been telling me that they wanted to give me my first spot on Dave's show, but they came and went so fleetingly that I never really hoped hard. *Late Night* was aloof in its hipness. Breaking the barriers of mystique was tough to do and I'd resigned myself to not making the grade. I kept trying to make my material the sort that I liked to hear, but still could not shake what I was: a young Southern woman who looked simple when she smiled and cussed to spite expectation.

I felt like I had three acts working at once. I was capable of doing the kind of unremarkable, observational comedy that would probably get me on TV, so I had those five-minute sets of clean, sweet stuff. Then there were the times I just talked and said true things about what I thought about and where I came from. But the third comedian was the dark one, the one who ran and railed and fought hard to be listened to, being profane or abrasive if the occasion called for it while still trying to be funny. For a long time, I think I got booked because I was, at least, interesting. But I was beginning to get anxious about when all the parts of me would come together.

Then McCawley rang and asked me to fly out to Los Angeles so he could go over my act with me. I scraped up money for the ticket and stayed with a girlfriend who had moved out there the year before. All I remember about LA the first time was that it was very bright and the air was a room that hadn't been dusted. It was tough playing rooms where no one knew me. After a couple of years in New York, I at least felt like I belonged and had earned my stripes. But when I got there, the audiences did not seem to like my slow speech and dark fast lines. Crowds are like horses: they sense fear and will not let you ride them. McCawley was very patient and understood my disorientation. "Don't worry," he'd tell me after so-so sets. "We're still putting the set together."

Once I got back to New York, however, he didn't seem in as big a hurry to get me on the show. On March 9, 1987, Mike Wilson, the talent booker on David Brenner's show, called to see if I could do the show the next day. Someone had dropped out and they needed me. I said yes. I called Jim and told him I was going to do Brenner's show. He gave me a hard time, reminding me that "Johnny likes to give comedians their first national exposure." All I could think was that old "bird in the hand" thing and told him so. Besides, I argued amiably, this would make me better when Johnny saw me on his show. It would be good practice. Jim relented, but was still unhappy with my decision. I was left feeling less than positive about my chances of being on *The Tonight Show* in the near future.

The great thing about short notice is that I didn't have time to think. I thrive on certain kinds of stress, and comedy is one of them. I had *The Tonight Show* set planned for a month, so I just dished it out over the phone to one of Brenner's producers.

Seeing the tape of my first Brenner show is like seeing a girl I knew a long time ago and liked. My hair is shaggy and my clothes look like scrambled eggs on a cheap plane ride, but I'll never be that fresh or sweet again, at least not in that way. The set was better than I even hoped for. Since Brenner taped in New York, it was just like a club on a good night. As they say, I killed. People were screaming. I think that part of the reason they were on my side was that, in my introduction, Brenner told them that it was my first time on TV.

The next day, Rick DuBrow wrote a review of my appearance in *The Los Angeles Herald-Examiner*. It was the best press I've ever gotten. I sent him a note saying, in part, that while I didn't plan to make a habit of corresponding with critics, I wanted to thank him from the top of my new résumé. He wrote back with a letter that would also bring me to another level of The Business. He said that he was glad to hear from me because a friend of his, Marty Erlichman, was interested in contacting me. Casually he added that Marty was also Barbra Streisand's manager. BARBRA STREISAND'S MANAGER.

Before and since that time, I've had jolts of awareness that made me realize just how far I've come, but that day was one of the biggest. Did he know that I used to walk around like a redneck cabaret act singing "Don't Rain on My Parade" and just about every song Barbra sang before 1969? Didn't he know that this sort of thing just wasn't in the cards for a girl from Marietta, Georgia? Rick gave me Marty's number and said to call him. When I phoned, Marty gave me an explosive validation of my work. I am surprised that I heard him at all through my heartbeat. I expected him to be tough and abrasive. Instead, he offered nothing but support and advice. Thankfully, I'd been in the business long enough to be wary of great big smoke rings. But Marty offered no promises or paternalism. He said that the next time I was in Los Angeles to ring him up and we'd have dinner. Unlike many similar conversation enders before or since, he actually followed up on it.

The next week I received a surprising call from Jim McCawley. He said my Brenner set was great and offered me a date on *The Tonight Show*. I was so happy and called up my mother to tell her. She said, "Well, it's about time they came to their senses." I didn't mention that a comedian who was getting that shot usually had to wait longer than the four and a half years I'd been in the business. The day before I was to fly out to LA and do the show, someone from Catch a Rising Star called and said that they would like to manage me. As badly as I wanted to be represented by people who believed in me, I didn't want to sign with people whose interest was so precipitate. After all, these were the same people who watched me work night after night to get good, but didn't think I'd made the grade until a bigger fish bit. To her credit, the woman who made the call decided to fly out with me anyway so I wouldn't be at the show alone. *The Tonight Show* only paid for one ticket and we couldn't afford for Ken to go, too, so I was glad for the company.

Although May 14, 1987, was one of the most important days in my life, the first thing I remember about it is passing through a picket line to get into the studio. One of the technical unions was on strike and I slouched down in the limo trying to avert their gaze. What a long way I'd come, I thought wryly. The next thing I remember is waiting backstage to go on. The stage manager patted me on the back and asked if I was nervous. I said no, I felt ready. And I did. Ask any comic about the first time they did Carson. It is the comedian's equivalent to knowing where you were when Kennedy was shot.

Johnny Carson introduced me and I didn't fall down when I went out. So far, so good. The audience was generous and I waited until I got my first big laugh to breathe. When they clapped for the first time, I relaxed. I watched the tape last year and saw a complicated woman trying to do a simple thing, half pleased with herself for getting the desired response and half knowing it wasn't enough.

Something funny happened when I was preparing my set with McCawley. I used to have a joke in my act: "I look like a lesbian art teacher from Hartford, Connecticut. . . . I'm not a lesbian, I can't even do improv." I think people laughed because of the cadence of the words, the fact that it was a non sequitur, and the image of me roughly fitting this strange description. All I know is that it worked as well in Manhattan as it did in Mobile. Before the show, Jim said I couldn't do it. The afternoon of my appearance I said, "You've got to let me have that line." He looked at me earnestly, replying, "Brett, Johnny's crowd won't know where Hartford, Connecticut, is." I was flabbergasted. "You mean I can say 'lesbian,' but not 'Hartford'? Good grief, I'll change the line."

Now this bloody joke that McCawley didn't like was suddenly important to me. So when I started the joke, I just changed the name of the city to Santa Cruz. Out of the corner of my eye I could see Johnny lean over his desk and laugh. That's it, I thought, I made Johnny Carson laugh, so I can go home now. Then I did the part about, "I'm not a lesbian, I can't even do improv," and the band laughed.

I finished up, said good night, got the okay sign from Mr. Carson, and walked backstage. Before anyone got to me, I said, "Thank you," and I heard the words "You're welcome." No one spoke them, but I heard them, and that's all there is to it. I'd been performing for four years and finished a good spot on *The Tonight Show* much sooner than many comedians get to, and I had, in the process, forgotten one very important thing. . . .

We went back to the hotel and waited for the show to come on. Then the calls started coming in from the East Coast and everyone said how great it was and wasn't I happy. Hell, yes, I was happy. My friends left and I washed my face and went to bed. Just as I was about to drift off, I realized that while it was great to have a dream come true I hadn't bothered to dream past it. I hadn't planned on anything after *The Tonight Show*. I tried to imagine myself continuing to go on doing five-minute sets on anyone's show and be content with my life. I couldn't talk myself into it, but I wasn't trained for anything else. I guess I ended up raining on my own parade.

❧

When I got back to New York, and some more national spots increased my visibility, there were various people interested in me. I was approached by an agent. Her name was Nancy Curtis, and she was the first person to come up to me and tell me she thought I could act.

I was scared of acting. I always thought of it like one of those scenes in an old movie where someone accidentally pulls a book from a crowded shelf: suddenly the whole wall turns around and you are in a different part of the castle. I just hadn't figured out which book to pull.

Nancy told me that she worked for a theatrical agent, Bret Adams, and that they all wanted to meet with me. Even though I thought she was wrong about my ability to act, I liked her and stopped by her office. Once I was there, Nancy asked if I could perform a two-minute monologue the next day. She said it was a prerequisite to signing unknowns. As I was leaving, I said, "Now this monologue—does it have to be from my act?" She laughed and said, "Oh, Brett, you're so funny."

That night I worked hard preparing the two-minute piece and, by morning, felt ready to impress. I got to the office covered in anxious sweat and taxi dirt. The agents gathered to watch me expectantly, with some of the most tolerant expressions I've seen on any group since. I said, "I'm going to tell the story of my life in two minutes." Then I did.

It wasn't until later that I was able to translate the gazes of the agents who saw that performance. At first they were in shock, but then they paid attention. I suppose even a dull rendering would have been interesting, because I kept the juicy pieces. I think I really grabbed them with the story about getting out of the Army. When I was finished, they applauded. One of the agents grinned and said, "What's wrong? Don't you have a favorite monologue?" Then it hit me. I turned to find Nancy and said, "Oh, God! You meant I was supposed to do some scene from a play or something, didn't you?" I was so ignorant that I didn't even know what she meant when she told me to "do" a monologue. I just thought she'd want something other than my act, so I did the best I could. For some reason, they signed me anyway. I still wasn't ready to act, but I'll always be grateful to Nancy for thinking I was worth a shot.

I probably didn't wait long enough between my first and second appearances on *The Tonight Show*. I hadn't given myself the time to come up with another "perfect" five-minute set, but was so taken in by the momentum of the thing that I went ahead even when I doubted that I could do it right. Literally moments before I went on, I was struck by the asinine outfit I was wearing and thought the only way to save myself was to joke about it. I made some self-deprecating remark that involved Joan Collins without realizing that Johnny Carson had mentioned her both in his monologue and the sit-down piece he did before bringing me out. The sound of silence during what was supposed to be a comedy routine is louder than one might think. Then my feelings were hurt by another guest on the show. He was snide after my set and worse backstage afterward. I wouldn't have cared if I hadn't been such a fan of that person's comedy.

When I left the stage, McCawley came over to me and began complaining about my performance, cementing my hunches about the duration of loyalty in Hollywood. Actually, I didn't envy his position. When things went badly on the show, he would get yelled at, and that wasn't a job for a forty-year-old to have.

Being on *The Tonight Show* presents more problems than solutions after the initial flurry of excitement wears off. You begin the process of getting the hell over it. Right after my appearances, I was trying to book myself as usual, and what I was hearing was, "Just because you've done Carson doesn't make you a headliner." I would reply, "I know. Just let me keep middling." Then they'd give me another Catch-22. "Well, we can't middle you if you've done Carson, either." I couldn't get arrested, as they say. Marty Erlichman called to tell me that if I needed it, he'd send money. It was the opposite of what I thought would happen when I made it to TV.

Offers for smaller TV gigs began to come in. Stand-up was hitting its peak in the clubs, and it was natural that there would arise more forums for us on all kinds of shows. For almost two years straight, I was on some kind of TV show at least once a month. The quality of the shows didn't really matter to me. I was getting stage time and enough checks to make me eligible for AFTRA. I finally had health insurance from being a stand-up comedian.

I did almost every show except Letterman. At first I thought they weren't letting me on Dave's show because I'd done Carson first, but later I realized that I still wasn't cool enough for the *Late Night* audience. My accent kept getting in the way of the credibility I was trying to establish. I was getting edgier, darker, and went too far at times, especially in my live performances. I was still a five-year-old comedian and I think all of us go through transitions about that time.

I was twenty-nine in people years, though, and that was when the article came out about the odds being greater to be kidnapped by a terrorist than for a woman to be married if she was past thirty. I brought it up to Ken. He always said, "You know I'm not going to love you any more just because we get married." I believed him. . . . We had a small wedding.

It was held upstate at the weekend place his parents had. It was raining lightly, which everyone said was good luck, and the bride was hyperventilating. So was the officiant, my friend Barry Steiger, who, in addition to being an ordained minister, was also a good comedian literally on his way to a gig. He had a car idling in the driveway as our vows were being spoken. If anyone in Ken's family minded that he was marrying a non-Jew with a gay Baptist preacher presiding, they didn't let on. I did think I saw a few of them genuflecting, but it could have been my nerves.

Ken was right. He didn't love me any more. He didn't change at all, and that was the best part of my life.

Work was starting to be stressful in new ways. Comedy had turned from a joyous adventure into a competitive race I wasn't sure I wanted to win. Maybe my definition of winning was merely different from anyone else's. I was doing new kinds of material, things that were more personal at a time when the audience liked less of that stuff. The tidal wave of novelty performers was getting the loudest cheers, and those of us who hadn't found our "formulas" were feeling the squeeze. Late night sets in the city used to be for trying out new bits. Suddenly those sets were being scrutinized by the club bookers, whose jobs depended on finding that "new act" who would catapult to stardom, bringing them management commissions. Lately, some club owners have followed that trend too far. Now, many of the new acts cannot even go on stage without signing a piece of paper saying that the club owner is their manager. Everyone is afraid of missing a piece of the pie.

In the middle of this growth period, I was going

back and forth from New York to LA. The trips were getting more frequent and the stakes higher. In Los Angeles, I was always in clubs that were new to me, places that would never let me on stage at all except to appease the TV talent bookers who called the shots about whom they wanted to see. Under such circumstances it was rare to feel welcomed.

There was one club in particular, probably the most famous in LA, where the owner was notoriously demagogic. His opportunistic style was the butt of comics' jokes for years. The sad part is that he is devoid of either knowledge or conscience about any of it. For years, I could not even get on his stage at midnight, and now, if he sees me and I can't move away quickly enough, he'll swoop across the room to kiss me.

One night, years ago, a bunch of us had to sit at a dinner table with this man after we'd finished one of his gigs on a cruise ship. The poor man was speaking rather loudly about being honored as man of the year by an organization that hands out such tributes if you donate a lot of money and don't care who knows it. Within five minutes of watching him coronate himself as Humanitarian of the Century, he said, "I'm so upset. I asked for a Chinese butler and they sent me a black one." When he said this, I had been looking at my plate, so I sought his face to see if he was serious. He was. Later, those of us at the table talked of the different ways we had avoided vomiting after hearing his words.

My delight at having to audition for my third *Tonight Show* at his club was minimal. I was already nervous about McCawley seeing me again after my less-than-stellar performance on the show months before. Then the club owner bumped me so that I didn't get on until nearly midnight, an inopportune time for auditioning, both for the audience and anyone who comes to see you.

I tried out my new material, and when I got off, McCawley came up to me and asked, "What happened?" I started to say that I thought the set went okay, but maybe it was a late crowd. "No, that's not what I meant. I mean, what happened to the nice little Southern girl?" For a minute I thought he had met one of my cousins, but then realized that he was talking about me. I was aggravated. For almost thirty years I had not wanted to be called a nice little anything. Then he proceeded to tell me that my material had gotten too dark, too political, and thematically inconsistent. (Actually, if he'd used this last term, I'd at least feel like he'd been paying attention to the ways in which I was trying to grow.) I was discouraged. I wasn't interested in displaying a discernible persona anymore. It was like people thought my accent was a costume—you could only wear it to certain events. Beyond that, you were overstepping your bounds. I wanted to be able to convey complex bits and still be funny. And I couldn't figure out whether I just needed more guts, brains, or time to do it.

๛

Dolly Parton was starting a new variety show, and her producers were hiring performers. I auditioned for it and one producer, in particular, was quite helpful to me. I read for him, and when I finished my lines, he said, "That was fine. Now do it like you've been on stage killing for fifteen minutes." That was the best single piece of direction I've ever had. I figured out something important about a job that scared the hell out of me: acting. I didn't get the job, but some of the mystery of how to read at auditions began to clear up.

A few months later, they called me back. They were going to overhaul the show, I heard from my new agent. They wanted more Southern input. Alarms went off in my head, but I ignored them. So what if I'd worked for years to be urban and political, despite my accent? So what if being categorized both as female and Southern was often derogatory and limiting? This was the big time, and compromises were called for. I choked on my objections and went West.

The new producer I met was Nick Vanoff. He was so calm, kind, and bright that I wondered if he knew what he was in for. I sat down with him and he said, "So what other shows have you written for?" I said none, and started to get my bag and head out. He laughed and said, "Sit back down. Could you write jokes for Dolly?" I thought about it and said, "I don't know. I'm a stand-up. Dolly's just sort of . . . well, Dolly. I would write things for her that only Dolly could do. She's an event. Put her someplace and I can try, I guess." "Good enough for me. Let's go meet Dolly." I almost jumped up. "You mean I get to meet Dolly?!" "Well, see if she likes you."

He smiled and took me by the hand and into the room next door. There she was. Other than Johnny Carson, whom I never actually met even though I was on his show twice, she was the biggest star I'd ever seen "up close," as we say back home. She jumped up and hugged me. To this day she is still one of the most remarkable people I've ever met. She told me that she was a fan of mine, so at least I would have something to tell my mom that night on the phone. When I left the room with Nick, he told me that I had the job writing for Dolly. I said, "You mean with the Writers Guild?" I thought the cachet of being a writer was far more elegant than being a stand-up. Nick said, "Sure. But we need you to perform, too." I got two jobs at the same place in one day.

The worst part was being away from Kenny for thirteen weeks. He was still in school and could only fly out some of the time. We saw each other at the Christmas hiatus and talked on the phone every night. I stayed at a place in Hollywood that houses transient show-biz folk and didn't mind it because some of my friends from New York were also out there trying to become famous.

At my first day on the job, I was introduced to the other writers. Jesus. They had over a hundred years of writing experience between them. I was intimidated until I saw how nice they were. My boss was Jack Burns. He was too funny to be anywhere. I turned in my first sketch, and he said, "Say there. That was great. Inventive, funny, smart, and different. Put it in the trash on your way out. We're writing for Dolly. This is variety. We aren't reinventing the wheel here." I knew he was being serious in a funny way.

That's when I found out something else about Hollywood. Wait. What I am about to say is probably just as true if someone works for the phone company or a car wash. But it happened to me in LA, so show business will have to take the hit. When we were sitting around with each other pitching ideas back and forth, I was uninhibited about what I said. After working alone all those years, it was a blast to toss around ideas with other funny people. It wasn't even like working except for the tension, long hours, and the fact that the show was in huge ratings trouble.

One of the writers was very nice. He was a quiet Southern fellow who did not seem to possess the manic energy of some of us, and I mistook these traits for decency. I'd tell him ideas I had and then listen in amazement as he pitched them to Dolly as his own. Now I know whoever has the biggest balls wins, but I was in shock. (Someone should have given me a copy of *What Makes Sammy Run?* around that time.)

Oddly, this happened more than once. I finally called him on it. I told him that it wasn't right, that stealing might be common among comedians, even though it went unpunished because the acts were hardly ever in the same town, but that I still found it despicable. And to do it as blatantly as he did was beyond rude. My ire was matched only by my naïveté. When he hurried to put me, however briefly, into a sketch, I realized that a little guilt was better than none. He was actually a pretty nice guy. Unlike me, he didn't have a job like stand-up to fall back on. Impressing Dolly was his ticket out of wherever he came from, and I can't say I blame him for wanting to leave.

Gradually, I realized that no one really *wanted* me to think of anything different. Despite everyone's insistence that I had been hired for "fresh blood," I ended up writing intros for bands and guest stars. When Dolly's audience was seated, I had to go around with a pen and paper and ask them to think of questions for her. But I was in the Guild with benefits, so I did it gladly.

If you saw the stand-up set I did on her show, you'd never believe I'd sent money to McGovern when I was fourteen years old. I wore a glitzy country shirt with a sequined yoke. My voice was even higher than my hair, a sure sign that I was not being myself. The show in which I participated was the most surreal of my career, before or since. First of all, Mary Hart sang and danced, and they wrote some kind of sketch around her based on the fact that her legs were insured for a million dollars by Lloyd's of London. She just wanted to sing, and they built just a bit too much around it. Merle Haggard was on, too, as well as Holly Dunn. Somehow we all ended up singing "Rolling in My Sweet Baby's Arms" with Dolly and, for the viewers at home, the words appeared on the screen. Even though it was a thrill to be singing, or even standing near Merle Haggard, the whole thing was bizarre.

A long time ago, when I was married to Mike and we were living in Lizella, Georgia, and I was staying up late stoned and timing the wine, speed, and pot, I heard a line from *Teahouse of the August Moon* that was so good that I stumbled for my pen and wrote it down. Glenn Ford's character said, "I want to make peace between my ambitions and my limitations." Now, after seeing the tape of me on *Dolly,* I'd wager I lost that scrap of paper I'd carried for all those years. On the other hand, I also thought I could write sketch comedy, and I wasn't exactly doing that, either. I was tired of Oz and wanted to go home.

While I was in LA doing nothing and getting paid, I was asked to do *The Hollywood Squares*. I didn't really see the point, but my agent said it would be good for me. Anyone who'd ever made me laugh on that show was dead, and this new version was a pitiful replacement for Wally Cox, Paul Lynde, and Charlie Weaver. Except for Joan Rivers, I couldn't understand how they could let the rest of us even take the seats. I sat next to Joan. She had just lost both her husband and her gig hosting on late-night television, and had taken the center square to regroup. During commercials, she appeared so frail, comforted by her dog Spike, but, by God, when the lights came back up, she was ready to fire. I was struck by her seriousness when off stage. In the few moments we had to speak, she talked about real things. Her intelligence made the show seem even dumber.

I began to squirm under the artificial lights and wanted to run away. Katy Segal, from *Married with Children,* did leave. We taped all five shows in one afternoon and I saw her heading out the door right before "Wednesday." "I want to go, too!" I called after her. "Come on!" she called back. Then I realized that she'd left Ed O'Neill, her TV husband, back in her square and was covered. There wasn't anyone to take my place and I had to stay long enough to hear the phrase that chased me away from Hollywood until I came out to do the pilot for something called *Grace Under Fire.*

If you watch the tape of my "week" on *The Holly-wood Squares,* you can see me change from a gleeful show-biz ingenue and eager participant into someone who's obviously biting her tongue to keep from saying what she's thinking. Somewhere in that brightly lit box, in between the high jinks of the other celebrities and our written-in-advance ad-libs, I began to re-member why I got into comedy, and none of it was to do what I was doing at that moment. The questions were inane and the answers were worse. One of the contestants, someone who had to look like he was hav-ing fun while fretting about winning desperately needed money, peered up at the nine flashing cubes and said, "I'll take Brett Butler to block." Perhaps it was the alliterative quality of his command or the fact that I wished I'd had the guts of Ms. Segal, who was by now probably resting her feet and happily telling her agent to go to hell. But at that moment I knew that I was going to leave Hollywood and not come back until I had a reason to be there.

It might sound as if that epiphany was as definite as Scarlett O'Hara's when she went out into her once-plentiful yard and bit into a bad carrot, swearing at the sky that she would do whatever it took "never to be hungry again." I'd love to say I was that determined. I just knew that I wasn't ready for prime time and that the only thing that would get me there was to keep doing comedy in clubs, and to keep writing.

꒐

I was happy to be back in New York with Ken. As soon as the season was over, the Writers Guild went on strike. Most of us doubted that *Dolly* would ever be picked up for the next year anyway, despite its two-year guarantee and multimillion-dollar promise from ABC. It just wasn't rating high enough. American audiences hadn't bought variety television for a long time, and even the mesmerizing force of Ms. Parton and her big-shot guest stars weren't changing their minds.

I resumed my stand-up, pretending that I hadn't gotten the fever for Big Time Show Business while I was on the other coast. Luckily, I didn't have to feign the extra confidence I felt after being hired, at least, to write for TV. And I only shuddered a bit whenever an emcee brought me to the stage crediting me with a stint on *The Hollywood Squares*.

Thanks to the superstar powers of Eddie Murphy, comedians were being sought for parts in movies. Producers were coming into the clubs again, buoyed by the success of comedians in profitable films. When they ran out of new talent, they made movies about comedians. It was exciting to go to a movie and see someone that you worked with catch a few good lines. When the audience laughed, you wanted to turn around and say, "Hey! I know her!" Then my colleagues started to get parts on situation comedies. From where I stood, they were gigs like my *Dolly* job, except that none of them, no matter how bad the show was, had to sing along with the words on the screen.

I kept working on my act and hoping that something would come of it. First, my pay got better. The top tier of female comedians were often out of the price range of most comedy clubs and were already opening acts for singers out in Vegas. So that left me. Headlining in comedy clubs with commensurate money finally moved me into a new level of performing energy. It was a fine feeling to be able to follow whatever they put on before me and still do the job. Sometimes I'd work with male middle acts who resented "girl" headliners. They would often do the most sexist, gross material they could think of, stirring up the crowd so that I might have my hands full once on stage. But the heels were in a minority.

Most of the comedians with whom I worked were just like me—people who wanted to be funny, get paid decent money for it, and eventually be discovered and make so much money that we could go back to LA, look up that mean club owner who wouldn't give us the time of day, and set his pants on fire. We laughed at each other's jokes, sometimes made friends with one another, and then moved on to the next job.

Some competitiveness began to rise up between female acts, as well. I am sure it was always there, but it was fed anew by the simple-minded club owners and bookers who wouldn't hire more than one woman at a time. Once, when considering a spot for me on his roster, a club owner actually said, "Gosh, I'd use you next week, but there's already a woman on the show." And I'm not sure how much we helped one another. One established woman comedian even went so far as to state in her contract that no other women could open for her. Whenever a female comic stole material from another comedian or treated a comic badly, I took it personally. After years of insisting that women comedians be treated the same as the men, it turned out that I held us to a higher, and perhaps unfair, standard.

When I started doing stand-up and received generous advice from older comedians, I swore that I would do the same when my time came. But I got tired of hearing women comics complain about being treated differently from men when the first thing they'd do when they went on stage was to start tearing men apart. It was no different to me than the piggy boys who spewed vitriol about "dumb broads." I was tired of being asked how to succeed when I didn't think I *had* succeeded. I would finally just say, "Look. We have a hard job and there aren't any books about how to do it

better. You just have to keep going out there and taping your show and writing it down and making the
phone calls to get work."

As far as the rest of my career went, I was in danger
of losing my representation. My agent stared at me
when I told him that I didn't want to audition for any
sitcoms or go to LA again, for that matter. "Well, what
do you want to do?" "I want to be a really good comedian. Then I'll see." That didn't seem to thrill him. Comedians who really *wanted* to do television were plen-
tiful enough. There just wasn't room for a doubting
purist like me. I realized that I was probably just as
scared of Los Angeles as of being asked to be on bad
television, so when the time came for my renewal papers with the agency to be signed, we both saved face
by agreeing that we'd see each other down the road.

~

Writing seemed so much "nobler" during the time I
was not solvent at comedy, much less successful. For
years, I would stay up late and try my hand at stories,
plays, miniature bits of prose, without any specific goal
other than to try and get better at it. I was a raging
dilettante, capable of flashes of goodness on stage or on
the page, but not enough of either for me to be excellent at anything.

About five years ago I thought I'd combine the two

and do one of those ubiquitous one-person shows that were all the rage in New York. I knew that my life was a unique one and was confident about my ability to portray it as such. Plus, time had given me perspective that would have made such a task impossible any earlier in my career. I figured that performing what I wrote on paper would get me, a step at a time, out of the comedy club scene. The clubs, as the old comics are quick to tell you, ain't what they used to be. Maybe they never were.

Not all comedians, despite the very public nature of the work, are extroverts. Some of the best and most famous are downright shy, and a few are outright misanthropes. (Funny, I am often friends with them.) Comedy was rarely as juicy and autobiographical as it was twenty or so years ago. When Lenny Bruce and Richard Pryor named and claimed their pain, often exorcising it in the process, audiences gasped and wanted more. Their most personal material reflected universal themes. Conversely, when they spoke of the political, they were telling us something very private about themselves. I do not go so far as to say that it is the duty of art to make one uncomfortable, but I need some of that in my own life to stay awake.

These are things I think about, and perhaps it is to digress from the large, tiny place where I've lived and the huge, small things I have done.

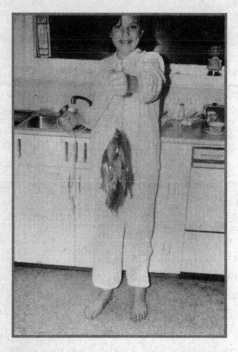

Heaven was ignoring my awkward phase by fishing, spending the night at Memaw's and getting to wear her pajamas to bed.

Marietta, '68

19.

You probably think that if another interesting thing never happened to me it'd be too soon. I will admit I have had more than my share of surprises. But, deep down, and maybe not so deep down, I've always wanted to know about my father. At one point I even considered seeing a psychic just to hear something different from—or added to—the refrain of abandonment that whirled around my head for years.

Thoughts of my father would enter my life suddenly like a splinter entering a running foot. The occasion was rarely familial, and he would be there not getting older, not as I was aging, his voice fading, growing tinny and distant and his face staying the same. He was running, too, as if in one of those movie sets designed to make the actor appear in motion while only a painted screen flashed by behind him. He was running and not moving, away from me and toward me at the same time, forever panting, forever young, as the poem says. I rarely mentioned him at all. My birthdays became marks of my own aging and also anniversaries of the distance between us.

Then, amidst comedy and late-night writing sessions, I got a call from my estranged sister, Toren. I knew for her to call me at all, it must be serious. She told me that she was down in Alabama, and that there was a crisis with Julia. She said that our grandmother, Andy's mother, had tried to kill herself by drowning in her tub. The poor woman had gotten into a tub filled with water, not stopping to think that the rubber stopper was as old as the house itself and would not hold a cup of water for more than five minutes. So they found her there, fully dressed, soaking wet, and mumbling, "Ah wasn't trying to kill myself. Ah just wanted somebody to pay attention to me." We did.

The next step was finding her a place to stay. The task fell to Toren, as well, and she was not too keen on it. Although we had not been close to Julia over the years, it was still sad and arduous to locate the right nursing home for her. No matter how hard Toren tried to see that there was nothing else to do, she felt as if she was just dumping the old lady off to die. Because Tana was out in California with a new baby and I was on the road working, Toren and the lawyer in charge of Julia's trust fund had to do all the work alone. A suitable "home" was located in Birmingham, and Julia seemed glad to be there. Many of her old Florida State College for Women and Ladies' Auxiliary pals were in there, too, and it appeared to be a favorite dropping-off point for the elderly social set of the area.

I was sorry that Julia's life was such that she wanted to die or get close to it. I'd never seen her even cry, although her letters to us since our childhood were filled with such continual apologizing that I grew up thinking they were crocodile tears. She spoke of her "broken heart at how things turned out." I'd seen her a few times since that day Mom and I had gone to Tuskegee, but they were short visits, which seemed to suit us both.

Most of the time, I went to see her at the urging of Memaw, who wanted me to remember my other grandmother with more than greeting cards. Our separateness was not borne of enmity, but was fixed just the same. When I drove to Tuskegee, she never wanted to go out to eat or anything, choosing instead to speak animatedly of whatever paper she was preparing to give at the next meeting of the Ladies' Auxiliary.

She specialized in dead generals and I recalled that the last time I'd been to her house, she showed me her voluminous notes on General "Black Jack" Pershing. Julia sparkled when she told of the generals' adventures, and an ignorant listener might have thought that she was either kin to them or else they had been on active duty the month before, so fresh were her biographies. We would astonish each other not at all and then kiss goodbye. I am not sure whether she gave a good impression of not being lonely or I just chose to believe it. Now that she was infirm, elderly, and being put away, for all practical purposes, I was ashamed of not keeping in better touch with her.

I pulled out a letter she had sent to me right after my first appearance on *The Tonight Show*. This is what it said:

> *Dearest Brett,*
>
> *I hope you receive this, as the last letter I wrote you came back; as we must have put the wrong zip or something.*
>
> *Anyway I wrote to congratulate you on being on the Johnny Carson show, as you were just darling; but I wouldn't have known it if Toren hadn't told me before and I'm so proud of you!*
>
> *Why haven't you written me about all these important things happening in your life?*

You know I love you girls more than anything in the world.

I couldn't help what happened in the past, and it nearly killed me too, because I couldn't do anything.

I didn't have a home you know as I was living with my mother in her house and she had the "say so"; and she wasn't very well either and required lots of care.

I never will get over what I missed in not being able to see you precious little girls grow up, but have tried to keep going some way.

Now, I didn't know about your marriage until Toren told me too; so please see if you can find it in your heart to forgive me, and write to me if you receive this letter.

Since you've married, I didn't know your address, or are you in the same place.

I want to mail you something, and I want to be sure you get it.

So I'll be looking forward to hearing from you right away. Dearest love to you and Kenny,

> *Julia*

I remember getting the letter and writing Julia back right away, telling her that I harbored no ill will toward her and that I was sorry that she thought so. I told her that I was also sorry for not keeping in touch, but that I didn't know if my job was the kind that would make some of the family proud of me. And I tried to make a joke out of a second marriage not being big news.

Although I was making an attempt to reassure her, I was sadder than I wanted to tell her. There I was, almost thirty years old, still wondering why she had hidden my father all those years, never stopping to consider that Julia was imprisoned, too, in a different way than I had been, but locked up just the same. I did not write, either, that I never knew she cared that much, that getting her letter so filled with emotion and apologies broke my heart. I felt worse than a bad granddaughter. I felt like half a person. And now she was running away from home in the only way she knew how.

So my sister began to pack away Julia's life. Our grandmother had lived for more than eighty years in the same house, and, for the last decade or more, alone. In the end, her only roommates were the clutter of misspent lives covered with chenille-like dust. Toren said that the entire place appeared to be on the verge of complete disintegration. I felt for Toren, too, because she was so orderly and cared well for her own possessions. She was an interior decorator, for God's sake, and the only one of us still living amid the image consciousness of Southern influence. Her shame at being related to this mess must have been immense. I could picture her down there in the heat, struggling with severe asthma and grim memories, and did not envy her this chore.

After a day of going through everything, she called to tell me that Andy's room was just as he had left it. His clothes and personal articles were there behind the closed door, and Toren said that she didn't know where to begin with it all. She said that beneath his bed lay an engaging panorama of asthma inhalers, cigarette cartons, and skin magazines. The walls, she continued, had obscene photographs of women with weird cartoon animal heads taped or glued on them.

I was fascinated. I didn't mind that the place was hideous or what secrets were hidden there. Years and miles lay between me, my father, and that house where he stayed for so long in the darkness. Then my sister told me, "There's a bunch of old books here, too, Brett. None of them look worth keeping because they are either filthy or rotting." She sighed, saying that maybe the best alternative for everything was to have a bonfire in the backyard. I caught my breath and asked her if she would send the books to me. Now, my sister is not a book burner in the Third Reichian sense at all. Although she uses the word "Satan" more than the rest of the family, I think the fact that the books were literally covered in grime and largely obscene—from her viewpoint—bothered her. They were not the sort of things she wanted her father to have read. She tried to warn me of the sheer volume of them, as well as their deteriorated state.

"There must be five hundred books, Brett, and nearly all paperback. The ones that are hardcover are about to fall off the spines. It's really not worth the trouble to keep them." I asked if she would ship them insured and I'd pay the costs. To this day, those books are probably the most important things I've ever gotten in my life.

About a week later, eight large boxes arrived from UPS. I don't know what happened to the furniture, jewelry, or antiques, and don't care. It's strange to think that but for coincidence and the possible lure of other relative "riches," the real treasures would be buried in a Macon County, Alabama, dump today.

I began to open the boxes, at first slowly, carefully, and then ripping the tops from the cartons like a madwoman. The sun was streaming in the blinds of our living room. Ken was there beside me as we watched the lost years of wondering roll out of the cardboard, the musty particles rising up and seeing light for the first time in decades. My questions began to be washed over in answers. . . .

My dad read like a sonofabitch! So *that* was how he spent the time in that ancillary womb in Alabama, the house of his mother—reading! My sister was right. There were at least five hundred books. For seventeen years, the same amount of time a locust stays in chrysalis, my father was a prisoner, chained in by forfeit and fear. All of the books, magazines, papers, and notebooks fell out on the wooden floor of our apartment. I wanted to see them all at once, to touch them. One of the first things I saw was an old *Holiday* magazine that was a special issue on New York City. It was like he was in the room with me.

The books ranged from the sublime to the ridiculous. I found classics, obscure novels, coffee-table art books, and foreign publications. There were biographies, references volumes, music magazines, and literary guides. He kept a manila envelope stuffed with hundreds of fillers from *The New Yorker*. He had snipped away at the magazines, saving them for ... what? He also left modern novels, sociological and political essays, poetry, short fiction, and cartoons. Perhaps thirty of the books were strictly about filmmaking and criticism. The authors were nearly all white guys, but among the best contemporary writers, from Thomas Wolfe to Tom Wolfe. He read Buckley, Mailer, Cheever, O'Hara, Updike, Henry Miller, Albee, Waugh, Pynchon, and Flannery O'Connor. And I cried when I found an ancient copy of *To Kill a Mockingbird*.

When I say that I didn't quite "get" my father, it might sound like a corpulent understatement. Actually, the traits in him that might mystify or repel the more conventional person are not hard for me to understand. Not at all. I may have resented those parts of him, but I could grasp them. I was stirred more than confounded. His thoughts about art, politics, literature, nearly everything in his frame of reference, were perhaps different than mine, but the similar interests were uncanny. I had never found a connection between us before, and now I had hundreds of them right in front of me.

Over the years, he had apparently become a supporter of civil-rights policies, as indicated by the articles on the subject. In one of his *World Almanac*s, however, I found a copy of the United States Constitution that was almost entirely underlined in red ink. In the margins, Andy had written an explanation: these were the parts of the document that LBJ had violated. It pertained mostly to Vietnam, I gathered, and it was both meticulous and amusing.

Also, I noticed that Andy had collected random misstatements of John Lindsay during the New York mayoral election in the sixties. His deification of William F. Buckley, Jr., and the near biblical reverence in which he held the man's quotations, were funny and cogently rendered.

I began to miss my father, with all of his opinions and misplaced principles. I missed his heterodoxy, his challenges, and his outrage. I even missed his insanity. I wanted to hear what he thought about the current crop of politicians, in particular, a notoriously inane senator who was rising very high on the ladder of American power. Despite his conservatism, my father always liked a good go at mediocrity.

My father was attracted to the literary equivalents of the comedians I liked: males, urban, often more ethnic than our white-bread Anglo selves; the ones who were enveloped in a mire of not understanding what branded them, ironically, ultimately, with complete sentience. I settled for urban comics who were either black, Jewish, or Italian, while Andy plowed through the best contemporary American fiction writers. The books lying dusty in his room were ones I had begun and tossed aside over the course of my own lifetime, the one I had spent away from him, and now I picked them up again, trying to find either a link between us or a cause for our separation. I found the fiction of lean emotional expectation, of grief and sorrow. Yet there was a splendid side effect—to know those feelings and untangle them somehow mitigated the pain of having them at all.

But I found more than books that other people had written. I noticed little pieces of paper sticking out from almost all of them. Opening them, I saw, for example, that my father would save a book review from *Time* magazine and would write the date of the issue on the review itself. Then, probably for financial reasons, he would wait until the book came out in paperback, buy it, and use the review as a bookmark. He underlined and placed little stars next to certain passages, and put his own notes in the margins in his tiny perfect print.

Then I found what was obscene, and not only within the parameters of the mega-Christian, either. Roland Decatur Anderson, Jr., had an impressive and oxymoronic collection of Victorian pornography and Eastern manuals of love. God only knows how he found them in Tuskegee, but I am damned glad that he did. I was a bit surprised, but then felt our kinship in disconcerting ways. Some of the books are funny and some are downright arousing. What an improper legacy! What utter joy!

My father, in a more innocent pastime, also collected cartoons. He seemed to have everything Charles Addams ever printed, hundreds of cartoons clipped from the pages of *The New Yorker,* plus a lot of old Charlie Brown and Andy Capp, along with "B.C.," too. There must have been fifty books of these amidst his headier fare. As if that were not enough of a coincidence for his stand-up daughter to find, Andy had dozens of biographies of comedians. Now I have books by and about everyone from Stan Laurel to Bob Hope. His favorites, computed from the number of books and articles on them, were Oscar Levant and W. C. Fields.

But the best parts of what was in those boxes were things scattered and scribbled, tucked away in tiny pieces of paper or in the margins of other books. Almost hidden, almost from himself, it seemed, I found comedy that my dad wrote. I do not mean one-liners rendered by TV comics, but twisted, pointy pieces for a wickedly erudite sort of person—perhaps just for himself. The "bits" were toxic blends of politically demented references, free-form rants, and oblique scatology that could keep a sloppy shrink busy for years. I realized that he had been dead for three years before I set foot on a stage to perform the one thing he apparently could not have enough of, especially in his lamentable life. My old man wanted to laugh.

Some of the material added to the mystery of my father's life and when I could not answer his secrets, I felt for his losses and brooded over my own. He'd placed asterisks beside the visa requirements for various Latin American countries, which were found in *World Almanac*s dated to the year of his death. And I found almost fifty articles about New York City. My mother told me that he'd never gotten to see the place. Thinking about a trip, Daddy? He drank in that room while he listened to symphonies, read editorials, and tried to be funny all by himself.

Then I saw the first thing that made me mad. The context of my anger surprised me, but there it was: starting in 1965, he had compiled more than a dozen spiral-bound notebooks filled with stats from the Crimson Tide, the University of Alabama football team. His charts and clippings were precise. I just wanted a fraction of the time he must have spent in keeping those records. What an obsessive bastard he was.

An odd postscript to this was that when I mentioned to Julia, after visiting her in the home, that I was thinking about giving all Andy's memorabilia to the Bear Bryant Museum, she became terribly upset. She pleaded, "Don't do that! The reporters will come here and start digging and asking questions and find out everything. Please, just let it be." Lord. I was just making small talk. She had been so long in the iron but lace-covered grip of convention that she was beginning to think her crazy son was actually illegal. I didn't press her, but thought I'd been quite polite in the past, too polite, never just coming right out and asking her, "Why in holy hell did you hide him out all those years? What on earth was he doing in the back of your house? What did y'all talk about? Where did he take your car at night?" But she's old and she's my grandmother and I'll leave her alone and wonder by myself. She'll take the answers to her grave with her and, if God's as funny as I think He is, she'll outlive us all.

I thought I could suddenly and simply civilize my father by putting his possessions in piles. Within the boxes, I also found more personal items: a notebook from his sixth-grade science class, a shoe brush, a calendar stopping at November of '79, smaller things, things that said, "I was alive once, if hidden." His mystery deepened, his enigma endured. There was still no human link. I had asked my mother more than I thought fair about the man she had not seen for as long as I. It was like I held pieces of him, only to have them slip away from my grasp.

After the initial excitement at finding this "father-lode," I began to catalog everything. In the days that followed, I read more carefully. Almost as an after-thought, I browsed through his fraternity newsletters. In spite of the *Kama Sutra, Last Exit to Brooklyn,* and the Marquis de Sade, the man who was Roland Decatur Anderson, Jr., wanted to keep abreast of his alma mater and his Greek kin. I wrote to the main office of the organization and asked for a list of the SAE men who had graduated with my father at Tuscaloosa nearly thirty years before. They sent it to me. I looked at the list and called my mother to ask if any of the names sounded familiar. I began to read them off to her. Almost immediately, since the list was in alpha-betical order, I read the name "Robert L. Brannon." My mother said, "That's your godfather."

It was tough getting up my nerve to call him. Mom filled me in on their relationship, telling me that my godfather, Robert L. Brannon, cared deeply for Andy despite my father's penchant for creating unnecessary crises with almost everyone close to him. I knew enough about my dad's behavior to imagine that he could've become tiresome after a certain amount of time. Then I recalled my recent contacts with the cousins in my father's family and figured that whatever happened in a call to Bobby Brannon could not be any more disappointing, so I prepared what I was going to say.

Incidentally, I do not mean to say that these relatives were mean. They were not. Truthfully, they were more polite than the law allows. They cooed delightedly at hearing from me and could not get off the phone fast enough. I had mixed feelings about talking to them, too. In a way, I imagined that adopted people looking for their birth parents go through similar feelings: after all, I was loved and cared for by my mother and her family, so why look for strangers who hadn't bothered to locate me? But my curiosity won, and one Sunday afternoon I found myself speaking on the phone with an elderly cousin of Julia's. It was an enlightening conversation. Right away she asked if I kept in touch with Julia. I replied that I wrote to her every now and then, sometimes sent her things, and tried to see her when I was "down that way." Both her answer and the vociferousness of it surprised me. She said, "Well, I should hope so. That's your grandmother, you know." I paused, unsure of what direction to take. She continued, "And it's disrespectful to call her Julia." I sighed, finally realizing why my mother never encouraged contact with that side of her family. I said, "I mean no disrespect, ma'am. We've always called her that, at her request." Then, trying to lighten the moment, I added, "Besides, we called our mother's mother Memaw and Julia's mother Nana. Maybe we just ran out of names." She responded with a curt "That's no excuse."

Then I realized that the woman was afraid of me, of what I wanted. All she knew was that my father was crazy and that Julia was a sweet woman whose whole goddamn life wasn't one you'd wish on your worst enemy. She also knew that my father always wanted something from everyone, and had bled his own mama dry. And now, decades after you think it's all over, and all of the whispers have literally died down, the progeny of the malevolent Little Roland, the only truly shameful kin you can claim, calls you up out of the blue. I felt for her predicament and tried to speak lightly of it all. But she could not shake her mortification. She continued her inquiries into my suitability as a granddaughter and I was done listening.

I asked her when *she* had last seen Julia. She paused and said, "We sent her a card when Little Roland died." "Little Roland," aka Andy, aka my father, died in 1979. This was 1989. We faced off sternly, uncertain of one another's claim to proper indignation, and became adversaries over a corpse. We ended the call, but not without the true Southern woman sign-off: "It was good talking to you, too. Now you keep in touch, you hear?"

Not all of my calls shortened the lives of decent old

people. One woman found me after I started the television series. She's actually a "double cousin" and only a Mormon and anthropologist could figure out the exact linkage, but she's been terrific about getting me photos and pieces of our family's history. And I found another couple, elderly cousins of Julia's, who very kindly sent me a copy of the family tree, and gave me numbers of others I could call. They seemed happy to hear from me and wished me well in my career. But I don't intend to press my luck and will probably not "hunt down" any more lost relations.

The first talk I had with my godfather turned out to be more than I had hoped for. I phoned his home in Memphis, where he was living at the time. His wife answered and I said, "Mrs. Brannon? My name is Brett Anderson. I'm Andy Anderson's oldest daughter. Could I please speak with your husband?" Her shock was apparent, but she quickly moved toward genuine delight. "Well, I'll put him right on." I heard her calling for him, and a few long moments went by before my godfather got to the phone. I wanted him to know that I wasn't like my dad in all of the awful ways, like wanting something or being drunk and abusive. I tried to speak to him in the same laid-back, gentle tone that he was using with me. We spoke for about an hour. In the first few minutes, I detected an understandable caution in his voice. I did not solicit pity, nor did I retell the story of our abandonment. And I did not ask for just the hearts and flowers of his recollections. Once he realized that, we began to speak of the man who had been my father and his best friend.

This happened several years ago and my godfather has become one of the people I most trust in my life. We discuss the sort of things I'd like to think my father and I would have had things turned out differently—culture, art, politics, and just the things that are happening in our lives. Through time, we've found a bond surpassing the common thread of Andy, who must be pleased, wherever he is, to see us close. I do not think of Bobby as a replacement father, but I take the term "godfather" more literally that I would have once thought possible. He loved Andy, and I love him for that. Even though Bobby Brannon was around for some of Andy's saddest times and reprehensible deeds, he saw what Andy was and what he could have been. We have mourned him and never stooped to being maudlin in the process.

After our first talk, I sent him a letter and a tape of my first *Tonight Show*. Not long after that, he and his wife made the trip to New York and asked Kenny and me to dinner. Later that night, when we were back at our apartment, Ken told me that when I left the table for a minute Bobby turned to him and said, "When I watched that tape and saw Brett walk out on that stage, I could swear it was just like seeing Andy." I've since learned that Bobby is not given to hyperbole, and I like even more that he said this to Ken while they were alone.

Bobby has given me invaluable information about my father. He told me about Andy's dreams, opinions, and quirks, speaking kindly but realistically about his shortcomings. In an episode that was new to me, Bobby described the time he'd flown down to Houston to check on Andy not long after we'd all gone away. My godfather said, "He was just sitting there with the blinds drawn, filled with blame and almost to the point of madness. I told him emphatically that he must go see a psychiatrist. Andy got very upset and angry. He said, 'No! People would find out!' After that, he would call or write, usually asking for money. I didn't ever mind sending it to him, but the letters started not to make any sense at all after a while. Sometimes, though, I'd get one of his letters and see a flash of the Andy I used to know. It was almost sadder than not hearing from him at all. Damn. I wish I'd saved them so you could have them."

Bobby said that when he heard that Andy died, he went down to Alabama to look at his grave. He told me about the times he came to visit us in Houston when my sisters and I were small. "At first it was thrilling to see him so taken by something as he was with y'all. He'd finally found something that overjoyed and overwhelmed him. But he wasn't satisfied that you were all healthy and bright. He would get you to perform, to do parlor tricks of his own devising. Sometimes he'd get you to sing or recite parts of movies that he thought would be funny for a toddler to say."

He said that in these moments my father surpassed paternal pride and affection and became more like a maestro to his own offspring. Bobby's expression became sad when he explained, "You would all just watch him, never looking at anything else in the room. You were so eager to please, and were just trying to remember the things he had taught you. It wasn't like you were afraid of him, but you wanted so badly not to disappoint him that it was a kind of fear. I finally told Andy that I couldn't watch anymore. He seemed so surprised."

About a year and a half ago, as of this writing, my godfather and his lovely, kind wife, Marilyn, agreed to meet Mom and me for dinner. I was visiting Atlanta while on hiatus from *Grace Under Fire* and wanted to clear some things up for the writing of this book. Although the show was going well, I'd pretty much left Ken and my marriage in the lurch with the advent of fame and its attendant baggage. Those feelings of insecurity came in handy when my life was dull; now that it was stressful beyond belief, I was inundated by them. I felt like I was dancing on the edge of something spectacular and horrible at the same time. It was hard for me to talk about, much less understand, so being with family at home was the next best thing to actually doing anything about it. I looked forward to the dinner and maybe finding something out about my father that I had not known before, perhaps something that would help either of us make more sense to me.

While the tales flew past, some fine, some less so, I couldn't help blurting out to my godfather, "Why did you care so much about my father?" He paused and said, "Because I never knew anyone like him, before or since." I looked over at my mother and knew that she understood his answer. The two of them seemed to be seeing the same memory at different angles. He continued, "When I met your father at college, it was as if we thought the same things about books, music, philosophy, etc. He was more interesting than any professor, and, in the beginning, I thought his eccentricities were just that. Then I went home with him for a visit to his parents and saw what his life was like. It was crazy and none of them knew it. He was outright abusive to his own father. It went beyond rude. He insulted him in front of me, his mother, anyone who was present. He bragged about Julia's family and sneered whenever his father was in the same room. Big Roland was so beaten down by it that he just slunk around and tried to ignore it. It was sad seeing a man that big slouching in the wake of his own snotty kid."

My mother added, "Julia thought that having Andy would make up for marrying Roland. After Big Dad 'rescued' Roland from whatever it was that he did wrong, then they were forever in his debt. The only thing they could pay him back with was your daddy. She did everything she could to make both Andy and Big Daddy see how special that little boy was. She was right to be that way when he was little. All children need to hear that they are special and smart and wonderful.

"But then she started letting him get away with murder." (I thought about the time my dad broke all of the eggs in their car and told Julia, "No harm done!") Mom continued, "Big Daddy saw just enough of the monster that they were creating to put that codicil in the trust fund, right before he died, the one about Andy never getting any money until Julia died. Even then, he had to split it with any children he might have."

Mom was quiet for a moment. "Andy waited there just to get that money. He died waiting for it." Then none of us spoke.

Finally, Bobby's wife, Marilyn, who had not particularly cared for my father but kept her own counsel about it, remarked, "I'll bet Julia was relieved when he died."

I'd never thought of it that way before. Then I remembered the day Julia opened the door to us, exactly twenty years before, when Andy was in the back of the house and he was as close to "capture" as he had ever been. It had taken her half an hour to let us in. God knows what he was saying to her in that time. And I remembered that I thought she was going to faint when I said I was going to walk around in the rest of the house. She protected her son from life when he was small: there were so many things out there that could harm a smart, sensitive child. Then Andy developed asthma to advance their cause. And, when he became a man, his mother shielded him from the things that scared or angered him—even if those things were his own children. Her devotion persisted until he was middle-aged, even when she knew he should and wished he would take on his rightful responsibilities. His response was to force her to keep him as she had always done.

I was thinking not just about Andy, the man who had transformed my sisters and me into self-seeking missiles, but of the whole messy, familial quagmire born of greed and doubt and another feeling I knew well, one that was upon me as we sat there talking— the fear of not being good enough, a fear so strong that it resembles grandeur to those unaware of its true extent.

As our dinner ended and we were walking back to our cars, I remembered something. I turned to Bobby and asked, "Were you the friend Andy took to see William Faulkner that day back in college?" He chuckled. "You mean to give him *Gone With the Wind* with a pack of matches?" I nodded. "Brett, he made that up." For a second, Mom and I sat there with open mouths. One of our favorite anecdotes was being demoted to apocrypha before our eyes. The four of us laughed while muttering "Son of a bitch" in mostly affectionate tones. Bobby looked at me and said, "I do wish your father could see you now. He would be insufferably proud." I am glad he said that where my mother could hear it. He was giving credit where it was finally due.

That night was the most I've ever gotten to talk to anyone about my father. I dropped Mom off and went back to my hotel with plenty of feelings to keep me company. I was happy to have some things cleared up, things I'd wondered about for thirty years, but something was stirring inside of me, too, something difficult to face. . . . For all of the time since April 1, 1962, I had successfully fought any comparisons between me and my father. He was gone, failed, quit, dead. He ran out and left without reason or rhyme. That night I realized that I was living a parallel life, one with not enough room to do all the running away I wanted. Roland and I differed in that his dreams became a vortex and he became lost inside of them, and life, the real one that beckoned to be held and tended to, withered away and met him only at the end. Just because I was living a dream my father undoubtedly would have killed for didn't mean I couldn't end up the same—

alone and desperate. I shivered in the car on that hot Georgia night and went into my hotel and called my husband.

I asked Ken if there was anything I could do, if I had gone too far to come back. As lawyers on both sides had started to make flurried phone calls to one another, I worried that he wouldn't speak once I reached him. He said, yes, that we could talk. That was all I could hope for, but something felt right. It seemed that I wasn't going to lose myself scrambling for some damned dream that wasn't real in the first place. A few months later, we reconciled. Things have been different and better since then. I cannot say whether our separation—almost a year long—created the progress we've reached or if we would've gotten there eventually without me trying to pull the plug. I felt as if I'd been standing on the edge of an inherited abyss. Now I could understand what Julia meant when she said, "Ah wasn't trying to kill myself. Ah just wanted somebody to pay attention to me."

༄

The first time I visited Julia where she is now, I asked a nurse if anyone ever came to see her. The answer was no. Although it is nice as nursing homes go, it's sad to see rooms full of people alone together, some of them returned to the fetal position by the ungodly amount of time they've been alive, just wheeled in and out of sunlight in their chairs.

One day I walked in and didn't find Julia in her room. I walked past the other rooms and hardly any of the residents were in, either. Behind a cracked door in what appeared to be some sort of a recreation area, I got a glimpse of a row of old ladies lined up in chairs, looking straight ahead. A few were asleep, but most of them sat there smiling. I pushed open the door to greet my grandmother and looked over to see what television program amused them so. They were looking at a plain wall, one without even a painting on it. I stood there for a minute looking at it, too, and wondering how long I'd have to be alive before getting my very own memory-powered projection screen.

Julia and I walked slowly down the hall, chatting about nothing in particular. As she held on to my arm, she mentioned something about being on a diet. I couldn't help but laugh. After all, she was well into her eighties and was as vain as my great-grandmother, Torrie, who had passed on the decade before, but who flirted with the doctors up until her last breath. I was honestly jealous of Julia's figure. I was thankful for the height I inherited from the Andersons, but always coveted the slenderness of Julia and the Powells.

Once inside my grandmother's room, I noticed that her walls were bare. All of the other residents, mostly women, had pictures of their relatives everywhere.

Julia has three granddaughters and two great-grand-children and we were nowhere to be seen. I thought Roland, Sr., or Andy or even her father might at least be represented, but they weren't there either. The last time I'd been to see her, I asked if she wanted me to send her some more photos, joking that we'd all got-ten better looking and new ones had been taken. "Oooh! That would be wonderful." When they did not appear, I mentioned it to one of the nurses, and she said, "She likes to keep them in her closet. We tried to put some up and she didn't want us to." God bless her. Maybe she's had enough of all of us. But she does seem glad when we stop by. For some reason, she adores Ken and thinks he is a blood relative. How nice that her instincts crave someone normal in our midst.

In the first couple of visits to her, I politely tried to get her to talk about Andy. But then I realized that she felt safe in that nursing home, safe from scrutiny, mem-ories, safe from neighbors who would "talk about things," safe from the huge, horrible secrets that she had carried alone for so many years. I began to un-derstand how much she had carried and how little help she had doing it.

My father had died a week or so before any of us— my mother, sisters, or I—found out about it, and even then the obituary was seen in the paper quite by acci-dent as one of my mother's cousins was traveling that way. At the end of the burial notice, it said, "Survived by his mother, Mrs. Julia P. Anderson." His three daughters were not mentioned at all. For years I wondered how Julia could have just forgotten us or, worse, left us out intentionally. Now I wonder how she survived in the first place and how much of her got away at all.

Now that she was old and stuck in a prison of white walls and forgetting, I thought I could do something else for her. I decided to tell her funny things that Mom had told us about Andy. Julia was delighted by these tales. I kept them cheerful and clean, and since such anecdotes were scarce, eventually I started making them up. It wasn't hard. After all, I *am* his daughter.

The last time I saw Julia, she mistook me for someone else for a moment, but was still glad that someone else was there. We sat quietly for a time in the piano room and I said, out of the blue, surprising even myself, "Mama says that she is so glad she knew Andy because he taught her so much about so many things." Julia smiled her sweet smile, her always kind eyes shining over, and said, "Me, too! He taught me a lot, too."

So now I read my father's books. It was strange to see how many of them I had read before, but more of a delight to unearth some authors for the first time. If it were not for this inadvertent inheritance, I might never have read the likes of Stanley Elkin, Bruce Jay Friedman, Calder Willingham, Thomas Pynchon,

S. J. Perelman, or J. P. Donleavy. My father collected their early works and I've gotten the rest of them. One of my favorite discoveries has been James Agee, tragic in his own right, dying at the same age as my father—forty-six—who left behind one of the books my dad loved the most, *Let Us Now Praise Famous Men*.

Now that I think about it, what could my father have said to me that hot day so long ago, when he did not come out and see me when I was talking to him through a closed door? "Wow! Long time no see! Has it been—what?—a dozen years? Man, time flies when ..." When what, Daddy? When you're out of hope, but not brains? When the only voice you've heard for one hundred and forty-four months is that of your adoring yet tormented mother? When all you do is live for the beer store to be open or the latest Grove Press book to arrive at the college bookstore or wherever it is you go at night not to be drowned in what you did not become? I can only imagine how you felt as I spoke on the other side of that door. I had my own journey ahead of me, miles to go before I slept. That sort of thing. Were you waiting to hear that I'd made it through? Or were you just waiting until your mother died, so you could go where you wanted, wherever it was you thought you'd be safe from all of us?

A couple of summers after I got the books, I went to see my dad's grave for the first time. I didn't really plan to. There was another man in Andy's fraternity that

Bobby Brannon said I might look up, another one of Andy's friends. Bobby said the three of them were close during the time they were at college together. His name was Jon Will Pitts. He lived in Clanton, Alabama, and was in poor health. I wrote him from New York and introduced myself. He invited me down the next time I was in Atlanta.

I drove to his house and found someone who was a bit of a surprise. Jon Will was a retired attorney for the federal government, very religious and a lifelong student of Alabama history. We spent a few hours together, and just as I was leaving he asked me if I'd seen where Andy was buried. I told him no, but that I would one day. Jon Will got very excited. "Now then, Brett, you must go see it. Here, I've got a camera. It's an excellent one, and I think there's almost a whole roll of black-and-white film in it, which might be best for this sort of photography. Why don't you go on and take it? Just send it back to me and let me know what you find." There wasn't much I could say to that. I thought I was doing it to oblige him more than anything else. He was very kind and it seemed to matter so much to him. Tuskegee was only a couple of hours away and I didn't know the next time I'd be back through.

I pulled into town and drove past Julia's old house. It was the first time I'd ever driven past without stopping. Then, still wondering what the hell I was doing chasing the tomb of the unknown daddy, I just cruised around aimlessly until I spotted a large house with a sign out front that said FUNERAL HOME. It looked old and established, and in a place as small as Tuskegee I figured it had to be the best shot at finding the cemetery. I walked up to the porch and a man answered the door.

In that town, introducing myself as Young Roland's daughter is like saying you're half a ghost. I must say that the gentleman recovered very nicely. He looked at me for a moment and said, "Well, sure you are. You look a lot like him. Come inside, young lady." I walked in and sat in their cool parlor while the man excused himself to finish up some work. I realized that I had interrupted an embalming and wondered what it would be like to live in a house where the dead waited to be decked out amid the lives of the breathing. Sitting there, I reckoned that I was probably the latest visitor they'd ever had after the actual service. The proprietor returned and said, "Here's a map of how to get to the grave." He had drawn one that was quite easy to understand. "Why don't you let my wife go with you? She could help you find it faster. I just phoned her and she's coming right over." I thanked him anyway, but said I "best be going."

Before I could get to my car, she pulled up. I was impressed. She was one of the hip old women you hardly ever see that far south. She tucked wisps of silver hair back into a perfect French twist and apologized for her disheveled state, as she'd spent the day in her garden with the grandkids. She was casual, energetic, and elegant all at once. She didn't think it strange that I'd waited that long to come by. "Dear, dear. The whole thing with your father was so sad. Julia would get agitated whenever anyone asked about him. We'd drop her off things sometimes, just knowing Roland was in the back, pretending things were normal because that's how she wanted them to be. I hope you don't think there's something you think you should have done. No, that wouldn't do at all. There wasn't anyone who could change the game they were playing, I suppose." She asked where I lived and told me she'd attended Juilliard many years before. Unlike a lot of the townsfolk to whom I'd spoken about Andy, ones who often penalized me for the discomfort they felt at his memory, she and her husband were most accepting.

We got in her car and rolled up the hill to the cemetery. She drove slowly all the way to the back, and showed me the Powell family plot. I got out and saw Big Roland's grave first. My grandfather's resting place was not near the Powells, who had fancy tombstones, Bible passages, and flowers on them. There was just his name and the time he was on the planet. I remembered his slow laugh and the way he put ketchup on his eggs and the nasty cough from the Lucky Strikes that killed him.

I found myself wanting a cigarette myself about

then, thinking it might put off the emotions I was starting to push back. Then I saw Andy's grave. It was close to the gravel path, but far enough from the car so that I could kneel on the grass nearby. Seeing his tiny tombstone was overwhelming. So many secrets felt lost inside that small piece of ground. I realized that the woman waiting beside her car was the reason I did not weep aloud. I turned to look at her and said, "Thank you for coming here with me. For showing me where he was." She looked back at me and said in a very clear and calm voice, "You didn't need to come here by yourself." Good old Southern women. Helping each other bury that elephant in the living room.

I took some pictures. Jon Will was right. Black-and-white was a good way to remember that day. Sometimes when I read something funny that my dad wrote in one of his books, I think about going down there and putting up a bigger tombstone, something with an epitaph befitting his glories, ignoring his mistakes. Other days, I feel like putting up a ten-foot-tall statue of Elvis just to screw with him. But I'll leave him be.

When I was very young and still waiting for my father to come back to me—to us—I saw a Shirley Temple movie called *The Little Princess.* Shirley was my age and her father went to fight in some remote, exotic war and was severely wounded in battle. He could not speak or see, and since Shirley's mother was already dead, there was nothing for anyone to do but put her in an orphanage. There she made a friend who was, by the sound of her language and manners, well beneath Shirley on the socioeconomic ladder, and even called Shirley "Miss," as if to provide the cute little moppet her own lady-in-waiting.

The woman who ran the orphanage was, of course, cruel and cold-hearted, and the girls tried not to cry themselves to sleep at night. Through it all, Shirley was convinced that her father was alive. "Daddy wouldn't go off and leave me!" she insisted in her unaccountably American accent while those around her spoke either Cockney or the King's English. "No, mum, he'll come back and find us," her pal replied, though one could tell she was just trying to humor her friend.

Then a kindly, exceedingly rich neighbor with his very own East Indian valet began to take a paternal interest in Shirley and her friend. One night after the girls had cried themselves to sleep in their cold room without any food, the benevolent men spirited all sorts of goodies into their room: a built fire, embroidered quilts, scones, jam, hot tea, even embroidered pillows with silken fringe. When Shirley awoke, she went right to the fire, awed and properly grateful. Her friend went right for the food, another indicator of her lower breeding, I guess, and cried out in a voice I can still hear, "Oh, look, miss! Muffins!" I loved that. Screw the tapestries, the Gainsborough wannabe of the entire spread, this gal just wanted a fucking muffin and she was woman enough to cry with glee.

Now I know why this meant so much to me. But for thirty years I couldn't figure it out. I was—and am—nearly every person in that movie: I was the girl who knew her father would come home and that it was all a misunderstanding, that he was wounded across the miles and could not speak his love or claim her. "You'll see," I taunted the disbelievers. "When he gets home, you'll see, you'll all be sorry then." I was the pal who wanted the food first and thought finery was a blanket on the bed. And later, much later, I became the rich man across the way sending victuals in the night to the little girls who had almost given up.

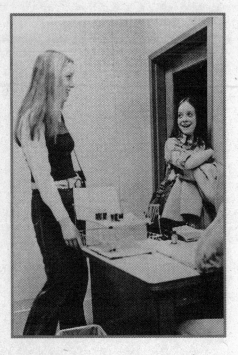

Undoubtedly saying something
terribly important — although I
was 16, with streaked hair,
bellbottoms and a macrame belt.
No wonder Toren is laughing...

Marietta, '74

MY FATHER MOVED THROUGH DOOMS OF

LOVE THROUGH SAMES OF AM THROUGH

HAVES OF GIVE

SINGING EACH MORNING OUT OF EACH

NIGHT

MY FATHER MOVED THROUGH THE DEPTHS

OF HEIGHT.

—e. e. cummings

20.

I have always written in books that are mine. I've heard it said that people who do such things do not respect books, but I don't agree. When I find something that I want to remember, I just mark it and then collect the page numbers I have noted in the back of the book. I started doing this with words I meant to look up, and it grew into all sorts of comments and comparisons. Eventually, my footnotes grew and I would buy note-books for my notes. When I noticed that my father did the same thing in his books, at least the nonfiction ones, I mentioned it to my mother, who said, "I know. You've done it since you were little. And your handwriting is like his, too." I looked more closely. She was right.

I started to see my father's notes as evidence, signs, as things he wanted us to see. Me to see. Sometimes, late at night, when I am reading one of the books he left behind, I will come across a note he left or a place he marked with his ubiquitous red felt pen, and I can see him sitting there, all those years ago, telling me to pay attention. There are those who would say that I assume much from scant evidence. I say to them: This is all of my father I have left. I am in the desert and these red lines are the only flask I have been given.

One of his books is *The Letters of F. Scott Fitzgerald*. My father wrote in the margins of this, in the letters Fitzgerald had written to his daughter, Frances Scott Fitzgerald, or Scottie. He hardly wrote at all in the rest of the book, only in the father-to-daughter letters. I cannot believe it's a coincidence that Andy chose specific passages from a father to his daughter across the miles. Nor do I doubt the turns of fate that led me to them, that led us to each other. In the introduction by Andrew Turnbull, my father put many red stars by the following reference, as well:

The letters to his daughter which begin the book are uniquely self-revealing and touching in their concern. As though reliving his life through her, Fitzgerald advises her from the depths of his conscience, and no American author of his stature has put so much of himself on paper for the sake of one of his offspring. His sternness, amounting almost to tyranny at times, sprang from an excess of love—an anxiety lest Scottie repeat his mistakes and fall short of her potential.

These are the things my father marked in the text of the book itself, in the letters from F. Scott Fitzgerald to Scottie:

I want you to be among the best of your race and not waste yourself on trivial aims. To be useful and proud—is that too much to ask? (July 1936)

༄

You have to have your own fences to jump and learn from experience. Nobody ever became a writer just by wanting to be one. If you have anything to say, anything you feel nobody has ever said before, you have got to feel it so desperately that you will find some way to say it that nobody has ever found before, so that the thing you have to say and the way of saying it blend as one matter—as indissolubly as if they were conceived together. (October, 1936)

க

When I was your age I lived with a great dream. The dream grew and I learned to speak of it and make people listen. Then the dream divided one day when I decided to marry your mother after all. . . . The mistake I made was in marrying her. We belonged to different worlds—she might have been happy with a kind simple man in a southern garden. She didn't have the strength for the big stage—sometimes she pretended, and pretended beautifully, but she didn't have it. She was soft when she should have been hard, and hard when she should have been yielding. She never knew how to use her energy—she's passed that failing on to you. . . . I want my energies and my earnings for people who talk my language. . . . You don't realize that what I

am doing here is the last tired effort of a man
who once did something finer and better.

꙳

Every girl your age in America will have the
experience of working for her living. To shut
your eyes to that is like living in a dream—to
say "I will do valuable and indispensable
work" is the part of wisdom and courage.
(July, 1938)

꙳

Besides the "cleverness" which you are vaguely
supposed to have "inherited," people will be
quick to deck you out with my sins. If I hear
of you taking a drink before you're twenty, I
shall feel entitled to begin my last and greatest non-stop binge. (September, 1938)

꙳

You and I have two very different ideas—
yours is to be immediately and overwhelm-
ingly attractive to as many boys as you can possibly meet, including Cro-Magnons, natural

born stevedores, future members of the Shriners and plain bums. My idea is that . . . you should be extremely attractive to a very limited amount of boys who will be very much heard of in the nation or who will at least know what it is all about. (Fall, 1938)

᳘

You must not ask me to wire you money—it is much harder to get than last summer. I owe thousands. . . . Sorry to close the letter this way but you must count your pennies. (June 12, 1940)

᳘

You haven't given me much idea of [your beau]. Would he object to your working— outside the house I mean? Excluding personal charm, which I assume, and the more conventional virtues which go with success in business, is he his own man? Has he any force of character? Or imagination or generosity? Does he read books? Has he any leaning toward the arts and sciences or anything beyond creature comfort or duck-shooting? In short, has he the possibilities of growth that would

make a lifetime with him seem attractive?
These things don't appear later—they are either there latently or they will never be there
at all. (August 24, 1940)

And the last place my father scored damn near killed
me to read:

I remember once a long time ago I had a
daughter who used to write me letters but now
I don't know where she is or what she is doing,
so I sit here listening to Puccini—"Someday
she'll write (Pigliano edda ciano)." (November
2, 1940)

F. Scott Fitzgerald died a month after this letter was
written to his nineteen-year-old daughter.

One early Saturday morning,
Mom got us together for this
picture. It was worth the trip
just to tickle Katy.

Marietta, '75

CLAY IS JUST DIRT WITH
QUENCHED THIRST.
I PICTURE IT SIPPING HIM
CAREFULLY.
AND THE TREES NEAR HIS COFFIN
BEND SWEETLY
TO SHADE HIS FEVERED SLEEP,
HIS INCOMPLETE VOYAGE.
SLEEP, DADDY, REST.
I FOUND WHAT YOU LEFT
THE THINGS YOU KEPT,
WHAT YOU WROTE—
YOUR BONES.
I FOUND THEM AND
I KNOW WHAT YOU MEAN
TO ME AT LAST.

21.

My father's life was such an unfulfilled one, both full
and empty at once, scattered with threads of truth and
huge immovable blocks of concrete opinion, too heavy
to carry into the demanding world of reality. Once I
found his books at least I knew part of what he had

been doing for all those years that he was gone, all those years in the back of that house. Several years ago I was given *A Confederacy of Dunces* by John Kennedy O'Toole. Except for the excess weight, I knew that my dad's literary prototype was Ignatius P. Reilly: for many years he existed with his mother, persecuting her from the vast ammunition of his own dysfunction, and they both complied to maintain such dependency.

What did they get out of it? Now I think I know. Julia got her boy, the man arising from the ether of the parlor, one who would never leave. It was such a shame that no one understood the genius that she had bred, but now she could just exist to be near him. Now that all of the other relatives were gone away, her son in her house was the next best thing to being married to kin—and without the mess of sex.

As for my father and what he gained from the safe haven of mommy's house: he simply had no other place to go. I believe he did love my mother and could do no better unless he found someone rich, as well. At least his mother put up with the knowledge of his insanity, gathered evidence that the world was too mediocre a place for all of his unfinished books, symphonies, and duties. They rowed forth, not looking back at the wreckage of my father's life, lest they turn into that proverbial pillar of salt, withering together. Just contemplating the remainder of that damned trust fund kept my father alive. It is the vision of my father, who waited so long for his very own Godot, that makes me move forward when it is not my nature to do so.

I dream that I could inherit his insanity like some physical disease passed from generation to generation, cropping up in adulthood, a lump in the breast of my soul, so to speak. Trying to gather what was wondrous in him and winnowing it from the ranting egomaniac is one of my tasks in this life. Now that I have learned about alcoholism, I know that he exhibited the symptoms of both the physical and mental aspects of the disease. When I think I have no control over how my life turns out, I remember that I've seen far sicker people get better. I also remember that I was one of them and that I still am, but that I do not have to live my life like a dying dreamer who accompanies herself into oblivion.

My father's spirit, if you will, seemed to me a troubled vapor between my own past and my future. Since the books arrived and I sighed the word "Daddy" for the first time in years, I know that our relationship has changed. It was hard to think of him as never loving me and my sisters, as never wanting to find or kiss us. Now I know that he could not. Too much time and too many inner promises had rushed past, and the best he could do was to die in the back of that house, and the best Julia could do was keep the mausoleum for us, his daughters, until we were prepared to be the archaeologists of our own paternity. In any case, I believe that

his soul was troubled, in the leftover hell of what he did
and did not do in life.

I also know that he is eased now. Some friends know
what I am talking about and there are others to whom
I've never mentioned this. When I moved West to start
taping the show, I would be up, still writing late at
night, and suddenly feel him around me, just watching. At first I did not think it was my father because
whoever it was, was content to watch me and be there
without criticizing or spewing forth any annihilating
criticism. My godfather used the phrase "insufferably
proud" to describe the way my dad might feel about me
today. Perhaps this is so. I also know that he would
second-guess my every major decision and even the
jokes I tell. My romanticism of how we would be if
things had been different, if he had lived or we had
grown up as part of the same family, is almost nil. I do
not suggest that the tragedy of our love has not played
itself out in my head in less than the saddest ways, but
at least time has cured me of wishing things had been
different. He will come back or not with lessons
learned, and if there is an afterlife, he will be bragging
to either the angels—or the succubi—of his children.

We are so fragmented, my sisters and I. It is next to
impossible for us to leave who we were and what we
did not get and be all right with one another. I wish
we could just laugh and remember the good parts of
our lives together, when we were children, before the

ropes holding us together frayed and we set out to sea on our own. I see my mother and father in all of us. I see where we are cursed with complexity and darkness that defies healing, but we do heal in our own ways. I also see our wit and capacity for joy that make our lives exceptional. Without science to support me, I think whatever rotten psychic inheritances we possessed can be voided via awareness. To be truthful, knowing who my father was and what he did and did not accomplish makes it possible for me to take what I want, as in sobriety, and leave the rest.

ROLAND D. ANDERSON, JR.
MAY 4, 1933
NOV. 8, 1979

The name Roland came from
one of Charlemagne's commanders.
In 778, Roland and his men,
ambushed by the Basques, were
massacred because he was
too proud to call for help.

Epilogue

One may wonder why I have written so candidly about my mother in a book that represents comparatively little of the rest of my family. My mother has been there for me for my entire life. She is the one who has encouraged me to write and to perform. She is the one who would say, after I finished with some hyperbolic account of one of my escapades, "Honey, you're going to be on television one day telling those stories and jokes." I always thought it odd, because what I had been talking about was usually too vulgar to turn up on television. Once I started doing comedy, and worried that a joke was "too much" of anything, she would say, "Do more. That's what makes you different." This would be remarkable if only for the fact that she had been raised in a place and time in which being "different" had little, if anything, to recommend it.

She is here every day in my heart and in my mind telling me, "I know I tried to be different and maybe things didn't work out for the best, but that wasn't the only way to be unique. Go and do this thing, not stopping until *you* decide to." I guess my mother paid the price for being different for a long time. When she and I speak about anything—what goes on in the day, mistakes of the afternoon or of life itself, she does so with an openness and humor that often belie the subject. I am just trying to say that she has given me permission to write about us, about her. There may be those who will judge us both for what we did and did not do. Whatever anyone else says, I honor and adore my mother for her relentless support, love, and encouragement. I do not wish to take equal liberties with other family members. My sisters know that I love them and what they mean to me. I would be surprised if they wanted to be included here for any other mention than these. . . .

Tana is brilliant and able to do so many things well. When she did not stop piano lessons and went on to learn more than one musical instrument, I knew she could couple being gifted with discipline and I have been jealous since. She writes fine fiction and poetry. She can draw, cook, do calligraphy, make astrology charts, and sing. In addition to these things, she does amazingly funny impressions of people, whether famous or the ones we grew up with. She raises my niece with wisdom and joy and an abiding sense of responsibility to the planet.

Toren is a force of nature. She is captivating, psychic (although she'd probably not like to be called that), and torrentially empathetic. Her wit is self-denigrating, yet powerful. Like Tana, she is multitalented and possesses a rare blend of the earthy and the holy, which makes for very interesting dinner conversation. She is still that caring person who worried about the homeless man at Christmas more than twenty years ago. She contains multitudes. Sometimes she has been my friend.

Kristen and Katy are my youngest sisters. Although we have different fathers, I don't think of them as half-sisters at all. They are complete sisters in all senses of the word, unstinting in their teasing and devotion, and they have not changed the ways in which they've treated me since This Whole Thing Happened. And if they were not my sisters, I'd want to be their friend. Either of them could run a large nation or family, and if they did not live so far away, I would want them to run the relatively placid domain of my life, for I would trust them with it.

A therapist I had when I moved to Manhattan from Georgia once told me that she was surprised I had gotten "this far." I asked her what she meant. She said, "Most women like you, with a past like yours, would have ended up as a clerk at Woolworth's." I asked, bowing to her superior wisdom, why she thought that I had avoided such a diminished occupation. She said, after pondering for a moment, "I guess your mother must have let you know you were loved. Somehow. But I don't think you'll get better, that you'll ever really be happy, until you admit that she abused you." I told her that I thought I'd be all right anyway and never went back to see her. Besides, I didn't need to think she would always envision me in a light blue shift, pushing keys, bagging badly made sundries, there, by the grace of God, in her $80-an-hour world.

I know this is not about my mother, per se, but she taught me important lessons—not least among them unconditional love. No matter how hard my personal life became, I knew that she believed in me and supported the things I thought I could do. Because of her influence, I was always able to keep track of, and care about, art, books, politics, the rest of the world.

I cherish my mother's ability to listen and accept. She always wanted to know about our day, and listened to our problems or whatever else five daughters had to talk about. As much as anything, I appreciate that she instilled in each of us an abhorrence of prejudice. Especially when I remember that my mother grew up years before the words "civil rights" existed in the minds of Americans am I impressed with her response to the intolerance in the world.

I owe my mother for getting us out alive. And keeping herself that way even if she didn't always know why. I owe her for keeping us with her as long as she could, as well as she could.

You may know someone with a story as odd as this one. All of us have those random moments in our lives that shape us for better or for worse for the rest of the time we inhabit our bodies before we go on to whatever else is beyond this. Most of the time, endurance is not an option. One day we find ourselves faced with a disturbing moment or series of moments and must decide what path to take to get the hell away from it. Sometimes lots of these moments must transpire before we realize that no one else has the key. And as contemptible as what we get away from seems at the time, often we can look back at that space, that second, and know that living through it made us stronger.

I send this to my sisters, the other children he left behind.

I send this to my mother, who stayed in as many

ways as she knew how. Who brought us forth and saved us from what he would eventually do to himself.

I send this to my father in hopes that in some better world he will be able to see and he will say, "Of course she's all right. That's my daughter there."

I send this to anyone who's ever been left without getting what you needed when you needed it—and for finding it anyway—other brothers and sisters I have never met.

I send this to my comrades who have guided me along the way. From the time I was very young to this moment I have known dear companions and teachers who have lit the road for me. In this life—and I think others—I've been counseled by the finest people anyone could ever imagine knowing, whose souls, strength, and wit were given freely so that I might find my own. My gratitude is boundless, both to them and to the Fates that arranged their gifts when I needed them most. I have been loved. I hope that fact is as apparent as the other things that have happened in my life, those things that bring notoriety, but that cannot measure the distance I have come by having such magnificent friends.

Mostly, though, I send this to myself, for all the unfinished journeys, good intentions, and times I meant to be kinder, work harder, try longer. I send it for exploring all the subsolar whims and valleys and places with thin air, all the times I tried to run away, and stayed instead to find some truth.

ॐ

Like our dead, we, too, will build
the beauty of days to come for other eyes to see,
and in this drunken spirit of freedom
spreading through the streets, swaying the trees
blowing smoke from fires
let our dead be with us—
        fulfilled
            happy
                always living.

—GIOCONDA BELLI,
Patria Libre, July 19, 1979

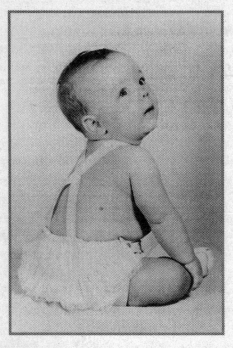

This picture of me, covered in
plastic, was the only one found
in my father's wallet nearly
ten years after he died.

Montgomery, '58

Acknowledgments

I am grateful to the following people for being so much to me not just during the writing of this book, but in my life: First, my mother, Carol O'Quinn, whose belief in her children was the well from which I drank when my own ran dry.

My wonderful grandparents, Eugene Robinson Parker and Elizabeth Mitchell Parker, whose love and support ensured our survival in so many ways.

My amazing sisters Tana, Toren, Kristen, and Katy,

who have given me the greatest laughs I've known since they were born.

Art and Pat Zeiger for being parents and friends to us both.

Blake and Malaika for giving me hope.

Robert Brannon for keeping Roland alive and for encouraging this work.

Christine and David Martin for holding it all together with such grace.

Special thanks to Daria Paris, for organizing and typing the manuscript.

And deep appreciation to Bob Miller, for helping me find the right book to make the wall turn around.

Many thanks, also, to the following people for reasons they understand: Larry Amoros, the irrepressible Sonya Gay Bourn, Marcy Carsey, Libby Carter, Courtney Conte, Abby Davis, Frank Dines, Nick DiPaolo, Elvis O. Ellis, Gil Goldberg, Robyn Golightly, Ginny and Mike Hatcher, Nancy Hernandez, Jonathan Karp, Mary Johnson, Levi Laub, Michael Lessac, Paul Malone, Jim Baker Moss, Eileen Motter, my Posse at *Grace Under Fire*, Colin Quinn, Randy Schutz, George Schlatter, Ron Shock, Beth Stansfield, Barry Steiger, Martha Terrill, Irene Souprake, Kate Wendel, Tom Werner, Sharon Wilson, and, in a class by himself, Mister Robert Dolan Smith.